1990

DR. JOHNSON AND FANNY BURNEY

For Betty and Ian Wood

Dr. Johnson
and
Fanny Burney

with an Introduction and Notes

by

Nigel Wood

Bristol Classical Press

Introduction and notes © Nigel Wood, 1989
Selection based on the 1912 edition of Chauncey Brewster Tinker

First published 1989 by
Bristol Classical Press, 226 North Street, Bedminster, Bristol

Printed in Great Britain by
Antony Rowe Ltd, Chippenham, Wiltshire

British Library Cataloguing in Publication Data

Burney, Fanny, 1752-1840
    Dr. Johnson and Fanny Burney.
    1. English literature. Johnson, Samuel,
    1709-1784 – Biographies – Early works
    I. Title
    828'.609

    ISBN 1-85399-066-3

Contents

Introduction   vii

Note on the Text   xii

Dr. Johnson and Fanny Burney   1

List of Abbreviations   122

Notes   126

Introduction

> ...to write by rule, to compose by necessity, to make the understanding, nature's first gift, subservient to interest, that meanest offspring of art! – when weary, listless, spiritless, to rack the head for invention, the memory for images, and the fancy for ornament and allusion;...Heavens! what a life of struggle between the head and the heart! how cruel, how unnatural a war between the intellects and the feelings!

Belfield's diatribe against a life of writing in Fanny Burney's second completed novel, *Cecilia*, suggests strain and unnatural motives, where inspiration and the spirit are wrung dry. However, it is characteristic of the writer of the *Journals* as well as the novels that there is also an attempt to put this self-indulgence by. After all, the chapter in which it occurs is entitled 'A Prating', and Cecilia, who is also detained by Hobson's ponderous advice on the life of business, is immediately 'tired of these interruptions, and impatient to be gone' (Book X, ch. vi, p. 883). Here is a sense of purpose as well as an appreciation of what it costs, the Fanny Burney who in secret sat up writing *Evelina* into the early hours and who burnt her first novel (almost completed), *The History of Caroline Evelyn*, because, as she confessed in the 'Introduction' to *The Wanderer* (1814), she had ever 'fastened degradation to this class of composition'.

This contradiction is rarely resolved not just for Fanny Burney but also for many of her sister novelists of the 1770s and 1780s. Publication involved the merciless exposure of the self as well as one's writing. For Fanny Burney, this often produced a crisis of identity as well as vocation. When about to commence her diary at the age of fifteen, to 'open [her] whole heart', the only *confidante* to whom she feels she can be 'wholly unreserved' and self-revealing is 'Nobody' (*Diary*, 1:19). When she realises that her authorship of *Evelina* has become an open secret, she becomes acutely self-conscious and almost chokes on a biscuit, obliging her to leave the room, when the venerable Rev. Michael Lort reads *Evelina* in her presence (pp. 28-30). When she discovers a satire against her in January, 1779, the Rev. Huddesford's *Warley: a Satire*, she goes 'for more than a week unable to eat, drink, or sleep, for vehemence of vexation...' and was 'strongly tempted to empty the whole contents of [her] bureau into the fire, and to vow never again to fill it' (pp. 49-50).

Patricia Meyer Spacks has illuminated this basic fear in her chapter on Fanny Burney in *Imagining A Self: Autobiography and Novel in Eighteenth-Century England* (1976), where she identifies this hold on a central 'informing purpose' as a form of self-defence: 'The force of public opinion has for her the status of a concrete reality with high potential for personal damage. By avoiding impropriety, she can avoid notice and consequently threat' (p. 165) and yet writing constituted a form of freedom, an escape from a reality of decorous confinement for one of the very few arenas for her where truth-telling was possible.

It must have seemed that Samuel Johnson, on meeting Fanny in 1778, was the polar opposite both in temperament and achievement, and yet, just over ten years before, the Thrales had come upon him at Bolt Court, on his knees before the Rev. Dr. John Delap, imploring God 'to continue to him the use of his understanding' (*Misc.*, 1:423). Streatham had become a place of succour and belonging, where he was forced no longer to earn friendship by an incessant parade of wit. When trying to coax Fanny's Johnsoniana from her for his *Life* in 1790, Boswell believed that the world had seen him 'long enough upon stilts' – an image that he was consequently at pains to uphold – and that he wanted to provide a glance at more unbuttoned moments, to 'entwine a wreath of the graces across his brow' (p. 104). The years 1778-84 that are covered by this selection seem, with hindsight and in the larger view, to be triumphant for Fanny Burney and vespertinal, even elegiac, ones for the Doctor. Looked at more closely, however, these images seem not to tally consistently with the experiences recorded in the journal-letters to Susan Burney or 'Daddy' Crisp. We may now regard Burney's talents as self-evident, and Johnson's sense of well-being as fated, but the privileged focus these documents provide is centred on a friendship that was born out of a radical insecurity on both sides: for the young author, the desire to escape the world whilst entering it and, for the established arbiter of taste, the fear of loneliness and rejection. For a short time, and at Streatham, we see these more perennial doubts held at bay, and, to echo Boswell, the stilts discarded.

For Johnson, the easy familiarity with the Thrales and Fanny Burney enabled him to return from the conflicts of composition and the demands of patrons or the book trade to more basic (and so scarcely recorded) pleasures. On the other hand, it would be wrong to feel that he lost his sharper perspectives or opinions on such visits. The clashes with Sir William Weller Pepys and Sir Philip Jennings-Clerke (pp. 64-7, 52-4) exemplify the opinion which Fanny Burney immediately formed of him, namely, that he was capable of decided judgements on people as well as books and that they could bring forth astringent commentary: 'Indeed, the freedom with which Dr. Johnson condemns whatever he disapproves, is astonishing; and the strength of words he uses would, to most people, be intolerable;...' (p. 13). At times such urgency would be followed by instant regret, where the demands of charity soothed exasperation, and yet we only occasionally get glimpses of the often scabrous press he almost daily received. The disapproval from Elizabeth Montagu's salon of his *Life of Lyttelton*, Chatterton's vicious denunciations in 1770 of his pensioned and hackneyed Muse and Charles Churchill's depiction of 'Pomposo' in *The Ghost* (1762) are graphic instances of what he regularly had to bear. With collections such as James Boulton's *Samuel Johnson: The Critical Heritage* (1971) and Helen Louise McGuffie's *Samuel Johnson in the British Press, 1749-1784* (1976) we can perhaps only now appreciate the extent of his celebrity and also the vitriol it excited. McGuffie records some 4,000 references in the period not just to his work but also to his appearance, political opportunism, possible sexual misadventures and his frigid (impotent?) taste in literature.

His fulsome praise of *Evelina* has, however, produced the instinctive critical reaction of regarding such occasions as olde-worlde gallantry to 'poor, dear Fanny'. This is wide of the mark. Throughout the 1780s into the next century no male novelist rivalled the achievement of Fanny Burney or Maria Edgeworth (1768-1849). In Dale Spender's timely and corrective study of *Mothers of the Novel* (1986) works such as *Evelina* or *Castle Rackrent* (1800) appear innovative in their own right, not merely as footnotes to a 'feminization' of Fielding's robustness or a development of Richardson's epistolary style. A survey of the first critical notices that *Evelina* and *Cecilia* received is instructive. For example, the anonymous reviewer of *Cecilia* in *The Gentlemen's Magazine*, for October, 1782, expected a Romance. Instead, he encountered incisive polemic: 'Cecilia holds up a mirror to the gay and dissipated of both sexes, in which they may see themselves and their deformities at full length, and exhibits more knowledge of the world, or *ton*, than could be expected from the years of the fair authoress' (Vol. 52, p. 485). The *Critical Review* was captivated in 1778 by the realism of *Evelina*, and summed up the performance as deserving 'no common praise, whether we consider it in a moral or literary light. It would have disgraced neither the head nor the heart of Richardson' (Vol. XLVI, p. 204), whereas *The Monthly Review* noted its 'great variety of natural incidents, some of the comic stamp, [which rendered] the narrative extremely interesting'. It was simply 'one of the most sprightly, entertaining, and agreeable productions' of its kind 'which has of late fallen under our notice' (Vol. LVIII, p. 316). Here there is the poise of the decorous satirist and the varied realist at a time when Fielding and Smollett were beginning to seem coarse and Richardson breathless and overblown.

One of Spender's more general comments, on the other hand, seems extreme. When stressing the validity of both Burney's and Edgeworth's sense of vocation as a novelist, she finds them 'serious women who did not see fiction as frivolous diversion but who placed their writing firmly within the honourable tradition of letters' (p. 272). This apparent generic ease minimises the challenge to the 'honourable tradition' that they both posed and which was also a current critical posture. Jane Austen, for example, enters the narrative in *Northanger Abbey* (1803; pub. 1818) to bewail 'the ungenerous and impolitic custom so common with novel writers, of degrading by their contemptuous censure the very performances, to the number of which they are themselves adding'. This crisis of confidence arises from ouside the ranks as well: 'Let us leave it to the Reviewers to abuse such effusions of fancy at their leisure, and over every new novel to talk in threadbare strains of the trash with which the press now groans. Let us not desert one another; we are an injured body' (ch. v, pp. 57-8; ed. Anne Henry Ehrenpreis [1972]). Recent commentators have indeed questioned the now traditional literary historical assumptions that the rise of the novel was safe in the hands of an emergent middle class. D.T. Laurenson and A. Swingewood claim that 'an urban middle class', and its ideological self-consciousness, actually militated against widespread novelistic experimentation, 'through its insatiable need for entertainment' (*The Sociology of Literature* [1972], pp. 184-5). More recently, Lennard C. Davis has found the 'intentionality' behind the evolution of the form a literary historical myth (*Factual Fictions:The Origins of the English Novel* [1983], pp. 192-3; see also Clive Probyn, *English Fiction of the Eighteenth Century, 1700-1789* [1987], pp. 149-81, and Gary Kelly, *English Fiction of the Romantic Period, 1789-1830* [1988], pp. 1-23).

The more we read in and on the period's writing the more we should be convinced that literary fame was dearly bought, and that both Samuel Johnson and Fanny Burney strove hard to pay their dues. For Fanny Burney, there was as much immediate risk in the delineation of characters such as the Harrels (*vide* the suicide) and Albany's clarion-calls for charity and justice (so nearly 'unrealistic') from *Cecilia*, and the savagery of Capt. Mirvan's baiting of Mme. Duval and Mr. Lovel from *Evelina*, as there was in the trenchant judgements in Johnson's *Lives of the Poets*. The hope is that the full context for such work can only be provided by the informal table talk recorded in this selection: rare sketches of that inhuman struggle between the head and heart and the determination to rise above it.

Any commentator on the friendship between Fanny Burney and Samuel Johnson is indebted to the early editorial skills of C.B. Tinker, Charlotte Barrett and Austin Dobson. As Tinker selected all but a few insignificant episodes of the growing relationship between the two for his compilation, it would be surprising if it bore no relationship to this one, but there are some significant departures. I have tried to supply more instances of Fanny Burney's guilty knowledge of Mrs. Thrale's attachment to Piozzi as well as her private anguish at the possible notoriety of authorship. Thanks to the invaluable labours of Joyce Hemlow, Katharine Balderston and W.J. Bate we also know far more about the motives and culture of the time plus the reactions of its main protagonists. Consequently, the order and range of annotation here assembled has only recently been possible. I owe special thanks for help in plugging various gaps to Julia Dashwood, Anne McDermott and Shearer West, and to the staff of the New York Public Library for their time and efforts at such short notice.

Note on the Text

As indicated in the text, the extracts are taken from four sources, Annie Raine Ellis' edition of Frances Burney's *Early Diary* (1889), Charlotte Barrett's edition of the Journal and Diaries, (1904), the Queeney *Letters* edited by the Marquis of Lansdowne (1934) and Mme. D'Arblay's edition of her father's *Memoirs* (1832). Whilst these versions may be taken as authoritative, there still remain certain *caveats* both about the Diary accounts and Charles Burney's *Memoirs*.

Ellis and Barrett worked from Burney's MSS., now split between the Berg Collection at the New York Public Library and Egerton MSS. 3690-3708 at the British Library (the Barrett Collection) with a few (later) entries in the Osborn Collection at Yale. (For the fullest account of the location of the MSS., see Hemlow, Appendix: 'The Burney Manuscripts: A Tentative Summary', pp. 496-502.) Whilst Burney claimed that the journal-letters were preserved for her son and heirs, there are obvious signs in the MSS. of extensive holograph editorial work. Joyce Hemlow discusses the difficulties in establishing the provenance of the Berg documents in the first volume of *The Journals and Letters of Fanny Burney (Madame d'Arblay)* (12 vols [1972-84], 1:xxxvi-lvi). The attempt to decipher the precise status of each of the annotations in the MSS. involves not only the separation of Burney's own second thoughts from her first, but also the identification of what may be Barrett's imposition of order or that of the editorial staff assembled by Henry Colborn who helped publish the first seven-volume *Diary and Letters* (1842-62). Until the completion of the Burney Papers Project directed by Lars Troide at McGill University any analysis (however detailed in part) must be provisional. The same order of problem arises in the extracts from Charles Burney's *Memoirs*, for, on her own admission, they are the fruit of Mme. D'Arblay's distant retrospective view (of nearly sixty years) and its inevitable re-ordering.

I have attempted to simplify the representation of this state of affairs by using square brackets in the *Early Diary* to indicate where there have been additions or where the original is indecipherable. As the account in *Memoirs* often provides parallels to many of the events in the *Early Diary*, I have occasionally interpolated the 1832 wording where necessary. The square brackets in the *Diary* extracts indicate passages present in the fuller first impression of the Barrett/Colborn edition but which were omitted from the second.

Dr. Johnson and Fanny Burney

28th March [1777]

My Dear Daddy,[1]

My dear father seemed well pleased at my returning to my time; and that is no small consolation and pleasure to me. So now, to our Thursday morning party.

Mrs. and Miss Thrale, Miss Owen, and Mr. Seward came long before *Lexiphanes*.[2] Mrs. Thrale is a very pretty woman still; she is extremely lively and chatty; has no supercilious or pedantic airs, and is really gay and agreeable. Her daughter[3] is about twelve years old, [stiff and proud], I believe, [or else shy and reserved: I don't yet know which]. Miss Owen, who is a relation, is good-humoured and *sensible enough;* she is a sort of butt, and, as such, a general favourite; for those sort of characters are prodigiously useful in drawing out the wit and pleasantry of others. Mr. Seward[4] is a very polite, agreeable young man.

My sister Burney[5] was invited to meet and play to them. The conversation was supported with a good deal of vivacity (N.B. my father being at home) for about half an hour, and then Hetty and *Sukey* for the first time *in public*, played a duet; and in the midst of this performance Dr. Johnson was announced. He is, indeed, very ill-favoured; is tall and stout; but stoops terribly; he is almost bent double. His mouth is almost [continually opening and shutting],[6] as if he was chewing. He has a strange method of frequently twirling his fingers, and twisting his hands. His body is in continual agitation, *see-sawing* up and down; his feet are never a moment quiet; and, in short, his whole person is in *perpetual motion*. His dress, too, considering the times, and that he had meant to put on his *best becomes*,[7] being engaged to dine in a large company, was as much out of the common road as his figure; he had a large wig, snuff-colour coat, and gold buttons, but no ruffles to his shirt, [doughty fists, and black worsted stockings.[8]] He is shockingly near-sighted, and did not, till she held out her hand to him, even know Mrs. Thrale.[9] He *poked his nose* over the keys of the harpsichord, till the duet was finished, and then my father introduced Hetty to him as an old acquaintance, and he [cordially] kissed her! When she was a little girl, he had made her a present of *The Idler*.

1

His attention, however, was not to be diverted five minutes from the books, as we were in the library; he pored over them, [shelf by shelf,] almost touching the backs of them with his eye-lashes, as he read their titles. At last, having fixed upon one, he began, without further ceremony, to read [to himself,] all the time standing at a distance from the company. We were [all] very much provoked, as we perfectly languished to hear him talk; but it seems he is the most silent creature, when not particularly drawn out,[10] in the world.

My sister then played another duet with my father; but Dr. Johnson was so deep in the *Encyclopédie* that, as he is very deaf, I question if he even knew what was going forward.[11] When this was over, Mrs. Thrale, in a laughing manner, said, "Pray, Dr. Burney, can you tell me what that song was and whose, which Savoi sung last night at Bach's[12] Concert, and which you did not hear?" My father confessed himself by no means so good a diviner, not having had time to consult the stars, though in the house of Sir Isaac Newton.[13] However, wishing to draw Dr. Johnson into some conversation, he told him the question. The Doctor, seeing his drift, good-naturedly put away his book, and said very drolly, "And pray, Sir, *who is Bach*? is he a piper?" Many exclamations of surprise, you will believe, followed this question. "Why you have read his name often in the papers," said Mrs. Thrale; and then [she] gave him some account of his Concert, and the number of fine performances she had heard at it.

"Pray," said he, [gravely,] "Madam, what is the expence?"

"O!" answered she, "much trouble and solicitation, to get a Subscriber's Ticket; — or else, half a Guinea."

"Trouble and solicitation," said he, "I will have nothing to do with; but I would be willing to give eighteen pence."[14]

[Ha! ha!]

Chocolate being then brought, we adjourned to the dining-room.[15] And here, Dr. Johnson being taken from the books, entered freely and most cleverly into conversation; though it is remarkable he never speaks at all, but when spoken to; nor does he ever *start*, though he so admirably *supports*, any subject.

The whole party was engaged to dine at Mrs. Montagu's.[16] Dr. Johnson said he had received the most flattering note he had ever read, or [that] any body else had ever read, by way of invitation. "Well! so have I too," cried Mrs. Thrale; "so if a note from Mrs. Montagu is to be boasted of, I beg mine may not be forgot."

"*Your* note," cried Dr. Johnson, "can bear no comparison with *mine*; I am *at the head of the Philosophers*, she says."

"And I," cried Mrs. Thrale, "*have all the Muses in my train!*"

"A fair battle," said my father. "Come, compliment for compliment, and see who will hold out longest."

"O! I am afraid for Mrs. Thrale," cried Mr. Seward; "for I know Mrs. Montagu exerts all her forces, when she attacks Dr. Johnson."

"Oh, yes!" said Mrs. Thrale, "she has often, I know, flattered *him*, till he has been ready to faint."

"Well, ladies," said my father, "you must get him between you to-day, and see which can lay on the paint thickest, Mrs. Thrale or Mrs. Montagu."

"I had rather," cried the Doctor, [drily,] "go to Bach's Concert!"

After this, they talked of Mr. Garrick and his late exhibition before the King, to whom and [to] the Queen and Royal Family he read Lethe[17] *in character, c'est à dire*, in different voices, and theatrically. Mr. Seward gave us an account of a Fable, which Mr. Garrick had written, by way of prologue or Introduction, upon the occasion. In this he says, that a blackbird, grown old and feeble, droops his wings, etc. etc., and gives up singing; but being called upon by the eagle, his voice recovers its powers, his spirits revive, he sets age at defiance, and sings better than ever. The application is obvious.

"There is not," said Dr. Johnson, "much of the spirit of *fabulosity* in this Fable; for the *call* of an eagle never yet had much tendency to restore the voice of a *black-bird*! Tis true that the fabulists frequently make the *wolves* converse with the *lambs*; but, when the conversation is over, the *lambs* are sure to be eaten! And so the *eagle* may entertain the *blackbird*; but the entertainment always ends in a feast for the *eagle*."

"They say," cried Mrs. Thrale, "that Garrick was extremely hurt at the coolness of the King's applause, and did not find his reception such as he expected."

"He has been so long accustomed," said Mr. Seward, "to the thundering approbation of the Theatre, that a mere 'Very well,' must necessarily and naturally disappoint him."

"Sir," said Dr. Johnson, "he should not, in a Royal apartment, expect the hallowing and clamour of the One Shilling Gallery. The King, I doubt not, gave him as much applause, as was rationally his due; and, indeed, great and uncommon as is the merit of Mr. Garrick, no man will be bold enough to assert he has not had his just proportion both of fame and of profit. He has long reigned the unequalled favourite of the public; and therefore nobody will mourn his hard fate, if the King and the Royal Family were not transported into rapture, upon hearing him read Lethe. Yet Mr. Garrick will complain to his friends, and his friends will lament the King's want of feeling and taste; — and then Mr. Garrick will [kindly] *excuse* the King. He will say that [His Majesty] might be thinking of something else; that the affairs of America might occur to him; or some subject of more importance than Lethe; but, though he will say this himself, he will not forgive his friends, if they do not contradict him!"

But now that I have written this satire, it is but just both to Mr. Garrick and to Dr. Johnson, to tell you what he said of him afterwards, when he discriminated[18] his character with equal candour[19] and humour.

"Garrick," said he, "is accused of vanity; but few men would have borne such unremitting prosperity with greater, if with equal moderation. He is accused, too, of avarice; but, were he not, he would be accused of just the contrary; for he now lives rather as *a prince* than an actor; but the frugality[20] he practised, when he first appeared in the world, and which, even then was perhaps beyond his necessity, has marked his character ever since; and now, though his table, his equipage, and manner of living, are all the most expensive, and equal to those of a nobleman, yet the original stain still blots his name! Though, had he not fixed upon himself the charge of avarice, he would long since have been reproached with luxury and with living beyond his station in magnificence and splendour."

Another time he said of him, "Garrick never enters a room, but he regards himself as the object of general attention, from whom the entertainment of the company is expected; and true it is, that he seldom disappoints them; for he has infinite humour, a very just proportion of wit, and more convivial pleasantry, than almost any other man. But then *off*, as well as *on* the Stage, he is always an Actor; for he thinks it so incumbent upon him to be sportive, that his gaiety becomes mechanical [from being] habitual, and he can exert his spirits at all times alike, without consulting his real disposition to hilarity.

[*Early Diary*, ii, 152-8]

July 20... I have also had a letter from Susanne. She informs me that my father, when he took the books back to Streatham,21 actually acquainted Mrs. Thrale with my secret.[22] He took an opportunity, when they were alone together, of saying that upon her recommendation, he had himself, as well as my mother, been reading *Evelina*.

"Well!" cried she, "and is it not a very pretty book? and a very clever book? and a very comical book?"

"Why," answered he, " 'tis well enough; but I have something to tell you about it."

"Well? what?" cried she; "has Mrs. Cholmondeley[23] found out the author?"

"No," returned he, "not that I know of; but I believe *I* have, though but very lately."

"Well, pray let's hear!" cried she eagerly, "I want to know him of all things."

How my father must laugh at the *him*! He then, however, undeceived her in regard to that particular, by telling her it was "*our Fanny!*" for she knows all about all our family, as my father talks to her of his domestic concerns without any reserve.

A hundred handsome things, of course, followed; and she afterwards read some of the comic parts to Dr. Johnson, Mr. Thrale, and whoever came near her. How I should have quivered had I been there! but they tell me that Dr. Johnson laughed as heartily as my father himself did.

[*Diary*, i, 46]

August 3. — I have an immensity to write. Susan has copied me a letter which Mrs. Thrale has written to my father, upon the occasion of returning my mother two novels by Madame Riccoboni.[24] It is so honourable to me, and so sweet in her, that I must copy it for my faithful journal.

Wednesday, 22 [July], 1778,
"Streatham.

"Dear Sir — I forgot to give you the novels home in your carriage which I now send by Mr. Abingdon's. *Evelina* certainly excels *them* far enough, both in probability of story, elegance of sentiment, and general power over the mind, whether exerted in humour or pathos. Add to this, that Riccoboni is a veteran author, and all she ever can be; but I cannot tell what might not be expected from *Evelina*, was she to try her genius at Comedy. So far had I written of my letter, when Mr. Johnson returned home, full of the praises of the *Book* I had lent him, and protesting there were passages in it which might do *honour* to Richardson. We talk of it for ever, and he feels ardent after the *dénouement;* he could not get *rid* of the Rogue, he said! I lent him the second volume, and he is now busy with the other two (*sic*). You must be more a philosopher, and less a father, than I wish you, not to be pleased with this letter; — and the giving such pleasure yields to nothing but receiving it. Long my Dear Sir, may you live to enjoy the just praises of your children! and long may they live to deserve and delight such a parent! These are things that you would say in verse; but Poetry implies Fiction, and all this is naked truth.

"Give my letter to my little friend, and a warm invitation to come and eat fruit while the season lasts. My Compliments to Mrs. Burney, and kindest wishes to all your flock, etc."

[How sweet, how amiable in this charming woman is her desire of making my dear father satisfied with his scribbler's attempt! I do, indeed, feel the most grateful love for her.]

But Dr. Johnson's approbation! — it almost crazed me with agreeable surprise — it gave me such a flight of spirits, that I danced a jig to Mr. Crisp, without any preparation, music, or explanation — to his no small amazement and diversion. I left him, however, to make his own comments upon my friskiness, without affording him the smallest assistance.

Susan also writes me word, that when my father went last to Streatham, Dr. Johnson was not there, but Mrs. Thrale told him, that when he gave her the first volume of *Evelina,* which she had lent him, he said, "Why, madam, why, what a charming book you lent me!" and eagerly inquired for the rest. He was particularly pleased with the Snow-hill scenes, and said that Mr. Smith's vulgar gentility was admirably portrayed; and when Sir Clement joins them,[25] he said there was a shade of character prodigiously well marked. Well may it be said, that the greatest minds are ever the most candid to the inferior set! I think I should love Dr. Johnson for such lenity to a poor mere worm in literature, even if I were not myself the identical grub he has obliged.

Susan has sent me a little note which has really been less pleasant to me, because it has alarmed me for my future concealment. It is from Mrs. Williams,[26] an exceedingly pretty poetess, who has the misfortune to be blind, but who has, to make some amends, the honour of residing in the house of Dr. Johnson: for though he lives almost wholly at Streatham, he always keeps his apartments in town, and this lady acts as mistress of his house.

"July 25,

"Mrs. Williams sends compliments to Dr. Burney, and begs he will intercede with Miss Burney to do her the favour to lend her the reading of *Evelina.*"

[I was quite confounded at this request, which proves that Mrs. Thrale has told Dr. Johnson of my secret, and that he has told Mrs. Williams, and that she has told the person whoever it be, whom she got to write the note.

I instantly scrawled a hasty letter to town to entreat my father would be so good as to write to her, to acquaint her with my earnest and unaffected desire to remain unknown.

And yet,] though I am frightened at this affair, I am by no means insensible to the honour which I receive from the certainty that Dr. Johnson must have spoken very well of the book, to have induced Mrs. Williams to send to our house for it. [She has known my father indeed for some years, but not with any intimacy; and I never saw her, though the perusal of her poems has often made me wish to be acquainted with her.]

I now come to last Saturday evening, when my beloved father came to Chessington, in full health, charming spirits, and all kindness, openness, and entertainment.

[I inquired what he had done about Mrs. Williams. He told me he went to her himself at my desire, for if he had written she could not herself have read the note. She apologised very much for the liberty she had taken, and spoke highly of the book, though she had only heard the first volume, as she was dependent upon a lady's good nature and time for hearing any part of it; but she went so far as to say that "his daughter was certainly the first writer, in that way, now living!"]

In his way hither, he had stopped at Streatham, and he settled with Mrs. Thrale that he would call on her again in his way to town, and carry me with him! and Mrs. Thrale said, "We all long to know her."

I have been in a kind of twitter ever since, for there seems something very formidable in the idea of appearing as an authoress! I ever dreaded it, as it is a title which must raise more expectations than I have any chance of answering. Yet I am highly flattered by her invitation, and highly delighted in the prospect of being introduced to the Streatham society.

[*Diary*, i, 48-51]

London, August. — I have now to write an account of the most consequential day I have spent since my birth: namely, my Streatham visit.

Our journey to Streatham was the least pleasant part of the day, for the roads were dreadfully dusty, and I was really in the fidgets from thinking what my reception might be, and from fearing they would expect a less awkward and backward kind of person than I was sure they would find.

Mr. Thrale's house is white, and very pleasantly situated, in a fine paddock. Mrs. Thrale was strolling about, and came to us as we got out of the chaise.

["Ah," cried she, "I hear Dr. Burney's voice! And you have brought your daughter? — well, now you are good!"]

She then received me, taking both my hands, and with mixed politeness and cordiality welcoming me to Streatham. She led me into the house, and addressed herself almost wholly for a few minutes to my father, as if to give me an assurance she did not mean to regard me as a show, or to distress or frighten me by drawing me out. Afterwards she took me upstairs, and showed me the house, and said she had very much wished to see me at Streatham, and should always think herself much obliged to Dr. Burney for his goodness in bringing me, which she looked upon as a very great favour.

But though we were some time together, and though she was so very civil, she did not *hint* at my book, and I love her very much more than ever for her delicacy in avoiding a subject which she could not but see would have greatly embarrassed me.

When we returned to the music-room we found Miss Thrale was with my father. Miss Thrale is a very fine girl, about fourteen years of age, but cold and reserved, though full of knowledge and intelligence.

Soon after, Mrs. Thrale took me to the library; she talked a little while upon common topics, and then, at last, she mentioned *Evelina*.

"Yesterday at supper," said she, "we talked it all over, and discussed all your characters; but Dr. Johnson's favourite is Mr. Smith. He declares the fine gentleman *manqué* was never better drawn; and he acted him[27] all the evening, saying he was 'all for the ladies!' He repeated whole scenes by heart.[28] I declare I was astonished at him. Oh you can't imagine how much he is pleased with the book; he 'could not get rid of the rogue,' he told me. But was it not droll," said she, "that I should recommend it to Dr. Burney? and tease him, so innocently, to read it?"

I now prevailed upon Mrs. Thrale to let me amuse myself, and she went to dress. I then prowled about to choose some book, and I saw, upon the reading-table, *Evelina*. — I had just fixed upon the new translation of Cicero's Lælius[29] when the library-door was opened, and Mr. Seward entered. I instantly put away my book, because I dreaded being thought studious and affected. He offered his service to find anything for me, and then, in the same breath, ran on to speak of the book with which I had myself "favoured the world!"

The exact words he began with I cannot recollect, for I was actually confounded by the attack; and his abrupt manner of letting me know he was *au fait* equally astonished and provoked me. How different from the delicacy of Mr. and Mrs. Thrale!

When we were summoned to dinner, Mrs. Thrale made my father and me sit on each side of her. I said that I hoped I did not take Dr. Johnson's place; for he had not yet appeared.

"No," answered Mrs. Thrale, "he will sit by you, which I am sure will give him great pleasure."

Soon after we were seated, this great man entered. I have so true a veneration for him, that the very sight of him inspires me with delight and reverence, notwithstanding the cruel infirmities to which he is subject; for he has almost perpetual convulsive movements, either of his hands, lips, feet, or knees, and sometimes of all together.

Mrs. Thrale introduced me to him, and he took his place. We had a noble dinner, and a most elegant dessert. Dr. Johnson, in the middle of dinner, asked Mrs. Thrale what was in some little pies that were near him.

"Mutton," answered she, "so I don't ask you to eat any, because I know you despise it."

"No, madam, no," cried he; "I despise nothing that is good of its sort; I am too proud now to eat of it. Sitting by Miss Burney makes me very proud to-day!"

"Miss Burney," said Mrs. Thrale, laughing, "you must take great care of your heart if Dr. Johnson attacks it; for I assure you he is not often successless."

"What's that you say, madam?" cried he; "are you making mischief between the young lady and me already?"

A little while after he drank Miss Thrale's health and mine, and then added:

" 'Tis a terrible thing that we cannot wish young ladies well, without wishing them to become old women!"

"But some people," said Mr. Seward, "are old and young at the same time, for they wear so well that they never look old."

"No, sir, no," cried the Doctor, laughing; "that never yet was; you might as well say that they are at the same time tall and short. I remember an epitaph to that purpose, which is in —."

(I have quite forgot what, — and also the name it was made upon, but the rest I recollect exactly:)

> "——— lies buried here;
> So early wise, so lasting fair,
> That none, unless her years you told,
> Thought her a child, or thought her old."

Mrs. Thrale then repeated some lines in French, and Dr. Johnson some more in Latin. An epilogue of Mr. Garrick's to *Bonduca*[30] was then mentioned, and Dr. Johnson said it was a miserable performance, and everybody agreed it was the worst he has ever made.

"And yet," said Mr. Seward, "it has been very much admired; but it is in praise of English valour, and so I suppose the subject made it popular."

"I don't know, sir," said Dr. Johnson, "anything about the subject, for I could not read on till I came to it; I got through half a dozen lines, but I could observe no other subject than eternal dulness. I don't know what is the matter with David; I am afraid he is grown superannuated, for his prologues and epilogues used to be incomparable."[31]

"Nothing is so fatiguing," said Mrs. Thrale, "as the life of a wit: he and Wilkes[32] are the two oldest men of their ages I know; for they have both worn themselves out, by being eternally on the rack to give entertainment to others."

"David, madam," said the Doctor, "looks much older than he is; for his face has had double the business of any other man's; it is never at rest; when he speaks one minute, he has quite a different countenance to what he assumes the next; I don't believe he ever kept the same look for half an hour together, in the whole course of his life; and such an eternal, restless, fatiguing play of the muscles, must certainly wear out a man's face before its real time."

"Oh yes," cried Mrs. Thrale, "we must certainly make some allowance for such wear and tear of a man's face."[33]

The next name that was started, was that of Sir John Hawkins:[34] and Mrs. Thrale said, "Why now, Dr. Johnson, he is another of those whom you suffer nobody to abuse but yourself; Garrick is one, too; for if any other person speaks against him, you brow-beat him in a minute!"

"Why, madam," answered he, "they don't know when to abuse him, and when to praise him; I will allow no man to speak ill of David that he does not deserve; and as to Sir John, why really I believe him to be an honest man at the bottom: but to be sure he is penurious, and he is mean, and it must be owned he has a degree of brutality, and a tendency to savageness, that cannot easily be defended."

We all laughed, as he meant we should, at this curious manner of speaking in his favour, and he then related an anecdote that he said he knew to be true in regard to his meanness. He said that Sir John and he once belonged to the same club,[35] but that as he eat no supper after the first night of his admission, he desired to be excused paying his share.

"And was he excused?"

"Oh yes; for no man is angry at another for being inferior to himself! we all scorned him, and admitted his plea. For my part I was such a fool as to pay my share for wine, though I never tasted any.[36] But Sir John was a most *unclubable*[37] man!"

[How delighted was I to hear this master of languages so unaffectedly and socially and good-naturedly make words, for the promotion of sport and good-humour.]

"And this," continued he, "reminds me of a gentleman and lady with whom I travelled once; I suppose I must call them gentleman and lady, according to form, because they travelled in their own coach and four horses. But at the first inn where we stopped, the lady called for – a pint of ale! and when it came, quarrelled with the waiter for not giving full measure. – Now, Madame Duval[38] could not have done a grosser thing!"

Oh, how everybody laughed! and to be sure I did not glow at all, nor munch fast, nor look on my plate, nor lose any part of my usual composure! But how grateful do I feel to this dear Dr. Johnson, for never naming me and the book as belonging one to the other, and yet making an allusion that showed his thoughts led to it, and, at the same time, that seemed to justify the character as being natural! But, indeed, the delicacy I met with from him, and from all the Thrales, was yet more flattering to me than the praise with which I have heard they have honoured my book.

After dinner, when Mrs. Thrale and I left the gentlemen, we had a conversation that to me could not but be delightful, as she was all good-humour, spirits, sense and *agreeability*. Surely, I may make words, when at a loss, if Dr. Johnson does.[39]

[However I shall not attempt to write any more particulars of this day – than which I have never known a happier, because the chief subject

that was started and kept up, was an invitation for me to Streatham, and
a desire that I might accompany my father thither next week, and stay with
them some time.]

We left Streatham at about eight o'clock, and Mr. Seward, who
handed me into the chaise, added his interest to the rest, that my father
would not fail to bring me again next week to stay with them some time.
In short I was loaded with civilities from them all. And my ride home was
equally happy with the rest of the day, for my kind and most beloved father
was so happy in *my* happiness, and congratulated me so sweetly that he
could, like myself, think on no other subject: [and he told me that, after
passing through such a house as that, I could have nothing to
fear — meaning for my book, my honoured book.]

Yet my honours stopped not here; for Hetty, who with her *sposo*[40]
was here to receive us, told me she had lately met Mrs. Reynolds,[41] sister
of Sir Joshua; and that she talked very much and very highly of a new novel
called *Evelina*; though without a shadow of suspicion as to the scribbler;
and not contented with her own praise, she said that Sir Joshua, who
began it one day when he was too much engaged to go on with it, was so
much caught, that he could think of nothing else, and was quite absent all
the day, not knowing a word that was said to him: and, when he took it up
again, found himself so much interested in it, that he sat up all night to
finish it!

Sir Joshua, it seems, vows he would give fifty pounds to know the
author! I have also heard, by the means of Charles,[42] that other persons
have declared they *will* find him out!

This intelligence determined me upon going my-self to Mr.
Lowndes,[43] and discovering what sort of answers he made to such curious
inquirers as I found were likely to address him. But as I did not dare trust
myself to speak, for I felt that I should not be able to act my part well, I
asked my mother to accompany me.

                                                              [*Diary*, i, 53-61]

Streatham, Sunday, Aug. 23. — I know not how to express the fulness
of my contentment at this sweet place. All my best expectations are
exceeded, and you know they were not very moderate. If, when my dear
father comes, Susan and Mr. Crisp were to come too, I believe it would
require at least a day's pondering to enable me to form another wish.

Our journey was charming. The kind Mrs. Thrale would give courage
to the most timid. She did not ask me questions, or catechise me upon
what I knew, or use any means to draw me out, but made it her business
to draw herself out — that is, to start subjects, to support them herself, and
to take all the weight of the conversation, as if it behoved her to find me

entertainment. But I am so much in love with her, that I shall be obliged to run away from the subject, or shall write of nothing else.[44]

When we arrived here, Mrs. Thrale showed me my room, which is an exceedingly pleasant one, and then conducted me to the library, there to divert myself while she dressed.

Miss Thrale soon joined me: and I begin to like her. Mr. Thrale was neither well nor in spirits all day. Indeed, he seems not to be a happy man, though he has every means of happiness in his power. But I think I have rarely seen a very rich man with a light heart and light spirits.[45]

Dr. Johnson was in the utmost good humour.

There was no other company at the house all day.

After dinner, I had a delightful stroll with Mrs. Thrale, and she gave me a list of all her "good neighbours" in the town of Streatham, and said she was determined to take me to see Mr. T———,[46] the clergyman, who was a character I could not but be diverted with, for he had so furious and so absurd a rage for building, that in his garden he had as many temples, and summer houses, and statues as in the gardens of Stow, though he had so little room for them that they all seemed tumbling one upon another.

In short, she was all unaffected drollery and sweet good humour.

At tea we all met again, and Dr. Johnson was gaily sociable. He gave a very droll account of the children of Mr. Langton,[47]

"Who," he said, "might be very good children if they were let alone; but the father is never easy when he is not making them do something which they cannot do; they must repeat a fable, or a speech, or the Hebrew alphabet; and they might as well count twenty, for what they know of the matter: however, the father says half, for he prompts every other word. But he could not have chosen a man who would have been less entertained by such means."

"I believe not!" cried Mrs. Thrale: "nothing is more ridiculous than parents cramming their children's nonsense down other people's throats. I keep mine as much out of the way as I can."

"Yours, madam," answered he, "are in nobody's way; no children can be better managed or less troublesome; but your fault is, a too great perverseness in not allowing anybody to give them anything. Why should they not have a cherry or a gooseberry as well as bigger children?"

"Because they are sure to return such gifts by wiping their hands upon the giver's gown or coat, and nothing makes children more offensive. People only make the offer to please the parents, and they wish the poor children at Jericho when they accept it."

"But, madam, it is a great deal more offensive to refuse them. Let those who make the offer look to their own gowns and coats, for when you interfere, they only wish *you* at Jericho."

"It is difficult," said Mrs. Thrale, "to please everybody."

Indeed, the freedom with which Dr. Johnson condemns whatever he disapproves, is astonishing; and the strength of words he uses would, to most people, be intolerable; but, Mrs.Thrale seems to have a sweetness of disposition that equals all her other excellences, and far from making a point of vindicating herself, she generally receives his admonitions with the most respectful silence.

But I fear to say all I think at present of Mrs. Thrale, lest some flaws should appear by and by, that may make me think differently. And yet, why should I not indulge the *now*, as well as the *then*, since it will be with so much more pleasure? In short, I do think her delightful; she has talents to create admiration, good humour to excite love, understanding to give entertainment, and a heart which, like my dear father's, seems already fitted for another world. My own knowledge of her, indeed, is very little for such a character; but all I have heard, and all I see, so well agree, that I won't prepare myself for a future disappointment.

But to return. Mrs. Thrale then asked whether Mr. Langton took any better care of his affairs than formerly?[48]

"No, madam," cried the doctor, "and never will; he complains of the ill effects of habit, and rests contentedly upon a confessed indolence. He told his father himself that he had 'no turn to economy'; but a thief might as well plead that he had 'no turn to honesty.' "

Was not that excellent?

At night, Mrs. Thrale asked if I would have anything? I answered, "No"; but Dr. Johnson said,

"Yes: she is used, madam, to suppers; she would like an egg or two, and a few slices of ham, or a rasher — a rasher, I believe, would please her better."

How ridiculous! However, nothing could persuade Mrs. Thrale not to have the cloth laid: and Dr. Johnson was so facetious, that he challenged Mr. Thrale to get drunk!

"I wish," said he, "my master[49] would say to me, Johnson, if you will oblige me, you will call for a bottle of Toulon, and then we will set to it, glass for glass, till it is done; and after that, I will say, Thrale, if you will oblige me, you will call for another bottle of Toulon, and then we will set to it, glass for glass, till that is done: and by the time we should have drunk the two bottles, we should be so happy, and such good friends, that we should fly into each other's arms, and both together call for the third!"

I ate nothing, that they might not again use such a ceremony with me. Indeed, their late dinners forbid suppers, especially as Dr. Johnson made me eat cake at tea, for he held it till I took it, with an odd or absent complaisance.

He was extremely comical after supper, and would not suffer Mrs. Thrale and me to go to bed for near an hour after we made the motion.[50]

The Cumberland[51] family was discussed. Mrs. Thrale said that Mr. Cumberland was a very amiable man in his own house; but as a father mighty simple; which accounts for the ridiculous conduct and manners of his daughters, concerning whom we had much talk, and were all of a mind; for it seems they used the same rude stare to Mrs. Thrale that so much disgusted us at Mrs. Ord's: she says that she really concluded something was wrong, and that, in getting out of the coach, she had given her cap some unlucky cuff, — by their merciless staring.

I told her that I had not any doubt, when I had met with the same attention from them, but that they were calculating the exact cost of all my dress. Mrs. Thrale then told me that, about two years ago, they were actually hissed out of the playhouse, on account of the extreme height of their feathers!

Dr. Johnson instantly composed an extempore dialogue between himself and Mr. Cumberland upon this subject, in which he was to act the part of a provoking condoler:

"Mr. Cumberland (I should say), how monstrously ill-bred is a playhouse mob! How I pitied poor Miss Cumberlands about that affair!"

"What affair?" cries he, for he has tried to forget it.

"Why," says I, "that unlucky accident they met with some time ago."

"Accident? what accident, sir?"

"Why, you know, when they were hissed out of the playhouse — you remember the time — oh, the English mob is most insufferable! they are boors, and have no manner of taste!"

Mrs. Thrale accompanied me to my room, and stayed chatting with me for more than an hour...

...Now for this morning's breakfast.

Dr. Johnson, as usual, came last into the library; he was in high spirits, and full of mirth and sport. I had the honour of sitting next to him; and now, all at once, he flung aside his reserve, thinking, perhaps, that it was time I should fling aside mine.

Mrs. Thrale told him that she intended taking me to Mr. T———'s.[52]

"So you ought, madam," cried he; "'tis your business to be Cicerone[53] to her."

Then suddenly he snatched my hand, and kissing it,

"Ah!" he added, "they will little think what a tartar[54] you carry to them!"

"No, that they won't!" cried Mrs. Thrale; "Miss Burney looks so meek and so quiet, nobody would suspect what a comical girl she is; but I believe she has a great deal of malice at heart."

"Oh, she's a toad![55]" cried the doctor, laughing — "a sly young rogue! with her Smiths and her Branghtons!"

"Why, Dr. Johnson," said Mrs. Thrale, "I hope you are very well this morning! if one may judge by your spirits and good humour, the fever you threatened us with is gone off."

He had complained that he was going to be ill last night.

"Why no, madam, no," answered he, "I am not yet well; I could not sleep at all; there I lay restless and uneasy, and thinking all the time of Miss Burney. Perhaps I have offended her, thought I; perhaps she is angry; I have seen her but once, and I talked to her of a rasher! — Were you angry?"

I think I need not tell you my answer.

"I have been endeavouring to find some excuse," continued he, "and, as I could not sleep, I got up, and looked for some authority for the word; and I find, madam, it is used by Dryden: in one of his prologues, he says — 'And snatch a homely rasher from the coals.'[56] So you must not mind me, madam; I say strange things, but I mean no harm."

I was almost afraid he thought I was really idiot enough to have taken him seriously; but, a few minutes after, he put his hand on my arm, and shaking his head, exclaimed,

"Oh, you are a sly little rogue! — what a Holborn beau have you drawn!"

"Ay, Miss Burney," said Mrs. Thrale, "the Holborn beau is Dr. Johnson's favourite; and we have all your characters by heart, from Mr. Smith up to Lady Louisa."[57]

"Oh, Mr. Smith, Mr. Smith is the man!" cried he, laughing violently. "Harry Fielding never drew so good a character! — such a fine varnish of low politeness! — such a struggle to appear a gentleman! Madam, there is no character better drawn anywhere — in any book or by any author."

I almost poked myself under the table. Never did I feel so delicious a confusion since I was born! But he added a great deal more, only I cannot recollect his exact words, and I do not choose to give him mine.

"Come, come," cried Mrs. Thrale, "we'll torment her no more about her book, for I see it really plagues her. I own I thought for awhile it was only affectation, for I'm sure if the book were mine I should wish to hear of nothing else. But we shall teach her in time how proud she ought to be of such a performance."

"Ah, madam," cried the Doctor, "be in no haste to teach her that; she'll speak no more to us when she knows her own weight."

"Oh, but, sir," cried she, "if Mr. Thrale has his way, she will become our relation, and then it will be hard if she won't acknowledge us."

You may think I stared, but she went on,

"Mr. Thrale says nothing would make him half so happy as giving Miss Burney to Sir J———— L————."[58]

Mercy! what an exclamation did I give. I wonder you did not hear me to St. Martin's Street. However, she continued,

"Mr. Thrale says, Miss Burney seems more formed to draw a husband to herself, by her humour when gay, and her good sense when serious, than almost anybody he ever saw."

"He does me much honour," cried I: though I cannot say I much enjoyed such a proof of his good opinion as giving me to Sir J———— L————; but Mr. Thrale is both his uncle and his guardian, and thinks, perhaps, he would do a mutual good office in securing me so much money, and his nephew a decent companion. Oh, if he knew how little I require with regard to money—how much to even bear with a companion! But he was not brought up with such folks as my father, my Daddy Crisp, and my Susan, and does not know what indifference to all things but good society such people as those inspire.

"My master says a very good speech," cried the doctor, "if Miss Burney's husband should have anything in common with herself; but I know not how we can level her with Sir J———— L————, unless she would be content to put her virtues and talents in a scale against his thousands: and poor Sir J———— must give cheating weight even then! However, if we bestow such a prize upon him, he shall settle his whole fortune on her."

Ah! thought I, I am more mercenary than you fancy me, for not even that would bribe me high enough.

Before Dr. Johnson had finished his *éloge*,[59] I was actually on the ground, for there was no standing it, — or sitting it, rather: and Mrs. Thrale seemed delighted for me.

"I assure you," she said, "nobody can do your book more justice than Dr. Johnson does: and yet, do you remember, sir, how unwilling you were to read it? He took it up, just looked at the first letter, and then put it away, and said, 'I don't think I have any taste for it!'—but when he was going to town, I put the first volume into the coach with him; and then, when he came home, the very first words he said to me were 'Why, Madam, this Evelina is a charming creature!'— and then he teased me to know who she married, and what became of her,—and I gave him the rest. For my part, I used to read it in bed, and could not part with it: I laughed at the second, and I cried at the third; but what a trick was that of Dr. Burney's, never to let me know whose it was till I had read it! Suppose it had been something I had not liked! Oh, it was a vile trick!"

"No, madam, not at all!" cried the doctor, "for, in that case, you would never have known;—all would have been safe, for he would neither have told you who wrote it, nor Miss Burney what you said of it."

Some time after the Doctor began laughing to himself, and then, suddenly turning to me, he called out, "Only think, Polly! Miss has danced with a lord!"[60]

"Ah, poor Evelina!" cried Mrs. Thrale, "I see her now in Kensington Gardens. What she must have suffered! Poor girl! what fidgets she must have been in! And I know Mr. Smith, too, very well; — I always have him before me at the Hampstead Ball, dressed in a white coat, and a tambour waistcoat, worked in green silk.[61] Poor Mr. Seward! Mr. Johnson made him so mad t'other day! 'Why, Seward,' said he, 'how smart you are dressed! why, you only want a tambour waistcoat to look like Mr. Smith.' But I am very fond of Lady Louisa; I think her as well drawn as any character in the book; so fine, so affected, so languishing; and, at the same time so insolent!"

She then ran on with several of her speeches.

Some time after, she gave Dr. Johnson a letter from Dr. Jebb,[62] concerning one of the gardeners who is very ill. When he had read it, he grumbled violently to himself, and put it away with marks of displeasure.

"What's the matter, sir!" said Mrs. Thrale; "do you find any fault with the letter?"

"No, madam, the letter's well enough, if the man knew how to write his own name; but it moves my indignation to see a gentleman take pains to appear a tradesman.[63] Mr. Branghton would have written his name with just such beastly flourishes."

"Ay, well," said Mrs. Thrale, "he is a very agreeable man, and an excellent physician, and a great favourite of mine, and so he is of Miss Burney's."

"Why, I have no objection to the man, madam, if he would write his name as he ought to do."

"Well, it does not signify," cried Mrs. Thrale; "but the commercial fashion of writing gains ground every day, for all Miss Burney abuses it, with her Smiths and her Branghtons. Does not the great Mr. Pennant[64] write like a clerk, without any pronouns? and does not everybody flourish their names till nobody can read them?"

After this they talked over a large party of company who are invited to a formal and grand dinner for next Monday, and among others Admiral Montague[65] was mentioned. The doctor, turning to me, with a laugh, said,

"You must mark the old sailor, Miss Burney; he'll be a character."

"Ah!" cried Mrs. Thrale, who was going out of the room, "how I wish you would hatch up a comedy between you! do, fall to work!"

A pretty proposal! to be sure Dr. Johnson would be very proud of such a fellow-labourer!

As soon as we were alone together, he said,

"These are as good people as you can be with; you can go to no better house; they are all good nature; nothing makes them angry."

As I have always heard from my father that every individual at Streatham spends the morning alone, I took the first opportunity of absconding to my room, and amused myself in writing till I tired. About noon, when I went into the library, book hunting, Mrs. Thrale came to me.

We had a very nice confab about various books, and exchanged opinions and imitations of Baretti; [66] she told me many excellent tales of him, and I, in return, related my stories.

She gave me a long and very entertaining account of Dr. Goldsmith, who was intimately known here; but in speaking of "The Goodnatured Man", when I extolled my favourite Croaker, I found that admirable character was a downright theft from Dr. Johnson. Look at the *Rambler*, and you will find Suspirius is the man, and that not merely the idea, but the particulars of the character, are all stolen thence![67]

While we were yet reading this *Rambler*, Dr. Johnson came in: we told him what we were about.

"Ah, madam!" cried he, "Goldsmith was not scrupulous; but he would have been a great man had he known the real value of his own internal resources."

"Miss Burney," said Mrs. Thrale, "is fond of his *Vicar of Wakefield*: and so am I; – don't you like it, sir?"

"No, madam, it is very faulty; there is nothing of real life in it, and very little of nature. It is a mere fanciful performance."[68]

He then seated himself upon a sofa, and calling to me, said, "Come, – Evelina, – come and sit by me."

I obeyed; and he took me almost in his arms, – that is, one of his arms, for one would go three times, at least, round me, – and, half-laughing, half-serious, he charged me to "be a good girl!"

"But, my dear," continued he with a very droll look, "what makes you so fond of the Scotch? I don't like you for that; I hate these Scotch, and so must you. I wish Branghton had sent the dog to jail! That Scotch dog Macartney."[69]

"Why, sir," said Mrs. Thrale, "don't you remember he says he would, but that he should get nothing by it?"

"Why, ay, true," cried the doctor, see-sawing very solemnly, "that, indeed, is some palliation for his forbearance. But I must not have you so fond of the Scotch, my little Burney; make your hero what you will but a Scotchman. Besides, you write Scotch – you say 'the one,' – my dear, that's not English. Never use that phrase again."

"Perhaps," said Mrs. Thrale, "it may be used in Macartney's letter, and then it will be a propriety."[70]

"No, madam, no!" cried he; "you can't make a beauty of it; it is in the third volume; put it in Macartney's letter, and welcome! — that, or anything that is nonsense."

"Why, surely," cried I, "the poor man is used ill enough by the Branghtons."

"But Branghton," said he, "only hates him because of his wretchedness, — poor fellow! — But, my dear love, how should he ever have eaten a good dinner before he came to England?"

And then he laughed violently at young Branghton's idea.

"Well," said Mrs. Thrale, "I always liked Macartney; he is a very pretty character, and I took to him, as the folks say."

"Why, madam," answered he. "I like Macartney myself. Yes, poor fellow, I liked the man, but I love not the nation."

And then he proceeded, in a dry manner, to make at once sarcastic reflections on the Scotch and flattering speeches to me, for Macartney's firing at the national insults of young Branghton: his stubborn resolution in not owning, even to his bosom friend, his wretchedness of poverty; and his fighting at last for the honour of his nation, when he resisted all other provocations; he said, were all extremely well marked.

We stayed with him till just dinner time, and then we were obliged to run away and dress; but Dr. Johnson called out to me as I went —

"Miss Burney, I must settle that affair of the Scotch with you at our leisure."

At dinner we had the company, or rather the presence, for he did not speak two words, of Mr. E———[71] the clergyman, I believe, of Streatham. And afterwards, Mrs. Thrale took the trouble to go with me to the T———'s.

[Dr. Johnson, who has a love of social converse that nobody, without living under the same roof with him, would suspect, quite begged us not to go till he went to town; but as we were hatted and ready, Mrs. Thrale only told him she rejoiced to find him so jealous of our companies, and then away we whisked, — she, Miss Thrale, and my ladyship.]

I could write some tolerable good sport concerning this visit, but that I wish to devote all the time I can snatch for writing, to recording what passes here[; themes of mere ridicule offer everywhere].

We got home late, and had the company of Mr. E———, and of Mr. Rose Fuller,[72] a young man who lives at Streatham, and is nephew of the famous Rose Fuller; and whether Dr. Johnson did not like them, or whether he was displeased that we went out, or whether he was not well, I know not; but he never opened his mouth, except in answer to a question, till he bid us good-night.

Saturday Morning. – Dr. Johnson was again all himself; and so civil to me! – even admiring how I dressed myself! Indeed, it is well I have so much of his favour; for it seems he always speaks his mind concerning the dress of ladies, and all ladies who are here obey his injunctions implicitly, and alter whatever he disapproves. This is a part of his character that much surprises me: but notwithstanding he is sometimes so absent, and always so near sighted, he scrutinises into every part of almost everybody's appearance. They tell me of a Miss Brown,[73] who often visits here, and who has a slovenly way of dressing. "And when she comes down in the morning," says Mrs. Thrale, "her hair will be all loose, and her cap half off; and then Dr. Johnson, who sees something is wrong, and does not know where the fault is, concludes it is in the cap, and says, 'My dear, what do you wear such a vile cap for?' 'I'll change it, sir,' cries the poor girl, 'if you don't like it.' 'Ay, do,' he says; and away runs poor Miss Brown; but when she gets on another, it's the same thing, for the cap has nothing to do with the fault. And then she wonders Dr. Johnson should not like the cap, for she thinks it very pretty. And so on with her gown, which he also makes her change; but if the poor girl were to change through all her wardrobe, unless she could put her things on better, he would still find fault."

When Dr. Johnson was gone, she told me of my mother's[74] being obliged to change her dress.

"Now," said she, "Mrs. Burney had on a very pretty linen jacket and coat, and was going to church; but Dr. Johnson, who, I suppose, did not like her in a jacket, saw something was the matter, and so found fault with the linen: and he looked and peered, and then said, 'Why, madam, this won't do! you must not go to church so!' So away went poor Mrs. Burney and changed her gown! And when she had done so, he did not like it, but he did not know why; so he told her she should not wear a black hat and cloak in summer! Oh, how he did bother poor Mrs. Burney! and himself too, for if the things had been put on to his mind, he would have taken no notice of them."

"Why," said Mr. Thrale, very drily, "I don't think Mrs. Burney a very good dresser."

"Last time she came," said Mrs. Thrale, "she was in a white cloak, and she told Dr. Johnson she had got her old white cloak scoured on purpose to oblige him! 'Scoured!' says he, 'ay, – have you, madam?' – so he see-sawed, for he could not for shame find fault, but he did not seem to like the scouring."

[So I think myself amazingly fortunate to be approved by him; for, if he disliked, alack-a-day, how could I change! But he has paid me some very fine compliments upon this subject.

I was very sorry when the doctor went to town, though Mrs. Thrale made him promise to return to Monday's dinner; and he has very affectionately invited me to visit him in the winter, when he is at home: and he talked to me a great deal of Mrs. Williams, and gave me a list of her works, and said I must visit them; — which I am sure I shall be very proud of doing.]

And now let me try to recollect an account he gave us of certain celebrated ladies of his acquaintance: an account which, had you heard from himself, would have made you die with laughing, his manner is so peculiar, and enforces his humour so originally.

It was begun by Mrs. Thrale's apologising to him for troubling him with some question she thought trifling — Oh, I remember! We had been talking of colours, and of the fantastic names given to them, and why the palest lilac should be called a *soupir étouffé;* and when Dr. Johnson came in she applied to him.

"Why, madam," said he with wonderful readiness, "it is called a stifled sigh because it is checked in its progress, and only half a colour."

I could not help expressing my amazement at his universal readiness upon all subjects, and Mrs. Thrale said to him,

"Sir, Miss Burney wonders at your patience with such stuff; but I tell her you are used to me, for I believe I torment you with more foolish questions than anybody else dares do."

"No, madam," said he, "you don't torment me; — you tease me, indeed, sometimes."

"Ay, so I do, Dr. Johnson, and I wonder you bear with my nonsense."

"No, madam, you never talk nonsense; you have as much sense, and more wit, than any woman I know!"

"Oh," cried Mrs. Thrale, blushing, "it is my turn to go under the table this morning, Miss Burney!"

"And yet," continued the doctor, with the most comical look, "I have known all the wits, from Mrs. Montagu down to Bet Flint!"[75]

"Bet Flint!" cried Mrs. Thrale; "pray, who is she?"

"Oh, a fine character, madam! She was habitually a slut and a drunkard, and occasionally a thief and a harlot."

"And, for Heaven's sake, how came you to know her?"

"Why, madam, she figured in the literary world, too! Bet Flint wrote her own life, and called herself Cassandra, and it was in verse; — it began:

'When Nature first ordained my birth,
A diminutive I was born on earth:

And then I came from a dark abode
Into a gay and gaudy world.'

"So Bet brought me her verses to correct; but I gave her half a crown, and she liked it as well. Bet had a fine spirit; — she advertised for a husband, but she had no success, for she told me no man aspired to her! Then she hired very handsome lodgings and a footboy; and she got a harpsichord, but Bet could not play; however she put herself in fine attitudes, and drummed."

Then he gave an account of another of these geniuses, who called herself by some fine name, I have forgotten what.

"She had not quite the same stock of virtue," continued he, "nor the same stock of honesty as Bet Flint; but I suppose she envied her accomplishments, for she was so little moved by the power of harmony, that while Bet Flint thought she was drumming very divinely, the other jade had her indicted for a nuisance!"

"And pray what became of her, sir?"

"Why, madam, she stole a quilt from the man of the house, and he had her taken up: but Bet Flint had a spirit not to be subdued; so when she found herself obliged to go to jail, she ordered a sedan chair and bid her footboy walk before her. However, the boy proved refractory, for he was ashamed, though his mistress was not."

"And did she ever get out of jail again, sir?"

"Yes, madam; when she came to her trial the judge acquitted her.[76] 'So now,' she said to me, 'the quilt is my own, and now I'll make a petticoat of it.' Oh, I loved Bet Flint!"

Oh, how we all laughed! Then he gave an account of another lady, who called herself Laurinda, and who wrote verses and stole furniture; but he had not the same affection for her, he said, though she too "was a lady who had high notions of honour."

Then followed the history of another, who called herself Hortensia, and who walked up and down the park repeating a book of Virgil.

"But," said he, "though I know her story, I never had the good fortune to see her."

After this he gave us an account of the famous Mrs. Pinkethman.[77] "And she," he said, "told me she owed all her misfortunes to her wit; for she was so unhappy as to marry a man who thought himself also a wit, though I believe she gave him not implicit credit for it, but it occasioned much contradiction and ill-will."

"Bless me, sir!" cried Mrs. Thrale, "how can all these vagabonds contrive to get at *you*, of all people?"[78]

"Oh, the dear creatures!" cried he, laughing heartily, "I can't but be glad to see them!"

"Why, I wonder, sir, you never went to see Mrs. Rudd[79] among the rest?"

"Why, madam, I believe I should," said he, "if it was not for the newspapers; but I am prevented many frolics that I should like very well, since I am become such a theme for the papers."

Now would you ever have imagined this? Bet Flint, it seems, once took Kitty Fisher[80] to see him, but to his no little regret he was not at home. "And Mrs. Williams," he added, "did not love Bet Flint, but Bet Flint made herself very easy about that."

How Mr. Crisp would have enjoyed this account! He gave it all with so droll a solemnity, and it was all so unexpected, that Mrs. Thrale and I were both almost equally diverted.

Streatham, August 26. — My opportunities for writing grow less and less, and my materials more and more. After breakfast, I have scarcely a moment that I can spare all day.

Mrs. Thrale I like more and more. Of all the people I have ever seen since I came into the "gay and gaudy world,"[81] I never before saw the person who so strongly resembles our dear father. I find the likeness perpetually; she has the same natural liveliness, the same general benevolence, the same rare union of gaiety and of feeling in her disposition. And so kind is she to me! She told me at first that I should have all my mornings to myself, and therefore I have actually studied to avoid her, lest I should be in her way; but since the first morning she seeks me, sits with me, saunters with me in the park, or compares notes over books in the library; and her conversation is delightful; it is so entertaining, so gay, so enlivening, when she is in spirits, and so intelligent and instructive when she is otherwise, that I almost as much wish to record all she says, as all Dr. Johnson says.

Proceed — no! Go back, my muse, to Thursday.

Dr. Johnson came home to dinner.

In the evening he was as lively and full of wit and sport as I have ever seen him; and Mrs. Thrale and I had him quite to ourselves; for Mr. Thrale came in from giving an election dinner[82] (to which he sent two bucks and six pine apples) so tired, that he neither opened his eyes nor mouth, but fell fast asleep. Indeed, after tea he generally does.

Dr. Johnson was very communicative concerning his present work of the *Lives of the Poets*;[83] Dryden is now in the press, and he told us he had been just writing a dissertation upon Hudibras.

He gave us an account of Mrs. Lenox.[84] Her *Female Quixote* is very justly admired here. But Mrs. Thrale says that though her books are generally approved, nobody likes her. I find she, among others, waited on Dr. Johnson upon her commencing writer, and he told us that, at her request, he carried her to Richardson.

"Poor Charlotte Lenox!" continued he; "when we came to the house, she desired me to leave her, 'for,' says she 'I am under great restraint in your presence, but if you leave me alone with Richardson I'll give you a very good account of him': however, I fear poor Charlotte was disappointed, for she gave me no account at all!"

He then told us of two little productions of our Mr. Harris,[85] which we read; they are very short and very clever: one is called *Fashion*, the other *Much Ado*, and they are both of them full of a sportive humour, that I had not suspected to belong to Mr. Harris, the learned grammarian.

Some time after, turning suddenly to me, he said, "Miss Burney, what sort of reading do you delight in? History? – travels? – poetry? – or romances?"

"Oh, sir!" cried I, "I dread being catechised by you. I dare not make any answer, for I fear whatever I should say would be wrong!"

"Whatever you should say – how's that?"

"Why, not whatever I should – but whatever I could say."

He laughed, and to my great relief spared me any further questions upon the subject. Indeed, I was very happy I had the presence of mind to evade him as I did, for I am sure the examination which would have followed, had I made any direct answer, would have turned out sorely to my discredit.

"Do you remember, sir," said Mrs. Thrale, "how you tormented poor Miss Brown[86] about reading?"

"She might soon be tormented, madam," answered he, "for I am not yet quite clear she knows what a book is."

"Oh, for shame!" cried Mrs. Thrale, "she reads not only English, but French and Italian. She was in Italy a great while."

"Pho!" exclaimed he; "Italian, indeed! Do you think she knows as much Italian as Rose Fuller does English?"

"Well, well," said Mrs. Thrale, "Rose Fuller is a very good young man, for all he has not much command of language, and though he is silly enough, yet I like him very well, for there is no manner of harm in him."

Then she told me that he once said, "Dr. Johnson's conversation is so instructive that I'll ask him a question. 'Pray, sir, what is Palmyra? I have often heard of it, but never knew what it was.' 'Palmyra, sir?' said the doctor; 'why, it is a hill in Ireland, situated in a bog, and has palm-trees at the top, when it is called Palm mire.' "[87]

Whether or not he swallowed this account, I know not yet.

"But Miss Brown," continued she, "is by no means such a simpleton as Dr. Johnson supposes her to be; she is not very deep, indeed, but she is a sweet, and a very ingenuous girl, and nobody admired Miss Streatfield more. But she made a more foolish speech to Dr. Johnson than she would have done to anybody else, because she was so frightened and embarrassed that she knew not what she said. He asked her some question about reading, and she did, to be sure, make a very silly answer; but she was so perplexed and bewildered, that she hardly knew where she was, and so she said the beginning of a book was as good as the end, or the end as good as the beginning, or some such stuff; and Dr. Johnson told her of it so often, saying, 'Well, my dear, which part of a book do you like best now?' that poor Fanny Brown burst into tears!"

"I am sure I should have compassion for her," cried I; "for nobody would be more likely to have blundered out such, or any such speech, from fright and terror."

"You?" cried Dr. Johnson. "No; you are another thing; she who could draw Smiths and Branghtons, is quite another thing."

Mrs. Thrale then told some other stories of his degrading opinion of us poor fair sex; I mean in general, for in particular he does them noble justice. Among others, was a Mrs. Somebody who spent a day here once, and of whom he asked, "Can she read?"

"Yes, to be sure," answered Mrs. Thrale; "we have been reading together this afternoon."

"And what book did you get for her?"

"Why, what happened to lie in the way, Hogarth's *Analysis of Beauty*."[88]

"Hogarth's *Analysis of Beauty*! What made you choose that?"

"Why, sir, what would you have had me take?"

"What she could have understood — *Cow-hide*, or *Cinderella*!"

"Oh, Dr. Johnson!" cried I; " 'tis not for nothing you are feared!"

"Oh, you're a rogue!" cried he, laughing, "and they would fear *you* if they knew you!"

"That they would," said Mrs. Thrale; "but she's so shy they don't suspect her. Miss P——— gave her an account of all her dress, to entertain her, t'other night! To be sure she was very lucky to fix on Miss Burney for such conversation! But I have been telling her she must write a comedy;[89] I am sure nobody could do it better. Is it not true, Dr. Johnson?"

I would fain have stopt her, but she was not to be stopped, and ran on saying such fine things! though we had almost a struggle together; and she said at last:

"Well, authors may say what they will of modesty; but I believe Miss Burney is really modest about her book, for her colour comes and goes every time it is mentioned."

I then escaped to look for a book which we had been talking of, and Dr. Johnson, when I returned to my seat, said he wished Richardson had been alive.

"And then," he added, "she should have been introduced to him — though I don't know neither — Richardson would have been afraid of her."[90]

"Oh yes! that's a likely matter," quoth I.

"It's very true," continued he; "Richardson would have been really afraid of her; there is merit in *Evelina* which he could not have borne. No; it would not have done! unless, indeed, she would have flattered him prodigiously. Harry Fielding, too, would have been afraid of her; there is nothing so delicately finished in all Harry Fielding's works, as in *Evelina*!"[91] Then shaking his head at me, he exclaimed, "Oh, you little character-monger, you!"

Mrs. Thrale then returned to her charge, and again urged me about a comedy; and again I tried to silence her, and we had a fine fight together; till she called upon Dr. Johnson to back her.

"Why, madam," said he, laughing, "she *is* writing one. What a rout[92] is here, indeed! she is writing one upstairs all the time. Who ever knew when she began *Evelina*? She is working at some drama, depend upon it."

"True, true, O king!" thought I.

"Well, that will be a sly trick!" cried Mrs. Thrale; "however, you know best, I believe, about that, as well as about every other thing."

Friday was a very full day. In the morning we began talking of *Irene*, and Mrs. Thrale made Dr. Johnson read some passages which I had been remarking as uncommonly applicable to the present times. He read several speeches, and told us he had not ever read so much of it before since it was first printed.[93]

"Why, there is no making you read a play," said Mrs. Thrale, "either of your own, or any other person. What trouble had I to make you hear Murphy's *Know your own Mind*![94] 'Read rapidly, read rapidly,' you cried, and then took out your watch to see how long I was about it![95] Well, we won't serve Miss Burney so, sir; when we have her comedy we will do it all justice."...

...The day was passed most agreeably. In the evening we had, as usual, a literary conversation. I say we, only because Mrs. Thrale will make me take some share, by perpetually applying to me; and, indeed, there can be no better house for rubbing up the memory, as I hardly ever read, saw, or heard of any book that by some means or other has not been mentioned here.

Mr. Lort[96] produced several curious MSS. of the famous Bristol Chatterton;[97] among others, his will, and divers verses written against Dr. Johnson,[98] as a placeman and pensioner; all which he read aloud, with a steady voice and unmoved countenance.

I was astonished at him; Mrs. Thrale not much pleased; Mr. Thrale silent and attentive; and Mr. Seward was slily laughing. Dr. Johnson himself, listened profoundly and laughed openly. Indeed, I believe he wishes his abusers no other than a good dinner, like Pope.

Just as we had got our biscuits and toast-and-water, which make the Streatham supper, and which, indeed, is all there is any chance of eating after our late and great dinners, Mr. Lort suddenly said,

"Pray, ma'am, have you heard anything of a novel that runs about a good deal, called *Evelina?*"

What a ferment did this question, before such a set, put me in!

I did not know whether he spoke to me, or Mrs. Thrale; and Mrs. Thrale was in the same doubt, and as she owned, felt herself in a little palpitation for me, not knowing what might come next. Between us both, therefore, he had no answer.

"It has been recommended to me," continued he; "but I have no great desire to see it, because it has such a foolish name. Yet I have heard a great deal of it, too."

He then repeated *Evelina* — in a very languishing and ridiculous tone.

My heart beat so quick against my stays that I almost panted with extreme agitation, from the dread either of hearing some horrible criticism, or of being betrayed; and I munched my biscuit as if I had not eaten for a fortnight.

I believe the whole party were in some little consternation; Dr. Johnson began see-sawing; Mr. Thrale awoke; Mr. E————[99], who I fear has picked up some notion of the affair from being so much in the house, grinned amazingly; and Mr. Seward, biting his nails and flinging himself back in his chair, I am sure had wickedness enough to enjoy the whole scene.

Mrs. Thrale was really a little fluttered, but without looking at me, said,

"And pray what, Mr. Lort, what have you heard of it?"

[Now, had Mrs. Thrale not been flurried, this was the last question she should have ventured to ask before me. Only suppose what I must feel when I heard it.]

"Why, they say," answered he, "that it's an account of a young lady's first entrance into company, and of the scrapes she gets into; and they say there's a great deal of character in it, but I have not cared to look in it, because the name is so foolish — *Evelina!*"

"Why foolish, sir?" cried Dr. Johnson. "Where's the folly of it?"

"Why, I won't say much for the name myself," said Mrs. Thrale, "to those who don't know the reason of it, which I found out, but which nobody else seems to know."

She then explained the name from Evelyn, according to my own meaning.[100]

"Well," said Dr. Johnson, "if that was the reason, it is a very good one."

"Why, have you had the book here?" cried Mr. Lort, staring.

"Ay, indeed, have we," said Mrs. Thrale; "I read it when I was last confined, and I laughed over it, and I cried over it!"

"Oh, ho!" said Mr. Lort, "this is another thing! If you have had it here, I will certainly read it."

"Had it? ay," returned she; "and Dr. Johnson, who would not look at it at first, was so caught by it when I put it in the coach with him that he has sung its praises ever since, — and he says Richardson would have been proud to have written it."

"Oh, ho! this is a good hearing!" cried Mr. Lort; "if Dr. Johnson can read it, I shall get it with all speed."

"You need not go far for it," said Mrs. Thrale, "for it's now upon yonder table."

I could sit still no longer; there was something so awkward, so uncommon, so strange in my then situation, that I wished myself a hundred miles off; and, indeed, I had almost choked myself with the biscuit, for I could not for my life swallow it; and so I got up, and, as Mr. Lort went to the table to look at *Evelina*, I left the room, and was forced to call for water to wash down the biscuit, which literally stuck in my throat.

I heartily wished Mr. Lort at Jerusalem. Notwithstanding all this may read as nothing, because all that was said was in my favour, yet at the time, when I knew not what might be said, I suffered the most severe trepidation.

I did not much like going back, but the moment I recovered breath I resolved not to make bad worse by staying longer away: but at the door of the room I met Mrs. Thrale, who, asking me if I would have some water, took me into a back room, and burst into a hearty fit of laughter.

"This is very good sport!" cried she; " the man is as innocent about the matter as a child, and we shall hear what he says to it to-morrow at breakfast. I made a sign to Dr. Johnson and Seward not to tell him."

When she found I was not in a humour to think it such good sport as she did, she grew more serious, and, taking my hand, kindly said—

"May you never, Miss Burney, know any other pain than that of hearing yourself praised! and I am sure *that* you must often feel."

[When I told her how much I dreaded being discovered, and besought her not to betray me any further, she again began laughing, and openly declared she should not consult me about the matter. I was really uneasy — nay, quite uncomfortable, — for the first time I have been so

since I came thither, but as we were obliged soon to return, I could not
then press my request with the earnestness I wished. But she told me that
as soon as I had left the room when Mr. Lort took up *Evelina*, he
exclaimed contemptuously, "Why, it's printed for Lowndes!" and that Dr.
Johnson then told him there were things and characters in it more than
worthy of Fielding.

"Oh ho!" cried Mr. Lort, "what, is it better than Fielding?"

"Harry Fielding," answered Dr. Johnson, "knew nothing but the shell
of life."

"So you, ma'am," added the flattering Mrs. Thrale, "have found the
kernel."[101]

Are they all mad? or do they want to make me so?]

When we returned, to my great joy, they were talking of other
subjects, yet I could not sufficiently recover myself the whole evening to
speak one word but in answer; [for the dread of the criticisms which Mr.
Lort might innocently make the next day, kept me in a most
uncomfortable state of agitation.]

When Mrs. Thrale and I retired, she not only, as usual, accompanied
me to my room, but stayed with me at least an hour, talking over the affair.
I seized with eagerness this favourable opportunity of conjuring her not
merely not to tell Mr. Lort my secret, but ever after never to tell anybody.
For a great while she only laughed, saying –

"Poor Miss Burney! so you thought just to have played and sported
with your sisters and cousins, and had it all your own way; but now you
are in for it! But if you will be an author and a wit, you must take the
consequences!"

But when she found me seriously urgent and really frightened, she
changed her note, and said,

"Oh, if I find you are in earnest in desiring concealment, I shall quite
scold you; for if such a desire does not proceed from affectation, 'tis from
something worse."

"No, indeed," cried I, "not from affectation; for my conduct has been
as uniform in trying to keep snug as my words, and I never have wavered:
I never have told anybody out of my own family, nor half the bodies in it.
And I have so long forborne making this request to you for no other
reason in the world but for fear you should think me affected."

"Well, I won't suspect you of affectation," returned she – "nay, I
can't, for you have looked like your namesake in the *Clandestine
Marriage*[102] all this evening, 'of fifty colours, I wow and purtest'; but when
I clear you of that, I leave something worse."

"And what, dear madam, what can be worse?"

"Why, an over-delicacy that may make you unhappy all your life.[103]
Indeed you must check it – you must get the better of it: for why should

you write a book, print a book, and have everybody read and like your book, and then sneak in a corner and disown it!"

"My printing it, indeed," said I, "tells terribly against me to all who are unacquainted with the circumstances that belonged to it, but I had so little notion of being discovered, and was so well persuaded that the book would never be heard of, that I really thought myself as safe, and meant to be as private, when the book was at Mr. Lowndes's, as when it was in my own bureau."

"Well, I don't know what we shall do with you! But indeed you must blunt a little of this delicacy, for the book has such success, that if you don't own it, somebody else will!"

Yet notwithstanding all her advice, and all her encouragement, I was so much agitated by the certainty of being known as a scribbler, that I was really ill all night and could not sleep.

When Mrs. Thrale came to me the next morning, she was quite concerned to find I had really suffered from my panics.

"Oh, Miss Burney," cried she, "what shall we do with you? This must be conquered; indeed this delicacy must be got over."

"Don't call it delicacy," cried I, "when I know you only think it folly."

"Why, indeed," said she, laughing, "it is not very wise!"

"Well," cried I, "if, indeed, I am in for it, why I must seriously set about reconciling myself—yet I never can!"

"We all love you," said the sweet woman, "we all love you dearly already; but the time will come when we shall all be proud of you – so proud, we shall not know where to place you! You must set about a comedy; and set about it openly; it is the true style of writing for you: but you must give up all these fears and this shyness; you must do it without any disadvantages; and we will have no more of such sly, sneaking, private ways!"

[I told her of my fright while at Chessington concerning Mrs. Williams, and of the letter I wrote to beg my father would hasten to caution her.

"And did he?" said she.

"Oh yes! directly."

"Oh, fie! I am ashamed of him! how can he think of humouring you in such maggots?[104] If the book had not been liked, I would have said nothing to it. But it is a sweet book, and the great beauty of it is that it reflects back all our own ideas and observations; for everybody must have met with some thing similiar to almost all the incidents."]

In short, had I been the child of this delightful woman, she could not have taken more pains to reconcile me to my situation: even when she laughed, she contrived, by her manner, still to reassure or to soothe me.

[We went down together. My heart was in my mouth as we got to the library, where all the gentlemen were waiting. I made Mrs. Thrale go in before me.

Mr. Lort was seated close to the door, *Evelina* in his hand. Mrs. Thrale began with asking how he found it? — I could not, if my life had depended on it, I am sure I could not, at that moment, have followed her in, and therefore, I skipped into the music-room.

However foolish all this may seem, the foolery occasioned me no manner of fun, for I was quite in an agony. However, as I met with Miss Thrale, in a few minutes we went into the library together.]

Dr. Johnson was later than usual this morning, and did not come down till our breakfast was over, and Mrs. Thrale had risen to give some orders, I believe: I, too, rose, and took a book at another end of the room. Some time after, before he had yet appeared, Mr. Thrale called out to me,

"So, Miss Burney, you have a mind to feel your legs before the doctor comes?"

"Why so?" cried Mr. Lort.

"Why, because when he comes she will be confined."

"Ay? — how is that?"

"Why, he never lets her leave him, but keeps her prisoner till he goes to his own room."

"Oh, ho!" cried Mr. Lort, "she is in great favour with him."

"Yes," said Mr. Seward, "and I think he shows his taste."

"I did not know," said Mr. Lort, "but he might keep her to help him in his *Lives of the Poets*, if she's so clever."

"And yet," said Mrs. Thrale, "Miss Burney never flatters him, though she is such a favourite with him; — but the tables are turned, for he sits and flatters her all day long."

"I don't flatter him," said I, "because nothing I could say would flatter him."

Mrs. Thrale then told a story of Hannah More,[105] which I think exceeds, in its severity, all the severe things I have yet heard of Dr. Johnson's saying.

When she was introduced to him, not long ago, she began singing his praise in the warmest manner, and talking of the pleasure and the instruction she had received from his writings, with the highest encomiums. For some time he heard her with that quietness which a long use of praise has given him: she then redoubled her strokes, and, as Mr. Seward[106] calls it, peppered still more highly: till, at length, he turned suddenly to her, with a stern and angry countenance, and said, "Madam, before you flatter a man so grossly to his face, you should consider whether or not your flattery is worth his having."

Mr. Seward then told another instance of his determination not to mince the matter, when he thought reproof at all deserved. During a visit of Miss Brown's to Streatham, he was inquiring of her several things that she could not answer; and, as he held her so cheap in regard to books,[107] he began to question her concerning domestic affairs — puddings, pies, plain work, and so forth. Miss Brown, not at all more able to give a good account of herself in these articles than in the others, began all her answers with, "Why, sir, one need not be obliged to do so, — or so," whatever was the thing in question. When he had finished his interrogatories, and she had finished her "need nots," he ended the discourse with saying, "As to your needs, my dear, they are so very many, that you would be frightened yourself if you knew half of them."...

...After breakfast on Friday, or yesterday, a curious trait occurred of Dr. Johnson's jocosity. It was while the talk ran so copiously upon their urgency that I should produce a comedy. While Mrs. Thrale was in the midst of her flattering persuasions, the doctor, see-sawing in his chair, began laughing to himself so heartily as to almost shake his seat as well as his sides. We stopped our confabulation, in which he had ceased to join, hoping he would reveal the subject of his mirth; but he enjoyed it inwardly, without heeding our curiosity, — till at last he said he had been struck with a notion that "Miss Burney would begin her dramatic career by writing a piece called 'Streatham'."

He paused, and laughed yet more cordially, and then suddenly commanded a pomposity to his countenance and his voice, and added, "Yes! 'Streatham — a Farce'."

[How little did I expect from this Lexiphanes,[108] this great and dreaded lord of English literature, a turn for burlesque humour.]

Streatham, September. — Our journey hither proved, as it promised, most sociably cheerful, and Mrs. Thrale opened still further upon the subject she began in St. Martin's Street, of Dr. Johnson's kindness towards me. To be sure she saw it was not totally disagreeable to me; though I was really astounded when she hinted at my becoming a rival to Miss Streatfield[109] in the doctor's good graces.

"I had a long letter," she said, "from Sophy Streatfield t'other day, and she sent Dr. Johnson her elegant edition of the 'Classics'; but when he had read the letter he said, 'She is a sweet creature, and I love her much; but my little Burney writes a better letter.' Now," continued she, "that is just what I wished him to say of you both."...

[*Diary*, i, 65-102]

...Before dinner, to my great joy, Dr. Johnson returned home from Warley Common.[110] I followed Mrs. Thrale into the library to see him, and he is so near-sighted that he took me for Miss Streatfield:[111] but he did not welcome me less kindly when he found his mistake, which Mrs. Thrale made known by saying, "No, 'tis Miss Streatfield's rival, Miss Burney."

At tea-time the subject turned upon the domestic economy of Dr. Johnson's own household. Mrs. Thrale has often acquainted me that his house is quite filled and overrun with all sorts of strange creatures, whom he admits for mere charity, and because nobody else will admit them – for his charity is unbounded – or, rather, bounded only by his circumstances.

The account he gave of the adventures and absurdities of the set was highly diverting, but too diffused for writing, though one or two speeches I must give. I think I shall occasionally theatricalise my dialogues.

Mrs. Thrale. – Pray, sir, how does Mrs. Williams like all this tribe?

Dr. Johnson. – Madam, she does not like them at all; but their fondness for her is not greater. She and De Mullin[112] quarrel incessantly; but as they can both be occasionally of service to each other, and as neither of them have any other place to go to, their animosity does not force them to separate.

Mrs. T. – And pray, sir, what is Mr. Macbean?[113]

Dr. J. – Madam, he is a Scotchman: he is a man of great learning, and for his learning I respect him, and I wish to serve him. He knows many languages, and knows them well; but he knows nothing of life. I advised him to write a geographical dictionary; but I have lost all hopes of his ever doing anything properly, since I found he gave as much labour to Capua as to Rome.

Mr. T. – And pray who is clerk of your kitchen, sir?

Dr. J. – Why, sir, I am afraid there is none; a general anarchy prevails in my kitchen, as I am told by Mr. Levat,[114] who says it is not now what it used to be!

Mrs. T. – Mr. Levat, I suppose, sir, has the office of keeping the hospital in health? for he is an apothecary.

Dr. J. – Levat, madam, is a brutal fellow, but I have a good regard for him; for his brutality is in his manners, not his mind.

Mr. T. – But how do you get your dinners drest?

Dr. J. – Why, De Mullin has the chief management of the kitchen; but our roasting is not magnificent, for we have no jack.

Mr. T. – No jack? Why, how do they manage without?

Dr. J. – Small joints, I believe, they manage with a string, and larger are done at the tavern. I have some thoughts (with a profound gravity) of buying a jack, because I think a jack is some credit to a house.

Mr. T. – Well, but you'll have a spit, too?

Dr. J. – No, sir, no; that would be superfluous; for we shall never use it; and if a jack is seen, a spit will be presumed!

Mrs. T. – But pray, sir, who is the Poll you talk of?[115] She that you used to abet in her quarrels with Mrs. Williams, and call out, "At her again, Poll! Never flinch, Poll"?

Dr. J. – Why, I took to Poll very well at first, but she won't do upon a nearer examination.

Mrs. T. – How came she among you, sir?

Dr. J. – Why, I don't rightly remember, but we could spare her very well from us. Poll is a stupid slut; I had some hopes of her at first; but, when I talked to her tightly and closely, I could make nothing of her; she was wiggle-waggle, and I could never persuade her to be categorical. I wish Miss Burney would come among us; if she would only give us a week, we should furnish her with ample materials for a new scene in her next work.

A little while after he asked Mrs. Thrale, who had read *Evelina* in his absence?

"Who?" cried she, – "why, Burke! – Burke sat up all night to finish it;[116] and Sir Joshua Reynolds is mad about it, and said he would give fifty pounds to know the author. But our fun was with his nieces – we made them believe I wrote the book,[117] and the girls gave me the credit of it at once."

"I am very sorry for it, madam," cried he, quite angrily, – "you were much to blame; deceits of that kind ought never to be practised; they have a worse tendency than you are aware of."[118]

Mr. T. – Why, don't frighten yourself, sir; Miss Burney will have all the credit she has a right to, for I told them whose it was before they went.

Dr. J. – But you were very wrong for misleading them for a moment; such jests are extremely blamable; they are foolish in the very act, and they are wrong, because they always leave a doubt upon the mind. What first passed will be always recollected by those girls, and they will never feel clearly convinced which wrote the book, Mrs. Thrale or Miss Burney.

Mrs. T. – Well, well, I am ready to take my Bible oath it was not me; and if that won't do, Miss Burney must take hers too.

I was then looking over the *Life of Cowley,* which he had himself given me to read, at the same time that he gave to Mrs. Thrale that of Waller. They are now printed, though they will not be published for some time.[119] But he bade me put it away.

"Do," cried he, "put away that now, and prattle with us; I can't make this little Burney prattle, and I am sure she prattles well; but I shall teach her another lesson than to sit thus silent before I have done with her."

"To talk," cried I, "is the only lesson I shall be backward to learn from you, sir."

"You shall give me," cried he, "a discourse upon the passions: come, begin! Tell us the necessity of regulating them, watching over and curbing them! Did you ever read Norris's *Theory of Love?*"[120]

"No, sir," said I, laughing, yet staring a little.

Dr. J.—Well, it is worth your reading. He will make you see that inordinate love is the root of all evil: inordinate love of wealth brings on avarice; of wine, brings on intemperance; of power, brings on cruelty; and so on. He deduces from inordinate love all human frailty.

Mrs. T.—To-morrow, sir, Mrs. Montagu dines here, and then you will have talk enough.

Dr. Johnson began to see-saw, with a countenance strongly expressive of inward fun, and after enjoying it some time in silence, he suddenly and with great animation, turned to me and cried,

"Down with her, Burney!—down with her!—spare her not!—attack her, fight her, and down with her at once! You are a rising wit, and she is at the top; and when I was beginning the world, and was nothing and nobody, the joy of my life was to fire at all the established wits;[121] and then everybody loved to halloo me on. But there is no game now; everybody would be glad to see me conquered: but then, when I was new, to vanquish the great ones was all the delight of my poor little dear soul! So at her, Burney—at her, and down with her!"

Oh, how we were all amused! By the way I must tell you that Mrs. Montagu is in very great estimation here, even with Dr. Johnson himself, when others do not praise her improperly. Mrs. Thrale ranks her as the first of women in the literary way. I should have told you that Miss Gregory, daughter of the Gregory[122] who wrote the *Letters*, or *Legacy of Advice*, lives with Mrs. Montagu, and was invited to accompany her.

"Mark now," said Dr. Johnson, "if I contradict her to-morrow. I am determined, let her say what she will, that I will not contradict her."

Mrs. T.—Why, to be sure, sir, you did put her a little out of countenance last time she came. Yet you were neither rough, nor cruel, nor ill-natured; but still, when a lady changes colour, we imagine her feelings are not quite composed.

Dr. J.—Why, madam, I won't answer that I shan't contradict her again, if she provokes me as she did then; but a less provocation I will withstand. I believe I am not high in her good graces already; and I begin (added he, laughing heartily) to tremble for my admission into her new house.[123] I doubt I shall never see the inside of it.

(Mrs. Montagu is building a most superb house.)

Mrs. T.—Oh, I warrant you, she fears you, indeed; but that, you know, is nothing uncommon; and dearly I love to hear your disquisitions; for certainly she is the first woman for literary knowledge in England, and if in England, I hope I may say in the world.

Dr. J. — I believe you may, madam. She diffuses more knowledge in her conversation than any woman I know, or, indeed, almost any man.

Mrs.T. — I declare I know no man equal to her, take away yourself and Burke, for that art. And you who love magnificence, won't quarrel with her, as everybody else does, for her love of finery.

Dr. J. — No, I shall not quarrel with her upon that topic. (Then, looking earnestly at me), "Nay," he added, "it's very handsome!"

"What, sir?" cried I, amazed.

"Why, your cap: — I have looked at it some time, and I like it much. It has not that vile bandeau[124] across it, which I have so often cursed."

Did you ever hear anything so strange? nothing escapes him. My Daddy Crisp is not more minute in his attentions: nay, I think he is even less so.

Mrs. T. — Well, sir, that bandeau you quarrelled with was worn by every woman at court the last birthday,[125] and I observed that all the men found fault with it.

Dr. J. — The truth is, women, take them in general, have no idea of grace. Fashion is all they think of. I don't mean Mrs. Thrale and Miss Burney, when I talk of women! — they are goddesses! — and therefore I except them.

Mrs. T. — Lady Ladd[126] never wore the bandeau, and said she never would, because it is unbecoming.

Dr. J. — (laughing). — Did not she? Then is Lady Ladd a charming woman, and I have yet hopes of entering into engagements with her!

Mrs. T. — Well, as to that I can't say; but to be sure, the only similitude I have yet discovered in you, is in size: there you agree mighty well.

Dr. J. — Why, if anybody could have worn the bandeau, it must have been Lady Ladd; for there is enough of her to carry it off; but you are too little for anything ridiculous; that which seems nothing upon a Patagonian, will become very conspicuous upon a Lilliputian, and of you there is so little in all, that one single absurdity would swallow up half of you.

Some time after, when we had all been a few minutes wholly silent, he turned to me and said,

"Come, Burney, shall you and I study our parts against Mrs. Montagu comes?"

"Miss Burney," cried Mr. Thrale, "you must get up your courage for this encounter! I think you should begin with Miss Gregory; and down with her first."

Dr. J. — No, no, always fly at the eagle! down with Mrs. Montagu herself! I hope she will come full of *Evelina*!

Wednesday. — At breakfast, Dr. Johnson asked me, if I had been reading his *Life of Cowley*?

"Oh yes," said I.

"And what do you think of it?"

"I am delighted with it," cried I; "and if I was somebody, instead of nobody, I should not have read it without telling you sooner what I think of it, and unasked."

Again, when I took up Cowley's 'Life', he made me put it away to talk. I could not help remarking how very like Dr. Johnson is to his writing; and how much the same thing it was to hear or to read him;[127] but that nobody could tell that without coming to Streatham, for his language was generally imagined to be laboured and studied, instead of the mere common flow of his thoughts.

"Very true," said Mrs. Thrale, "he writes and talks with the same ease, and in the same manner; but, sir (to him), if this rogue is like her book, how will she trim[128] all of us by and by! Now, she dainties us up with all the meekness in the world; but when we are away, I suppose she pays us off finely."

"My paying off," cried I, "is like the Latin of Hudibras,

...who never scanted,
His learning unto such as wanted;[129]

for I can figure like anything when I am with those who can't figure at all."

Mrs. T. — Oh, if you have any *mag*[130] in you, we'll draw it out!

Dr. J. — A rogue! she told me that if she was somebody instead of nobody, she would praise my book!

F. B. — Why, sir, I am sure you would scoff my praise.

Dr. J. — If you think that, you think very ill of me; but you don't think it.

Mrs. T. — We have told her what you said to Miss More, and I believe that makes her afraid.[131]

Dr. Johnson. — Well, and if she was to serve me as Miss More did, I should say the same thing to her. But I think she will not. Hannah More has very good intellects, too; but she has by no means the elegance of Miss Burney.

"Well," cried I, "there are folks that are to be spoilt, and folks that are not to be spoilt, as well in the world as in the nursery; but what will become of me, I know not."

Mrs. T. — Well, if you are spoilt, we can only say, nothing in the world is so pleasant as being spoilt.

Dr. J. — No, no; Burney will not be spoilt: she knows too well what praise she has a claim to, and what not, to be in any danger of spoiling.

F. B. — I do, indeed, believe I shall never be spoilt at Streatham, for it is the last place where I can feel of any consequence.

Mrs. T. – Well, sir, she is *our* Miss Burney, however; we were the first to catch her, and now we have got her, we will keep her. And so she is all our own.

Dr. J. – Yes, I hope she is; I should be very sorry to lose Miss Burney.

F. B. – Oh, dear! how can two such people sit and talk such——

Mrs. T. – Such stuff, you think? but Dr. Johnson's love——

Dr. J. – Love? no, I don't entirely love her yet; I must see more of her first; I have much too high an opinion of her to flatter her. I have, indeed, seen nothing of her but what is fit to be loved, but I must know her more. I admire her, and greatly too.

F. B. – Well, this is a very new style to me! I have long enough had reason to think myself loved, but admiration is perfectly new to me.

Dr. J. – I admire her for her observation, for her good sense, for her humour, for her discernment, for her manner of expressing them, and for all her writing talents.

I quite sigh beneath the weight of such praise from such persons – sigh with mixed gratitude for the present, and fear for the future; for I think I shall never, never be able to support myself long so well with them.

We could not prevail with him to stay till Mrs. Montagu arrived...

[*Diary*, i, 111-20]

...When dinner was upon table, I followed the procession, in a tragedy step, as Mr. Thrale will have it, into the dining-parlour. Dr. Johnson was returned.

The conversation was not brilliant, nor do I remember much of it; but Mrs. Montagu behaved to me just as I could have wished, since she spoke to me very little, but spoke that little with the utmost politeness. But Miss Gregory, though herself a very modest girl, quite stared me out of countenance, and never took her eyes off my face.

When Mrs. Montagu's new house was talked of, Dr. Johnson, in a jocose manner, desired to know if he should be invited to see it.

"Ay, sure," cried Mrs. Montagu, looking well pleased; "or else I shan't like it: but I invite you all to a house warming; I shall hope for the honour of seeing all this company at my new house next Easter day: I fix the day now that it may be remembered."

Everybody bowed and accepted the invite but me, and I thought fitting not to hear it; for I have no notion of snapping at invites from the eminent. But Dr. Johnson, who sat next to me, was determined I should be of the party, for he suddenly clapped his hand on my shoulder, and called out aloud –

"Little Burney, you and I will go together!"

"Yes, surely," cried Mrs. Montagu, "I shall hope for the pleasure of seeing 'Evelina'."

"*Evelina*?" repeated he; "has Mrs. Montagu then found out *Evelina*?"

"Yes," cried she, "and I am proud of it; I am proud that a work so commended should be a woman's."

Oh, how my face burnt!

"Has Mrs. Montagu," asked Dr. Johnson, "read *Evelina*?"

"No, sir, not yet; but I shall immediately, for I feel the greatest eagerness to read it."

"I am very sorry, madam," replied he, "that you have not read it already, because you cannot speak of it with a full conviction of its merit: which, I believe, when you have read it, you will find great pleasure in acknowledging."

Some other things were said, but I remember them not, for I could hardly keep my place: but my sweet, naughty Mrs. Thrale looked delighted for me.

I made tea as usual, and Mrs. Montagu and Miss Gregory seated themselves on each side of me.

"I can see," said the former, "that Miss Burney is very like her father, and that is a good thing, for everybody would wish to be like Dr. Burney. Pray, when you see him, give my best respects to him; I am afraid he thinks me a thief with his *Linguet*;[132] but I assure you I am a very honest woman, and I spent full three hours in looking for it."

"I am sure," cried Mrs. Thrale, "Dr. Burney would much rather you should have employed that time about some other book."

They went away very early, because Mrs. Montagu is a great coward in a carriage. She repeated her invitation as she left the room. So now that I am invited to Mrs. Montagu's, I think the measure of my glory full!

When they were gone, how did Dr. Johnson astonish me by asking if I had observed what an ugly cap Miss Gregory had on? And then taking both my hands, and looking at me with an expression of much kindness, he said,

"Well, Miss Burney, Mrs. Montagu now will read *Evelina*."

To read it he seems to think is all that is wanted, and, far as I am from being of the same opinion, I dare not to him make disqualifying speeches, because it might seem impertinent to suppose her more difficult to please than himself.

"You are very kind, sir," cried I, "to speak of it with so much favour and indulgence at dinner; yet I hardly knew how to sit it then, though I shall be always proud to remember it hereafter."

"Why, it is true," said he, kindly, "that such things are disagreeable to sit, nor do I wonder you were distressed; yet sometimes they are necessary."

Was this not very kind? I am sure he meant that the sanction of his good opinion, so publicly given to Mrs. Montagu, would in a manner stamp the success of my book; and though, had I been allowed to preserve the snugness I had planned, I need not have concerned myself at all about its fate, yet now that I find myself exposed with it, I cannot but wish it insured from disgrace.

"Well, sir," cried I, "I don't think I shall mind Mrs. Montagu herself now; after what you have said, I believe I should not mind even abuse from any one."

"No, no, never mind them!" cried he; "resolve not to mind them: they can do you no serious hurt."

Mrs. Thrale then told me such civil things. Mrs. Montagu, it seems, during my retreat, inquired very particularly what kind of book it was?

"And I told her," continued Mrs. Thrale, "that it was a picture of life, manners, and characters. 'But won't she go on?' says she; 'surely she won't stop here?'

" 'Why,' said I 'I want her to go on a new path — I want her to write a comedy.'

" 'But,' said Mrs. Montagu, 'one thing must be considered; Fielding, who was so admirable in novelwriting, never succeeded when he wrote for the stage.' "

"Very well said," cried Dr. Johnson; "that was an answer which showed she considered her subject."

[*Diary*, i, 123-6]

...*Monday, September 21.* — I am more comfortable here than ever; Dr. Johnson honours me with increasing kindness; Mr. Thrale is much more easy and sociable than when I was here before; I am quite jocose, whenever I please, with Miss Thrale; and the charming head and life of the house, her mother, stands the test of the closest examination, as well and as much to her honour as she does a mere cursory view. She is, indeed, all that is excellent and desirable in woman.

I have had a thousand delightful conversations with Dr. Johnson, who, whether he loves me or not, I am sure seems to have some opinion of my discretion, for he speaks of all this house to me with unbounded confidence, neither diminishing faults, nor exaggerating praise. Whenever he is below stairs he keeps me a prisoner, for he does not like I should quit the room a moment; if I rise he constantly calls out, "Don't you go, little Burney!"

Last night, when we were talking of compliments and gross speeches, Mrs. Thrale most justly said that nobody could make either like Dr. Johnson. "Your compliments, sir, are made seldom, but when they are made they have an elegance unequalled; but then when you are angry, who dares make speeches so bitter and so cruel?"

Dr. J. – Madam, I am always sorry when I make bitter speeches, and I never do it but when I am insufferably vexed.

Mrs. T. – Yes, sir; but you suffer things to vex you, that nobody else would vex at. I am sure I have had my share of scolding from you!

Dr. J. – It is true, you have; but you have borne it like an angel, and you have been the better for it.

Mrs. T. – That I believe, sir: for I have received more instruction from you than from any man, or any book: and the vanity that you should think me worth instructing, always overcame the vanity of being found fault with. And you had the scolding, and I the improvement.

F. B. – And I am sure both make for the honour of both.

Dr. J. – I think so too. But Mrs. Thrale is a sweet creature, and never angry; she has a temper the most delightful of any woman I ever knew.

Mrs. T. – This I can tell you, sir, and without any flattery – I not only bear your reproofs when present, but in almost everything I do in your absence, I ask myself whether you would like it, and what you would say to it. Yet I believe there is nobody you dispute with oftener than me.

F. B. – But you two are so well established with one another, that you can bear a rebuff that would kill a stranger.

Dr. J. – Yes; but we disputed the same before we were so well established with one another.

Mrs. T. – Oh, sometimes I think I shall die no other death than hearing the bitter things he says to others. What he says to myself I can bear, because I know how sincerely he is my friend, and that he means to mend me; but to others it is cruel.

Dr. J. – Why, madam, you often provoke me to say severe things, by unreasonable commendation.[133] If you would not call for my praise, I would not give you my censure; but it constantly moves my indignation to be applied to, to speak well of a thing which I think contemptible.

F. B. – Well, this I know, whoever I may hear complain of Dr. Johnson's severity, I shall always vouch for his kindness, as far as regards myself, and his indulgence.

Mrs. T. – Ay, but I hope he will trim you yet, too!

Dr. J. – I hope not: I should be very sorry to say anything that should vex my dear little Burney.

F. B. – If you did, sir, it would vex me more than you can imagine. I should sink in a minute.

Mrs. T.—I remember, sir, when we were travelling in Wales,[134] how you called me to account for my civility to the people; "Madam," you said, "let me have no more of this idle commendation of nothing. Why is it, that whatever you see, and whoever you see, you are to be so indiscriminately lavish of praise?" "Why, I'll tell you, sir," said I, "when I am with you, and Mr. Thrale, and Queeny, I am obliged to be civil for four!"

There was a cutter[135] for you! But this I must say, for the honour of both—Mrs. Thrale speaks to Dr. Johnson with as much sincerity (though with greater softness), as he does to her...

[*Diary*, i, 128-30]

...*Streatham, September 26.*—I have, from want of time, neglected my journal so long, that I cannot now pretend to go on methodically, and be particular as to dates.

Messrs. Stephen and Rose Fuller[136] stayed very late on Monday; the former talking very rationally upon various subjects, and the latter boring us with his systems and "those sort of things." Yet he is something of a favourite, "in that sort of way," at this house, because of his invincible good humour, and Mrs. Thrale says she would not change him as a neighbour for a much wiser man. Dr. Johnson says he would make a very good Mr. Smith:[137] " Let him but," he adds, "pass a month or two in Holborn, and I would desire no better."

The other evening the conversation fell upon Romney,[138] the painter, who has lately got into great business, and who was first recommended and patronised by Mr. Cumberland.

"See, madam," said Dr. Johnson, laughing, "what it is to have the favour of a literary man! I think I have had no hero a great while; Dr. Goldsmith was my last; but I have had none since his time till my little Burney came!"

"Ay, sir," said Mrs. Thrale, "Miss Burney is the heroine now; is it not really true, sir?"

"To be sure it is, my dear!" answered he, with a gravity that made not only me, but Mr. Thrale laugh heartily.

Another time, Mr. Thrale said he had seen Dr. Jebb,[139] "and he told me he was afraid Miss Burney would have gone into a consumption," said he; "but I informed him how well you are, and he committed you to my care; so I shall insist now upon being sole judge of what wine you drink."

(*N.B.*—He had often disputed this point.)

Dr. J.—Why, did Dr. Jebb forbid her wine?

F. B.—Yes, sir.

Dr. J.—Well, he was in the right; he knows how apt wits are to transgress that way. He was certainly right!

In this sort of ridiculous manner he *wits* me eternally. But the present chief sport with Mrs. Thrale is disposing of me in the holy state of matrimony, and she offers me whoever comes to the house. This was begun by Mrs. Montagu, who, it seems, proposed a match for me in my absence, with Sir Joshua Reynolds! — no less a man, I assure you!

When I was dressing for dinner, Mrs. Thrale told me that Mr. Crutchley[140] was expected.

"Who's he?" quoth I.

"A young man of very large fortune, who was a ward of Mr. Thrale. Queeny, what do you say of him for Miss Burney?"

"Him?" cried she; "no, indeed; what has Miss Burney done to have him?"

"Nay, believe me, a man of his fortune may offer himself anywhere. However, I won't recommend him."

"Why then, ma'am," cried I, with dignity, "I reject him!"

This Mr. Crutchley stayed till after breakfast the next morning. I can't tell you anything of him, because I neither like nor dislike him.

Mr. Crutchley was scarce gone, ere Mr. Smith[141] arrived. Mr. Smith is a second cousin of Mr. Thrale, and a modest pretty sort of young man.

He stayed till Friday morning. When he was gone,

"What say you to him, Miss Burney?" cried Mrs. Thrale — "I am sure I offer you variety."

"Why, I like him better than Mr. Crutchley, but I don't think I shall pine for either of them."

"Dr. Johnson," said Mrs. Thrale, "don't you think Jerry Crutchley very much improved?"

Dr. J. — Yes, madam, I think he is.

Mrs. T. — Shall he have Miss Burney?

Dr. J. — Why, I think not; at least I must know more of him; I must inquire into his connections, his recreations, his employments, and his character, from his intimates, before I trust Miss Burney with him. And he must come down very handsomely with a settlement. I will not have him left to his generosity; for as he will marry her for her wit, and she him for his fortune, he ought to bid well; and let him come down with what he will, his price will never be equal to her worth.

Mrs. T. — She says she likes Mr. Smith better.

Dr. J. — Yes, but I won't have her like Mr. Smith without the money, better than Mr. Crutchley with it. Besides, if she has Crutchley, he will use her well, to vindicate his choice. The world, madam, has a reasonable claim upon all mankind to account for their conduct; therefore, if with his great wealth he marries a woman who has but little, he will be more attentive to display her merit than if she was equally rich, — in order to show that the woman he has chosen deserves from the world all the respect and admiration it can bestow, or that else she would not have been his choice.

Mrs. T. — I believe young Smith is the better man.

F. B. — Well, I won't be rash in thinking of either; I will take some time for consideration before I fix.

Dr. J. — Why, I don't hold it to be delicate to offer marriage to ladies, even in jest, nor do I approve such sort of jocularity; yet for once I must break through the rules of decorum, and propose a match myself for Miss Burney. I therefore nominate Sir J——— L———.[142]

Mrs. T. — I'll give you my word, sir, you are not the first to say that, for my master, the other morning, when we were alone, said, "What would I give that Sir J——— L——— was married to Miss Burney; it might restore him to our family." So spoke his uncle and guardian.

F. B. — He, he! Ha, ha! He, he! Ha, ha!

Dr. J. — That was elegantly said of my master, and nobly said, and not in the vulgar way we have been saying it. And where, madam, will you find another man in trade who will make such a speech — who will be capable of making such a speech? Well, I am glad my master takes so to Miss Burney; I would have everybody take to Miss Burney, so as they allow me to take to her most! Yet I don't know whether Sir J——— L——— should have her, neither. I should be afraid for her; I don't think I would hand her to him.

F. B. — Why, now, what a fine match is here broken off!

Some time after, when we were in the library, he asked me very gravely if I loved reading?

"Yes," quoth I.

"Why do you doubt it, sir?" cried Mrs. Thrale.

"Because," answered he, "I never see her with a book in her hand. I have taken notice that she never has been reading whenever I have come into the room."

"Sir," quoth I courageously, "I am always afraid of being caught reading, lest I should pass for being studious or affected, and therefore instead of making a display of books, I always try to hide them, as is the case at this very time, for I have now your *Life of Waller* under my gloves behind me. However, since I am piqued to it, I'll boldly produce my voucher."

And so saying, I put the book on the table, and opened it with a flourishing air. And then the laugh was on my side, for he could not help making a droll face; and if he had known Kitty Cooke,[143] I would have called out, "There I had you, my lad!"

"And now," quoth Mrs. Thrale, "you must be more careful than ever of not being thought bookish, for now you are known for a wit and a *bel esprit*, you will be watched, and if you are not upon your guard, all the misses will rise up against you."

Dr. J. – Nay, nay, now it is too late. You may read as much as you will now, for you are in for it, – you are dipped over head and ears in the Castalian stream,[144] and so I hope you will be invulnerable.

Another time, when we were talking of the licentiousness of the newspapers, Dr. Johnson said,

"I wonder they have never yet had a touch at little Burney."

"Oh, Heaven forbid!" cried I: "I am sure if they did, I believe I should try the depth of Mr. Thrale's spring-pond."[145]

"No, no, my dear, no," cried he kindly, "you must resolve not to mind them; you must set yourself against them, and not let any such nonsense affect you."

"There is nobody," said Mrs. Thrale, "tempers the satirist with so much meekness as Miss Burney."

Satirist, indeed! is it not a satire upon words, to call me so?

"I hope to Heaven I shall never be tried," cried l, "for I am sure I should never bear it. Of my book they may say what they will and welcome, but if they touch at me I shall be——"

"Nay," said Mrs. Thrale, "if you are not afraid for the book, I am sure they can say no harm of the author."

"Never let them know," said Dr. Johnson, "which way you shall most mind them, and then they will stick to the book; but you must never acknowledge how tender you are for the author."...

[*Diary*, i, 131-7]

...Monday was the day for our great party; and the doctor came home, at Mrs. Thrale's request, to meet them...

...Lady Ladd; I ought to have begun with her.[146] I beg her ladyship a thousand pardons – though if she knew my offence, I am sure I should not obtain one. She is own sister to Mr. Thrale. She is a tall and stout woman, has an air of mingled dignity and haughtiness, both of which wear off in conversation. She dresses very youthfully and gaily, and attends to her person with no little complacency. She appears to me uncultivated in knowledge, though an adept in the manners of the world, and all that. She chooses to be much more lively than her brother; but liveliness sits as awkwardly upon her as her pink ribbons. In talking her over with Mrs. Thrale, who has a very proper regard for her, but who, I am sure, cannot be blind to her faults, she gave me another proof to those I have already had, of the uncontrolled freedom of speech which Dr. Johnson exercises to everybody, and which everybody receives quietly from him. Lady Ladd has been very handsome, but is now, I think, quite ugly – at least she has a sort of face I like not. Well, she was a little while ago dressed in so showy a manner as to attract the doctor's notice, and when he had looked at her some time he broke out aloud into this quotation:

With patches, paint, and jewels on,
Sure Phillis is not twenty-one!
But if at night you Phillis see,
The dame at least is forty-three!

I don't recollect the verses exactly, but such was their purport.

"However," said Mrs. Thrale, "Lady Ladd took it very good-naturedly, and only said,

" 'I know enough of that forty-three—I don't desire to hear any more of it!' "...

...In the evening the company divided pretty much into parties, and almost everybody walked upon the gravel-walk before the windows. I was going to have joined some of them, when Dr. Johnson stopped me, and asked how I did.

"I was afraid, sir," cried I, "you did not intend to know me again, for you have not spoken to me before since your return from town."

"My dear," cried he, taking both my hands, "I was not sure of you, I am so near-sighted,[147] and I apprehended making some mistake."

Then drawing me very unexpectedly towards him, he actually kissed me!

To be sure, I was a little surprised, having no idea of such facetiousness from him. However, I was glad nobody was in the room but Mrs. Thrale, who stood close to us, and Mr. Embry,[148] who was lounging on a sofa at the farthest end of the room, Mrs. Thrale laughed heartily, and said she hoped I was contented with his amends for not knowing me sooner.

A little after she said she would go and walk with the rest, if she did not fear for my reputation in being left with the doctor.

"However, as Mr. Embry is yonder, I think he'll take some care of you," she added.

"Ay, madam," said the doctor, "we shall do very well; but I assure you I shan't part with Miss Burney!"

And he held me by both hands; and when Mrs. Thrale went, he drew me a chair himself facing the window, close to his own; and thus *tête-à-tête* we continued almost all the evening. I say *tête-à-tête*, because Mr. Embry kept at an humble distance, and offered us no interruption. And though Mr. Seward soon after came in, he also seated himself in a distant corner, not presuming, he said, to break in upon us! Everybody, he added, gave way to the doctor.

Our conversation chiefly was upon the Hebrides, for he always talks to me of Scotland, out of sport; and he wished I had been of that tour[149] – quite gravely, as I assure you!

Tuesday morning our breakfast was delightful. We had Mr. Seward, Mr. Embry, and Lady Ladd added to our usual party, and Dr. Johnson was quite in a sportive humour. But I can only write some few speeches, wanting time to be prolix, not inclination.

"Sir," said Mrs. Thrale to Dr. Johnson, "why did you not sooner leave your wine yesterday, and come to us? we had a Miss who sung and played like anything!"

"Ay, had you?" said he drolly; "and why did you not call me to the rapturous entertainment?"

"Why, I was afraid you would not have praised her, for I sat thinking all the time myself whether it were better to sing and play as she sang and played, or to do nothing. And at first I thought she had the best of it, for we were but stupid before she began; but afterwards she made it so long, that I thought *nothing* had all the advantage. But, sir, Lady Ladd has had the same misfortune you had, for she has fallen down and hurt herself woefully."

"How did that happen, madam?"

"Why, sir, the heel of her shoe caught in something."

"Heel?" replied he; "nay, then, if her ladyship, who walks six foot high" (*N.B.* this is a fact), "will wear a high heel, I think she almost deserves a fall."

"Nay, sir, my heel was not so high!" cried Lady Ladd.

"But, madam, why should you wear any? That for which there is no occasion, had always better be dispensed with. However, a fall to your ladyship is nothing," continued he, laughing; "you, who are light and little, can soon recover; but I who am a gross man, might suffer severely; with your ladyship the case is different, for

Airy substance soon unites again."[150]

Poor Lady Ladd, who is quite a strapper,[151] made no answer, but she was not offended. Mrs. Thrale and I afterwards settled, that not knowing his allusion from the *Rape of the Lock*, she only thought he had made a stupid sort of speech, and did not trouble herself to find a meaning to it.

"However," continued he, "if my fall does confine me, I will make my confinement pleasant, for Miss Burney shall nurse me – positively!" (and he slapped his hand on the table), "and then, she shall sing to me, and soothe my cares."

When public news was started, Mr. Thrale desired the subject might be waived till my father came, and could let us know what part of the late accounts were true.

Mr. Thrale then offered to carry Mr. Seward, who was obliged to go to town, in the coach with him, — and Mr. Embry also left us. But Dr. Johnson sat with Mrs. Thrale, Lady Ladd, and me for an hour or two.

The subject was given by Lady Ladd; it was the respect due from the lower class of the people.

"I know my place," said she, "and I always take it: and I've no notion of not taking it. But Mrs. Thrale lets all sort of people do just as they've a mind by her."

"Ay," said Mrs. Thrale, "why should I torment and worry myself about all the paltry marks of respect that consist in bows and courtesies? — I have no idea of troubling myself about the manners of all the people I mix with."

"No," said Lady Ladd, "so they will take all sorts of liberties with you. I remember, when you were at my house, how the hair-dresser flung down the comb as soon as you were dressed, and went out of the room without making a bow."

"Well, all the better," said Mrs. Thrale; "for if he had made me one, ten thousand to one if I had seen it. I was in as great haste to have done with him, as he could be to have done with me. I was glad enough to get him out of the room; I did not want him to stand bowing and cringing."

"If any man had behaved so insolently to me," answered she, "I would never again have suffered him in my house."

"Well," said Mrs. Thrale, "your ladyship has a great deal more dignity than I have! — Dr. Johnson, we are talking of the respect due from inferiors; — and Lady Ladd is of the same side you are."

"Why, madam," said he, "subordination is always necessary to the preservation of order and decorum."[152]

"I protest," said Lady Ladd, "I have no notion of submitting to any kind of impertinence: and I never will bear either to have any person nod to me, or enter a room where I am, without bowing."

"But, madam," said Dr. Johnson, "what if they will nod, and what if they won't bow? — how then?"

"Why, I always tell them of it," said she.

"Oh, commend me to that!" cried Mrs. Thrale; "I'd sooner never see another bow in my life, than turn dancing-master to hair-dressers."

The doctor laughed his approbation, but said that every man had a right to a certain degree of respect, and no man liked to be defrauded of that right.

"Well, sir," said Mrs. Thrale, "I hope you meet with respect enough!"

"Yes, madam," answered he, "I am very well contented."

"Nay, if you an't, I don't know who should be; for I believe there is no man in the world so greatly respected."

Soon after he went, I went and shut myself up in a sweet cool summer-house,[153] to read *Irene*: which, indeed, though not a good play, is a beautiful poem.

As my dear father spent the rest of the day here, I will not further particularise, but leave accounts to his better communication. He probably told you that the P———— family came in to tea; and, as he knows Mrs. P————, pray tell him what Dr. Johnson says of her. When they were gone Mrs. Thrale complained that she was quite worn out with that tiresome silly woman, who had talked of her family and affairs till she was sick to death of hearing her.

"Madam," said he, "why do you blame the woman for the only sensible thing she can do — talking of her family and her affairs? For how should a woman who is as empty as a drum, talk upon any other subject? — If you speak to her of the sun, she does not know it rises in the east; — if you speak to her of the moon, she does not know it changes at the full; if you speak to her of the queen, she does not know she is the king's wife; — how, then, can you blame her for talking of her family and affairs?"

[Diary, i, 140-7]

In short, not to spend my whole letter[154] in enigmatical preluding, just as I received your letter I had had information that my name had got into print, and what was yet worse, was printed in a new pamphlet.

I cannot tell you, and if I could you would perhaps not believe me, how greatly I was shocked, mortified, grieved, and confounded at this intelligence: I had always dreaded as a real evil my name's getting into print — but to be lugged into a pamphlet!

I must, however, now I have gone so far, tell you how it is, lest you should imagine matters worse. This vile pamphlet is called *Warley: a Satire*[155]; it is addressed to the first artist in Europe, who proves to be Sir Joshua Reynolds. Probably it is to to his unbounded partiality for *Evelina* that I owe this most disagreeable compliment, for he had been so eager to discover the author, that by what I had reason given me to conjecture, I fancy he has been not a little laughed at since the discovery, for divers *comique* sort of speeches which he had made while in the dark.

So now the murder's out! but, dear daddy, don't belabour me for my weakness, though I confess I was for more than a week unable to eat, drink, or sleep, for vehemence of vexation. I am now got tolerably stout again, but I have been furiously lectured for my folly (as I see everybody thinks it) by all who have known of it. I have, therefore, struggled against it with all my might, and am determined to aim at least at acquiring more strength of mind.

Yet, after all, I feel very forcibly that I am not — that I have not been — and that I never shall be, formed or fitted for any business with the public.

Yet now my best friends, and my father at their head, absolutely prohibit
a retreat; otherwise I should be strongly tempted to empty the whole
contents of my bureau into the fire, and to vow never again to fill it.

[*Diary*, i, 160-1]

...On Friday, I had a visit from Dr. Johnson! he came on purpose to
reason with me about this pamphlet, which he had heard from my father
had so greatly disturbed me.

Shall I not love him more than ever? However, Miss Young[156] was
just arrived, and Mr. Bremner[157] spent the evening here, and therefore he
had the delicacy and goodness to forbear coming to the point. Yet he said
several things that I understood, though they were unintelligible to all
others; and he was more kind, more good-humoured, more flattering to
me than ever. Indeed, my uneasiness upon this subject has met with more
indulgence from him than from anybody. He repeatedly charged me not
to fret; and bid me not repine at my success, but think of Floretta,[158] in
the Fairy Tale, who found sweetness and consolation in her wit sufficient
to counterbalance her scoffers and libellers! Indeed he was all good
humour and kindness, and seemed quite bent on giving me comfort as
well as flattery...

[*Diary*, i, 168-9]

...I shall now skip to the Thursday following, when I accompanied my
father to Streatham. We had a delightful ride, though the day was
horrible.

In two minutes we were joined by Mr. Seward, and in four, by Dr.
Johnson. Mr. Seward, though a reserved and cold young man, has a heart
open to friendship, and very capable of good-nature and goodwill, though
I believe it abounds not with them to all indiscriminately: but he really
loves my father, and his reserve once, is always, conquered. He seemed
heartily glad to see us both: and the dear Dr. Johnson was more kind,
more pleased, and more delightful than ever. Our several meetings in
town seem now to have quite established me in his favour, and I flatter
myself that if he were now accused of loving me, he would not deny it,
nor, as before, insist on waiting longer ere he went so far.[159]

["I hope, Dr. Burney," cried Mr. Seward, "you are now come to
stay?"

"No!" cried my father, shaking his head, "that is utterly out of my
power at present."

"Well, but this fair lady" – (*N.B.* – Fair and brown are synonymous
terms in conversation, however opposite in looks) "I hope will stay?"

"No, no, no!" was the response, and he came to me and pressed the
invitation very warmly; but Dr. Johnson, going to the window, called me
from him.]

"Well, my dear," cried he, in a low voice, "and how are you now? have you done fretting? have you got over your troubles?"

"Ah, sir," quoth I, "I am sorry they told you of my folly; yet I am very much obliged to you for bearing to hear of it with so much indulgence, for I had feared it would have made you hold me cheap ever after."

"No, my dear, no! What should I hold you cheap for? It did not surprise me at all; I thought it very natural; but you must think no more of it."

F. B. — Why, sir, to say the truth, I don't know, after all, whether I do not owe the affair in part to you!

Dr. J. — To me? how so?

F. B. — Why, the appellation of "little Burney," I think, must have come from you, for I know of nobody else that calls me so.

This is a fact, Susy,[160] and the "dear little Burney," makes it still more suspicious, for I am sure Sir Joshua Reynolds would never speak of me so facetiously after only one meeting.

Dr. Johnson seemed almost shocked, and warmly denied having been any way accessory.

"Why, sir," cried I, "they say the pamphlet was written by a Mr. Huddisford. Now I never saw, never heard of him before; how, therefore, should he know whether I am little or tall? he could not call me little by inspiration; I might be a Patagonian for anything he could tell."

Dr. J. — Pho! fiddle-faddle; do you suppose your book is so much talked of and not yourself? Do you think your readers will not ask questions, and inform themselves whether you are short or tall, young or old? Why should you put it on me?

After this he made me follow him into the library, that we might continue our confab without interruption; and just as we were seated, entered Mrs. Thrale. I flew to her, and she received me with the sweetest cordiality. They placed me between them, and we had a most delicious trio.

We talked over the visit at Sir Joshua's; and Dr. Johnson told me that Mrs. Cholmondeley[161] was the first person who publicly praised and recommended *Evelina* among the wits. Mrs. Thrale told me that at Tunbridge and Brightelmstone it was the universal topic; and that Mrs. Montagu had pronounced the dedication to be so well written, that she could not but suppose it must be the doctor's.

"She is very kind," quoth I, "because she likes one part better than another, to take it from me!"

"You must not mind that," said Dr. Johnson, "for such things are always said where books are successful. There are three distinct kind of judges upon all new authors or productions; the first are those who know no rules, but pronounce entirely from their natural taste and feelings; the second are those who know and judge by rules; and the third are those who know, but are above the rules. These last are those you should wish to satisfy. Next to them rate the natural judges; but ever despise those opinions that are formed by the rules."

[Mrs. Thrale wanted me much to stay all night, but it could not be...]

[*Diary*, i, 181-4]

...Last week I called on Mrs. Williams, and Dr. Johnson, who had just returned from Streatham, came down stairs to me, and was so kind! I quite dote on him; and I do really believe that, take away Mr. Crisp, there is no man out of this house who has so real and affectionate a regard for me: and I am sure, take away the same person, I can with the utmost truth say the same thing in return.

I asked after the Streathamites.

"Why;" said he, "we now only want you — we have Miss Streatfield, Miss Brown, Murphy, and Seward — we only want you! Has Mrs. Thrale called on you lately?"

"Yes, sir."

"Ah," said he, "you are such a darling!"

Mrs. Williams added a violent compliment to this, but concluded with saying,

"My only fear is lest she should put me in a book!"

"Sir Joshua Reynolds," answered Dr. Johnson, "says, that if he were conscious to himself of any trick, or any affectation, there is nobody he should so much fear as this little Burney!"

This speech he told me once before, so that I find it has struck him much...

[*Diary*, i, 184-5]

...*Streatham, February.* — I have been here so long, my dearest Susan, without writing a word, that now I hardly know where or how to begin. But I will try to draw up a concise account of what has passed for this last fortnight, and then endeavour to be more minute.

Mrs. Thrale and Dr. Johnson vied with each other in the kindness of their reception of me. Mr. Thrale was, as usual at first, cold and quiet, but soon, as usual also, warmed into sociality.

The next day Sir Philip Jennings Clerke[162] came. He is not at all a man of letters, but extremely well-bred, nay, elegant, in his manners, and sensible and agreeable in his conversation. He is a professed minority man, and very active and zealous in the opposition. He had, when I came, a bill in agitation concerning contractors — too long a matter to explain upon paper — but which was levelled against bribery and corruption in the ministry,[163] and which he was to make a motion upon in the House of Commons the next week.

Men of such different principles as Dr. Johnson and Sir Philip, you may imagine, cannot have much sympathy or cordiality in their political debates; however, the very superior abilities of the former, and the remarkable good breeding of the latter, have kept both upon good terms; though they have had several arguments, in which each has exerted his utmost force for conquest.

The heads of one of their debates I must try to remember, because I should be sorry to forget. Sir Philip explained his bill; Dr. Johnson at first scoffed it; Mr. Thrale betted a guinea the motion would not pass, and Sir Philip, that he should divide a hundred and fifty upon it.[164]

[I am afraid, my dear Susan, you already tremble at this political commencement, but I will soon have done, for I know your taste too well to enlarge upon this theme.]

Sir Philip, addressing himself to Mrs. Thrale, hoped she would not suffer the Tories to warp her judgment, and told me he hoped my father had not tainted my principles; and then he further explained his bill, and indeed made it appear so equitable, that Mrs. Thrale gave in to it, and wished her husband to vote for it. He still hung back; but, to our general surprise, Dr. Johnson, having made more particular inquiries into its merits, first softened towards it, and then declared it a very rational and fair bill, and joined with Mrs. Thrale in soliciting Mr. Thrale's vote.

Sir Philip was, and with very good reason, quite delighted. He opened upon politics more amply, and freely declared his opinions, which were so strongly against the Government, and so much bordering upon the Republican principles, that Dr. Johnson suddenly took fire; he called back his recantation, begged Mr. Thrale not to vote for Sir Philip's bill, and grew very animated against his antagonist.

"The bill," said he, "ought to be opposed by all honest men! in itself, and considered simply, it is equitable, and I would forward it; but when we find what a faction it is to support and encourage, it ought not to be listened to. All men should oppose it who do not wish well to sedition!"

These, and several other expressions yet more strong, he made use of; and had Sir Philip had less unalterable politeness, I believe they would have had a vehement quarrel. He maintained his ground, however, with calmness and steadiness, though he had neither argument nor wit at all equal to such an opponent.

Dr. Johnson pursued him with unabating vigour and dexterity, and at length, though he could not convince, he so entirely baffled him, that Sir Philip was self-compelled to be quiet — which, with a very good grace, he confessed.

Dr. Johnson then, recollecting himself, and thinking, as he owned afterwards, that the dispute grew too serious, with a skill all his own, suddenly and unexpectedly turned it to burlesque; and taking Sir Philip by the hand at the moment we arose after supper, and were separating for the night,

"Sir Philip," said he, "you are too liberal a man for the party to which you belong; I shall have much pride in the honour of converting you; for I really believe, if you were not spoiled by bad company, the spirit of faction would not have possessed you. Go, then, sir, to the House, but make not your motion! Give up your Bill, and surprise the world by turning to the side of truth and reason. Rise, sir, when they least expect you, and address your fellow-patriots to this purpose: — Gentlemen, I have, for many a weary day, been deceived and seduced by you. I have now opened my eyes; I see that you are all scoundrels — the subversion of all government is your aim. Gentlemen, I will no longer herd among rascals in whose infamy my name and character must be included. I therefore renounce you all, gentlemen, as you deserve to be renounced."

Then, shaking his hand heartily, he added,

"Go, sir, go to bed; meditate upon this recantation, and rise in the morning a more honest man than you laid down."

Now I must try to be rather more minute. On Thursday, while my dear father was here, who should be announced but Mr. Murphy;[165] the man of all other strangers to me whom I most longed to see.

He is tall and well made, has a very gentlemanlike appearance, and a quietness of manner upon his first address that, to me, is very pleasing. His face looks sensible, and his deportment is perfectly easy and polite.

When he had been welcomed by Mrs. Thrale, and had gone through the reception-salutations of Dr. Johnson and my father, Mrs. Thrale, advancing to me, said,

"But here is a lady I must introduce to you, Mr. Murphy: here is another F. B."

"Indeed!" cried he, taking my hand; "is this a sister of Miss Brown's?"

"No, no; this is Miss Burney."

"What!" cried he, staring, "is this — is this — this is not the lady that — that — "

"Yes, but it is," answered she, laughing.

"No, you don't say so? You don't mean the lady that — "

"Yes, yes, I do; no less a lady, I assure you."

He then said he was very glad of the honour of seeing me; and I sneaked away.

When we came upstairs, Mrs. Thrale charged me to make myself agreeable to Mr. Murphy.

"He may be of use to you, in what I am most eager for — your writing a play: he knows stage business so well; and if you will but take a fancy to one another, he may be more able to serve you than all of us put together.

My ambition is that Johnson should write your prologue, and Murphy your epilogue; then I shall be quite happy."

At tea-time, when I went into the library, I found Dr. Johnson reading, and Mrs. Thrale in close conference with Mr. Murphy.

"It is well, Miss Burney," said the latter, "that you have come, for we were abusing you most vilely; we were in the very act of pulling you to pieces."

"Don't you think her very like her father?" said Mrs. Thrale.

"Yes: but what a sad man is Dr. Burney for running away so! how long had he been here?"

Mrs. Thrale. – Oh, but an hour or two. I often say Dr. Burney is the most of a male coquet of any man I know; for he only gives one enough of his company to excite a desire for more.

Mr. Murphy. – Dr. Burney is, indeed, a most extraordinary man; I think I don't know such another: he is at home upon all subjects, and upon all so agreeable! he is a wonderful man!

And now let me stop this conversation, to go back to a similar one with Dr. Johnson, who, a few days since, when Mrs. Thrale was singing our father's praise, used this expression:

"I love Burney: my heart goes out to meet him!"

"He is not ungrateful, sir," cried I; "for most heartily does he love you."

"Does he, madam? I am surprised at that."

"Why, sir? why should you have doubted it?"

"Because, madam, Dr. Burney is a man for all the world to love: it is but natural to love him."

I could almost have cried with delight at this cordial unlaboured *éloge*. Another time, he said,

"I much question if there is, in the world, such another man as Dr. Burney."

But to return to the tea-table.

"If I," said Mr. Murphy, looking very archly, "had written a certain book – a book I won't name, but a book I have lately read – I would next write a comedy."

"Good," cried Mrs. Thrale, colouring with pleasure; "do you think so too?"

"Yes, indeed; I thought so while I was reading it; it struck me repeatedly."

"Don't look at me, Miss Burney," cried Mrs. Thrale, "for this is no doing of mine. Well, I do wonder what Miss Burney will do twenty years hence, when she can blush no more; for now she can never bear the name of her book."

Mr. Murphy. – Nay, I name no book; at least no author: how can I, for I don't know the author; there is no name given to it: I only say, whoever wrote that book ought to write a comedy. Dr. Johnson might write it for aught I know.

F. B. – Oh yes!

Mr. Murphy. – Nay, I have often told him he does not know his own strength, or he would write a comedy; and so I think.

Dr. Johnson (laughing). – Suppose Burney and I begin together?

Mr. Murphy. – Ah, I wish you would! I wish you would Beaumont and Fletcher us!

F. B. – My father asked me, this morning, how my head stood. If he should have asked me this evening, I don't know what answer I must have made.

Mr. Murphy. – I have no wish to turn anybody's head: I speak what I really think; – comedy is the forte of that book. I laughed over it most violently: and if the author – I won't say who (all the time looking away from me) – will write a comedy, I will most readily, and with great pleasure, give any advice or assistance in my power.

"Well, now you are a sweet man!" cried Mrs. Thrale, who looked ready to kiss him. "Did not I tell you, Miss Burney, that Mr. Murphy was the man?"

Mr. Murphy. – All I can do, I shall be very happy to do; and at least, I will undertake to say I can tell what the sovereigns of the upper gallery will bear: for they are the most formidable part of an audience. I have had so much experience in this sort of work, that I believe I can always tell what will be hissed at least. And if Miss Burney will write, and will show me –

Dr. Johnson. – Come, come, have done with this now; why should you overpower her? Let's have no more of it. I don't mean to dissent from what you say; I think well of it, and approve of it; but you have said enough of it.

Mr. Murphy, who equally loves and reverences Dr. Johnson, instantly changed the subject.

The rest of the evening was delightful. Mr. Murphy told abundance of most excellent stories; Dr. Johnson was in exceeding good humour; and Mrs. Thrale all cheerfulness and sweetness.

For my part, in spite of her injunctions, I could not speak; I was in a kind of consternation. Mr. Murphy's speeches, flattering as they were, made me tremble; for I cannot get out of my head the idea of disgracing so many people.[166]

After supper, Dr. Johnson turned the discourse upon silent folks – whether by way of reflection and reproof, or by accident, I know not; but I do know he is provoked with me for not talking more; and I was afraid he was seriously provoked; but, a little while ago, I went into the music-room, where he was *tête-à-tête* with Mrs. Thrale, and calling me to him, he took my hand, and made me sit next him, in a manner that seemed truly affectionate.

"Sir," cried I, "I was much afraid I was going out of your favour!"

"Why so? what should make you think so?"

"Why, I don't know — my silence, I believe. I began to fear you would give me up."

"No, my darling! — my dear little Burney, no. When I give you up — "

"What then, sir?" cried Mrs. Thrale.

"Why, I don't know; for whoever could give her up would deserve worse than I can say; I know not what would be bad enough."...

[*Diary*, i, 198-206]

... Yesterday, at night, I told Dr. Johnson the inquiry,[166] and added that I attributed it to my being at Streatham, and supposed the folks took it for granted nobody would be admitted there without knowing Latin, at least.

"No, my dear, no," answered he; "the man thought it because you have written a book — he concluded that a book could not be written by one who knew no Latin. And it is strange that it should — but, perhaps you do know it — for your shyness, and slyness, and pretending to know nothing, never took me in, whatever you may do with others. I always knew you for a toadling."

At our usual time of absconding, he would not let us go, and was in high good humour; and when, at last, Mrs. Thrale absolutely refused to stay any longer, he took me by the hand and said,

"Don't you mind her, my little Burney; do you stay whether she will or not."

So away went Mrs. Thrale, and left us to a *tête-à-tête*.

Now I had been considering that perhaps I ought to speak to him of my new castle,[168] lest hereafter he should suspect that I preferred the counsel of Mr. Murphy. I therefore determined to take this opportunity, and after some general nothings, I asked if he would permit me to take a great liberty with him?

He assented with the most encouraging smile. And then I said,

"I believe, sir, you heard part of what passed between Mr. Murphy and me the other evening, concerning — a — a comedy. Now, if I should make such an attempt, would you be so good as to allow me, any time before Michaelmas, to put it in the coach, for you to look over as you go to town?"

"To be sure, my dear! — What, have you begun a comedy, then?"

I told him how the affair stood. He then gave me advice which just accorded with my wishes, viz., not to make known that I had any such intention; to keep my own counsel; not to whisper even the name of it; to raise no expectations, which were always prejudicial, and finally to have it performed while the town knew nothing of whose it was.

I readily reassured him of my hearty concurrence in his opinion; but he somewhat distressed me when I told him that Mr. Murphy must be in my confidence, as he had offered his services, by desiring he might be the last to see it.

What I shall do, I know not, for he has, himself, begged to be the first. Mrs. Thrale, however, shall guide me between them. He spoke highly of Mr. Murphy, too, for he really loves him. He said he would not have it in the coach, but that I should read it to him; however, I could sooner drown or hang!

When I would have offered some apology for the attempt, he stopped me, and desired I would never make any.

"For," said he, "if it succeeds, it makes its own apology, if not — "

"If not," quoth I, "I cannot do worse than Dr. Goldsmith, when his play failed, — go home and cry!"[169]

He laughed, but told me repeatedly (I mean twice, which, for him, is very remarkable) that I might depend upon all the service in his power; and, he added, it would be well to make Murphy the last judge, "for he knows the stage," he said, "and I am quite ignorant of it."

Afterwards, grasping my hand with the most affectionate warmth, he said,

"I wish you success! I wish you well! my dear little Burney!"

When, at length, I told him I could stay no longer, and bid him good-night, he said, "There is none like you, my dear little Burney! there is none like you! — good-night, my darling!"...

...I forgot to mention that, when I told Dr. Johnson Mr. Murphy's kind offer of examining my plan, and the several rules he gave me, and owned that I had already gone too far to avail myself of his obliging intention, he said, "Never mind, my dear, — ah! you'll do without, — you want no rules."

[*Diary*, i, 207-10]

...And now I cannot resist telling you of a dispute which Dr. Johnson had with Mrs. Thrale, the next morning,[170] concerning me, which that sweet woman had the honesty and good sense to tell me. Dr. Johnson was talking to her and Sir Philip Jennings of the amazing progress made of late years in literature by the women. He said he was himself astonished at it, and told them he well remembered when a woman who could spell a common letter was regarded as all accomplished; but now they vied with the men in everything.

"I think, sir," said my friend Sir Philip, "the young lady we have here is a very extraordinary proof of what you say."

"So extraordinary, sir," answered he, "that I know none like her, — nor do I believe there is, or there ever was, a man who could write such a book so young."

They both stared — no wonder, I am sure! — and Sir Philip said,

"What do you think of Pope, sir? could not Pope have written such a one?"

"Nay, nay," cried Mrs. Thrale, "there is no need to talk of Pope; a book may be a clever book, and an extraordinary book, and yet not want a Pope for its author. I suppose he was no older than Miss Burney when he wrote *Windsor Forest*;[171] and I suppose *Windsor Forest* is equal to *Evelina*!"

"*Windsor Forest*," repeated Dr. Johnson, "though so delightful a poem, by no means required the knowledge of life and manners, nor the accuracy of observation, nor the skill of penetration, necessary for composing such a work as Evelina; he who could ever write *Windsor Forest*, might as well write it young or old.[172] Poetical abilities require not age to mature them; but *Evelina* seems a work that should result from long experience, and deep and intimate knowledge of the world; yet it has been written without either. Miss Burney is a real wonder. What she is, she is intuitively. Dr. Burney told me she had had the fewest advantages of any of his daughters, from some peculiar circumstances.[173] And such has been her timidity, that he himself had not any suspicion of her powers."

"Her modesty," said Mrs. Thrale (as she told me), "is really beyond bounds. It quite provokes me. And, in fact, I can never make out how the mind that could write that book could be ignorant of its value."

"That, madam, is another wonder," answered my dear, dear Dr. Johnson, "for modesty with her is neither pretence nor decorum; 'tis an ingredient of her nature; for she who could part with such a work for twenty pounds,[174] could know so little of its worth, or of her own, as to leave no possible doubt of her humility."

My kind Mrs. Thrale told me this with a pleasure that made me embrace her with gratitude; but the astonishment of Sir Philip Clerke at such an *éloge* from Dr. Johnson was quite, she says, comical.

Streatham, July 5. — I have hardly had any power to write, my dear Susy, since I left you, for my cold has increased so much that I have hardly been able to do anything.

Mr. Thrale, I think, is better,[175] and he was cheerful all the ride. Mrs. Thrale made as much of me as if the two days had been two months.

I was heartily glad to see Dr. Johnson, and I believe he was not sorry to see me: he had inquired very much after me, and very particularly of Mrs. Thrale whether she loved me as well as she used to do.

He is better in health than I have ever seen him before; his journey[176] has been very serviceable to him, and he has taken very good resolutions to reform his diet;[177] – so has my daddy Crisp. I wish I could pit them one against the other, and see the effect of their emulation.

I wished twenty times to have transmitted to paper the conversation of the evening, for Dr. Johnson was as brilliant as I have ever known him – and that's saying something; – but I was not very well, and could only attend to him for present entertainment.

July 10. – Since I wrote last, I have been far from well, – but I am now my own man again – *à peu-près*.

Very concise, indeed, must my journal grow, for I have now hardly a moment in my power to give it; however, I will keep up its chain, and mark, from time to time, the general course of things.

Sir Philip Jennings has spent three days here, at the close of which he took leave of us for the summer, and set out for his seat in Hampshire. We were all sorry to lose him; he is a most comfortable man in society, for he is always the same – easy, good-humoured, agreeable, and well-bred. He has made himself a favourite to the whole house, Dr. Johnson included, who almost always prefers the company of an intelligent man of the world to that of a scholar...

[Diary, i, 245-50]

...*July 20.* – What a vile journalist do I grow! – it is, however, all I can do to keep it at all going; for, to let you a little into the nature of things, you must know that my studies occupy almost every moment that I spend by myself. Dr. Johnson gives us a Latin lesson every morning. I pique myself somewhat upon being ready for him; so that really, when the copying my play, and the continual returning occurrences of every fresh day are considered, you will not wonder that I should find so little opportunity for scrawling letters.

What progress we may make in this most learned scheme I know not; but, as I have always told you, I am sure I fag[178] more for fear of disgrace than for hope of profit. To devote so much time to acquire something I shall always dread to have known, is really unpleasant enough, considering how many things there are I might employ myself in that would have no such drawback. However, on the other side, I am both pleased and flattered that Dr. Johnson should think me worth inviting to be his pupil, and I shall always recollect with pride and with pleasure the instructions he has the goodness to give me: so, since I cannot without dishonour alter matters,'tis as well to turn Frenchwoman, and take them in the *tant mieux* fashion...

[Diary, i, 252-3]

...Dr. Johnson has made resolutions exactly similar to yours,[179] and in general adheres to them with strictness, but the old Adam, as you say, stands in his way, as well as in his neighbours'. I wish I could pit you against each other for the sake of both. Yet he professes an aversion to you, because he says he is sure you are very much in his way with me! however, I believe you would neither of you retain much aversion if you had a fair meeting...

[Diary, i, 254-5]

...Do you know I have been writing to Dr. Johnson! I tremble to mention it; but he sent a message in a letter to Mrs. Thrale, to wonder why his pupils did not write to him,[180] and to hope they did not forget him: Miss Thrale, therefore, wrote a letter immediately, and I added only this little postscript:

"*P.S.* — Dr. Johnson's other pupil a little longs to add a few lines to this letter, — but knows too well that all she has to say might be comprised in signing herself his obliged and most obedient servant, F. B.: so that's better than a long rigmarole about nothing."...

[Diary, i, 300]

...*Thursday morning, April 13th.* — I am now come to the present time, and will try, however brief, to be tolerably punctual.

Dr. Johnson has sent a bitter reproach to Mrs. Thrale of my not writing to him,[181] for he has not yet received a scrawl I have sent him. He says Dr. Barnard, the provost of Eton,[182] has been singing the praises of my book, and that old Dr. Lawrence[183] has read it through three times within this last month! I am afraid he will pass for being superannuated for his pains!

"But don't tell Burney this," adds Dr. Johnson, "because she will not write to me, and values me no more than if I were a Branghton!"...

[Diary, i, 339]

Bath, May 28... I found my dear Mrs. Thrale so involved in business, electioneering,[184] canvassing, and letter-writing, that after our first *embrassades*, we hardly exchanged a word till we got into the chaise next morning.

Dr. Johnson, however, who was with her, received me even joyfully; and, making me sit by him, began a gay and spirited conversation, which he kept up till we parted, though in the midst of all this bustle.

The next morning we rose at four o'clock, and when we came downstairs, to our great surprise, found Dr. Johnson waiting to receive and breakfast with us; though the night before he had taken leave of us, and given me the most cordial and warm assurances of the love he has for me, which I do indeed believe to be as sincere as I can wish; and I failed not to tell him the affectionate respect with which I return it; though, as well as I remember, we never came to this open declaration before.

We, therefore, drank our coffee with him, and then he handed us both into the chaise. He meant to have followed us to Bath, but Mrs. Thrale discouraged him, from a firm persuasion that he would be soon very horribly wearied of a Bath life:[185] an opinion in which I heartily join...

[*Diary*, i, 371]

...I have not seen Dr. Johnson since the day you left me,[186] when he came hither, and met Mrs. Ord, Mr. Hoole, Mrs. Reynolds, Baretti, the Paradises, Pepys, Castles, Dr. Dunbar, and some others; and then he was in high spirits and good humour, talked all the talk, affronted nobody, and delighted everybody. I never saw him more sweet, nor better attended to by his audience. I have not been able to wait upon him since, nor, indeed, upon anybody, for we have not spent one evening alone since my return...

[*Diary*, i, 435]

...Since I wrote last I have drunk tea with Dr. Johnson.[187] My father took me to Bolt Court, and we found him, most fortunately, with only one brassheaded cane gentleman. Since that, I have had the pleasure to meet him again at Mrs. Reynolds's, when he offered to take me with him to Grub Street,[188] to see the ruins of the house demolished there in the late riots,[189] by a mob that, as he observed, could be no friend to the Muses! He inquired if I had ever yet visited Grub Street? but was obliged to restrain his anger when I answered "No," because he acknowledged that he had never paid his respects to it himself. "However," says he, "you and I, Burney, will go together; we have a very good right to go, so we'll visit the mansions of our progenitors, and take up our own freedom together"...

[*Diary*, i, 437-8]

...Well — *mal à propos* to all this[190] — Dr. Johnson, who expects nothing but what is good, and swallows nothing but what he likes, has delighted me with another volume of his *Lives*,[191] — that which contains Blackmore, Congreve, etc., which he tells me you have had. Oh what a writer he is! what instruction, spirit, intelligence, and vigour in almost every paragraph! Addison I think equal to any in the former batch; but he is rather too hard upon Prior,[192] and makes Gay, I think, too insignificant. Some of the little poems of Prior seem to me as charming as any little poems can be; and Gay's pastorals I had hoped to have seen praised more liberally.[193]...

[*Diary*, i, 443]

...Dr. Johnson, you know, came with my dear father the Thursday after our return.[194]

You cannot, I think, have been surprised that I gave up my plan of going to town immediately: indeed I had no heart to leave either Mr.

Thrale in a state so precarious,[195] or his dear wife in an agitation of mind
hardly short of a fever.

Things now went on tolerably smooth, and Miss Thrale and I renewed
our Latin exercises with Dr. Johnson, and with great *éclat* of praise. At
another time I could have written much of him and of Mr. Seward, for
many very good conversations past; but now I have almost forgot all about
them...

[Diary, i, 448]

...Dr. Johnson is very gay and sociable[196] and comfortable, and quite as
kind to me as ever; and he says the Bodleian librarian has but done his
duty,[197] and that when he goes to Oxford, he will write my name in the
books, my age when I writ them, and sign the whole with his own; "and
then," he says, "the world may know that we

> 'So mixed our studies, and so joined our fame'[198]

For we shall go down hand in hand to posterity!"...

[Diary, i, 450-1]

...Mrs. Thrale, in cutting some fruit, had cut her finger,[199] and asked me
for some black sticking-plaster, and as I gave it her out of my pocket-book,
she was struck with the beautiful glossiness of the paper of a letter which
peeped out of it, and rather *waggishly* asked me who wrote to me with so
much elegant attention?

"Mrs. Gast,"[200] answered I.

"Oh," cried she, "do pray then let me see her hand."

I showed it her, and she admired it very justly, and said,

"Do show it to Mr. Crutchley;[201] 'tis a mighty genteel hand indeed."

I complied, but took it from him as soon as he had looked at it. Indeed,
he is the last man in the world to have even desired to read any letter not
to himself.

Dr. Johnson now, who, too deaf to hear what was saying, wondered
what we were thus handing about, asked an explanation.

"Why, we are all," said Mrs. Thrale, "admiring the hand of Fanny's
Mr. Crisp's sister."

"And mayn't I admire it too?" cried he.

"Oh yes," said she; "show it him, Burney."

I put it in his hand, and he instantly opened and began reading it.
Now though there was nothing in it but what must reflect honour upon
Mrs. Gast, she had charged me not to show it; and, also, it was so *very*
flattering to me, that I was quite consternated at this proceeding, and
called out,

"Sir, it was only to show you the handwriting, and you have seen
enough for that."

"I shall know best myself," answered he, laughing, "when I have seen enough."

And he read on. The truth is I am sure he took it for granted they had all read it, for he had not heard a word that had passed.

I then gave Mrs. Thrale a reproachful glance for what she had done, and she jumped up, and calling out,

"So I have done mischief, I see!" and ran out of the room, followed by Queeny.[202] I stayed hovering over the doctor to recover my property...

...[Here Dr. Johnson returned me my letter, with very warm praise of its contents. Mrs. Gast would not only have forgiven me, but have been much delighted had she heard his approbation of all she had written to me...]

[*Diary*, i, 488-90]

...*Streatham, June.* – I found Dr. Johnson in admirable good-humour, and our journey hither was extremely pleasant. I thanked him for the last batch of his poets,[203] and we talked them over almost all the way.

Sweet Mrs. Thrale received me with her wonted warmth of affection, but shocked me by her own ill looks,[204] and the increasing alteration in her person, which perpetual anxiety and worry have made...

...We had a good cheerful day, and in the evening Sir Richard Jebb came; and nothing can I recollect, but that Dr. Johnson *forced* me to sit on a very small sofa with him, which was hardly large enough for himself; and which would have made a subject for a print by Harry Bunbury[205] that would have diverted all London: *ergo*, it rejoiceth me that he was not present...

[*Diary*, i, 496]

...*Wednesda*y. – We had a terrible noisy day. Mr. and Mrs. Cator[206] came to dinner, and brought with them Miss Collison, a niece. Mrs. Nesbitt[207] was also here, and Mr. Pepys.

The long war which has been proclaimed among the wits concerning Lord Lyttelton's *Life*,[208] by Dr. Johnson, and which a whole tribe of *blues,* with Mrs. Montagu, at their head, have vowed to execrate and revenge, now broke out with all the fury of the first actual hostilities, stimulated by long-concerted schemes and much spiteful information. Mr. Pepys, Dr. Johnson well knew, was one of Mrs. Montagu's steadiest abettors; and, therefore, as he had some time determined to defend himself with the first of them he met, this day he fell the sacrifice to his wrath.

In a long *tête-à-tête* which I accidentally had with Mr. Pepys before the company was assembled, he told me his apprehensions of an attack, and entreated me earnestly to endeavour to prevent it; modestly avowing he was no antagonist for Dr. Johnson; and yet declaring his personal friendship for Lord Lyttelton made him so much hurt by the *Life,* that he feared he could not discuss the matter without a quarrel, which, especially in the house of Mrs. Thrale, he wished to avoid.

It was, however, utterly impossible for me to serve him. I could have stopped Mrs. Thrale with ease, and Mr. Seward with a hint, had either of them begun the subject; but, unfortunately, in the middle of dinner it was begun by Dr. Johnson himself, to oppose whom, especially as he spoke with great anger, would have been madness and folly.

Never before have I seen Dr. Johnson speak with so much passion.

"Mr. Pepys," he cried, in a voice the most enraged, "I understand you are offended by my 'Life of Lord Lyttelton'. What is it you have to say against it? Come forth, man! Here am I, ready to answer any charge you can bring!"

"No, sir," cried Mr. Pepys, "not at present; I must beg leave to decline the subject. I told Miss Burney before dinner that I hoped it would not be started."

I was quite frightened to hear my own name mentioned in a debate which began so seriously; but Dr. Johnson made not to this any answer: he repeated his attack and his challenge, and a violent disputation ensued, in which this great but *mortal* man did, to own the truth, appear unreasonably furious and grossly severe. I never saw him so before, and I heartily hope I never shall again. He has been long provoked, and justly enough, at the *sneaking* complaints and murmurs of the Lytteltonians; and, therefore, his long-excited wrath, which hitherto had met no object, now burst forth with a vehemence and bitterness almost incredible.

Mr. Pepys meantime never appeared to so much advantage; he preserved his temper, uttered all that belonged merely to himself with modesty, and all that more immediately related to Lord Lyttelton with spirit. Indeed, Dr. Johnson, in the very midst of the dispute, had the candour and liberality to make him a personal compliment by saying,

"Sir, all that you say, while you are vindicating one who cannot thank you, makes me only think better of you than I ever did before. Yet still I think you do *me* wrong," etc., etc.

Some time after, in the heat of the argument, he called out,

"The more my Lord Lyttelton is inquired after, the worse he will appear; Mr. Seward has just heard two stories of him, which corroborate all I have related."

He then desired Mr. Seward to repeat them. Poor Mr. Seward looked almost as frightened as myself at the very mention of his name; but he quietly and immediately told the stories, which consisted of fresh instances, from good authorities, of Lord Lyttelton's illiberal behaviour to Shenstone;[209] and then he flung himself back in his chair and spoke no more during the whole debate, which I am sure he was ready to vote a bore.

One happy circumstance, however, attended the quarrel, which was the presence of Mr. Cator, who would by no means be prevented talking himself, either by reverence for Dr. Johnson, or ignorance of the subject in question; on the contrary, he gave his opinion, quite uncalled, upon everything that was said by either party, and that with an importance and pomposity, yet with an emptiness and verbosity, that rendered the whole dispute, when in his hands, nothing more than ridiculous, and compelled even the disputants themselves, all inflamed as they were, to laugh. To give a specimen — one speech will do for a thousand.

"As to this here question of Lord Lyttelton, I can't speak to it to the purpose, as I have not read his *Life,* for I have only read the 'Life of Pope'; I have got the books though, for I sent for them last week, and they came to me on Wednesday, and then I began them; but I have not yet read 'Lord Lyttelton'. 'Pope' I have begun, and that is what I am now reading. But what I have to say about Lord Lyttelton is this here: Mr. Seward says that Lord Lyttelton's steward dunned[210] Mr. Shenstone for his rent, by which I understand he was a tenant of Lord Lyttelton's. Well, if he was a tenant of Lord Lyttelton's, why should not he pay his rent?"

Who could contradict this?

When dinner was quite over, and we left the men to their wine, we hoped they would finish the affair; but Dr. Johnson was determined to talk it through, and make a battle of it, though Mr. Pepys tried to be off continually. When they were all summoned to tea, they entered still warm and violent. Mr. Cator had the book in his hand, and was reading the 'Life of Lyttelton', that he might better, he said, understand the cause, though not a creature cared if he had never heard of it.

Mr. Pepys came up to me and said,

"Just what I had so much wished to avoid! I have been crushed in the very onset."

I could make him no answer, for Dr. Johnson immediately called him off, and harangued and attacked him with a vehemence and continuity that quite concerned both Mrs. Thrale and myself, and that made Mr. Pepys, at last, resolutely silent, however called upon.

This now grew more unpleasant than ever; till Mr. Cator, having some time studied his book, exclaimed,

"What I am now going to say, as I have not yet read the 'Life of Lord Lyttelton' quite through, must be considered as being only said aside, because what I am going to say — "

"I wish, sir," cried Mrs. Thrale, "it had been *all* set aside; here is too much about it, indeed, and I should be very glad to hear no more of it."

This speech, which she made with great spirit and dignity, had an admirable effect. Everybody was silenced. Mr. Cator, thus interrupted in the midst of his proposition, looked quite amazed; Mr. Pepys was much gratified by the interference; and Dr. Johnson, after a pause, said,

"Well, madam, you *shall* hear no more about it; yet I will defend myself in every part and in every atom!"

And from this time the subject was wholly dropped. This dear violent Doctor was conscious he had been wrong, and therefore he most candidly bore the reproof.

Mr. Cator, after some evident chagrin at having his speech thus rejected, comforted himself by coming up to Mr. Seward, who was seated next me, to talk to him of the changes of the climates from hot to *could* in the countries he had visited; and he prated so much, yet said so little, and pronounced his words so vulgarly, that I found it impossible to keep my countenance, and was once, when most unfortunately he addressed himself to me, surprised by him on the full grin. To soften it off as well as I could, I pretended unusual complacency, and instead of recovering my gravity, I continued a most ineffable smile for the whole time he talked, which was indeed no difficult task. Poor Mr. Seward was as much off his guard as myself, having his mouth distended to its fullest extent every other minute.

When the leave-taking time arrived, Dr. Johnson called to Mr. Pepys to shake hands, an invitation which was most coldly and forcibly accepted.[211] Mr. Cator made a point of Mrs. Thrale's dining at his house soon, and she could not be wholly excused, as she has many transactions with him;[212] but she fixed the day for three weeks hence. They have invited me so often, that I have now promised not to fail making one.

Thursday morning. — Dr. Johnson went to town for some days, but not before Mrs. Thrale read him a very serious lecture upon giving way to such violence; which he bore with a patience and quietness that even more than made his peace with me; for such a man's confessing himself wrong is almost more amiable that another being steadily right...

[Diary, i, 496-503]

...*Wednesday, June 26.* — Dr. Johnson, who had been in town some days, returned, and Mr. Crutchley came also, as well as my father. I did not see the two latter till summoned to dinner; and then Dr. Johnson seizing my hand, while with one of his own he gave me a no very gentle tap on the shoulder, half drolly and half reproachfully called out,

"Ah, you little baggage, you! and have you known how long I have been here, and never to come to me?"

And the truth is, in whatever sportive mode he expresses it, he really likes not I should be absent from him half a minute whenever he is here, and not in his own apartment...

[Diary, ii, 2]

...Dr. Johnson, as usual when here, kept me in chat with him in the library after all the rest had dispersed; but when Mr. Crutchley returned again, he went upstairs...

[Diary, ii, 3]

Friday.[213] – The moment breakfast was over, Mr. Crutchley arose, and was taking leave; but Mrs. Thrale told him, with an arch laugh, he had better stay, for he would not get mended by going. He protested, however, that he must certainly go home.

"And why?" cried she; "what do you go for?"

"Nay," cried he, hesitating, "I don't know, I am sure!"

"Never mind him, madam," cried Dr. Johnson; "a man who knows not why he goes, knows not why he stays; therefore never heed him."

"Does anybody expect you?" said Mrs. Thrale. "Do you want to see anybody?"

"Not a soul!"

"Then why can't you stay?"

"No; I can't stay now; I'll meet you on Tuesday."

"If you know so little why you should either go or stay," said Dr. Johnson, "never think about it, sir; toss up – that's the shortest way. Heads or tails! – let that decide."

"No, no, sir," answered he; "this is but talk, for I cannot reduce it to that mere indifference in my own mind."

"What! must you go, then?" said Mrs. Thrale.

"I must go," returned he, "upon a system of economy."

"What! to save your horses coming again?"

"No; but that I may not weary my friends quite out."

"Oh, your friends are the best judges for themselves," said Mrs. Thrale; "do you think you can go anywhere that your company will be more desired?"

"Nay, nay," cried Dr. Johnson, "after such an excuse as that, your friends have a right to practise Irish hospitality, and lock up your bridle."

The matter was still undecided when Mrs. Thrale called him to walk out with her...

...At dinner, accordingly, he returned, and is now to stay till Tuesday...

...I have very often, though I mention them not, long and melancholy discourses with Dr. Johnson, about our dear deceased master, whom, indeed, he regrets incessantly;[214] but I love not to dwell on subjects of sorrow when I can drive them away, especially to you,[215] upon this account, as you were so much a stranger to that excellent friend, whom you only lamented for the sake of those who survived him...

[Diary, ii, 6-8]

... At dinner[216] we had a large party of old friends of Mrs. Thrale. Lady Frances Burgoyne,[217] a mighty erect old lady of the last age, lofty, ceremonious, stiff, and condescending.

Montague Burgoyne, her son, and as like any other son as ever you saw.

Mrs. Burgoyne, his wife, a sweet, pretty, innocent, simple young girl, just married to him.

Miss Burgoyne, his eldest sister, a good, sensible, prating old maid.

Miss Kitty Burgoyne, a younger sister, equally prating, and *not* equally sensible.

Mr. Ned Hervey, brother to the bride.

To these were added Mr. Pepys and Sophy Streatfield; the former as entertaining, the latter as beautiful, as ever. We had a very good day, but not of a writing sort.

Dr. Johnson, whom I had not seen since his Sunninghill expedition,[218] as he only returned from town to-day, gave me almost all his attention, which made me of no little consequence to the Burgoynes, who all stared amain[219] when they saw him make up to me the moment I entered the room, and talk to me till summoned to dinner.

Mr. Pepys had desired this meeting, by way of a sort of reconciliation after the Lyttelton quarrel; and Dr. Johnson now made amends for his former violence, as he advanced to him as soon as he came in, and holding out his hand to him, received him with a cordiality he had never shown him before. Indeed, he told me himself, that "he thought the better of Mr. Pepys for all that had passed." He is as great a *souled* man as a *bodied* one, and, were he less furious in his passions, he would be demi-divine.

Mr. Pepys also behaved extremely well, politely casting aside all reserve or coldness that might be attributed to a lurking ill-will for what had passed.

Streatham. — My poor journal is now so in arrears, that I forget wholly the date of what I sent you last. I have, however, minutes by me of things, though not of times, and, therefore, the chronology not being very important, take them, my dear girls, promiscuously. I am still, I know, in August, *et voilà tout.*

We have now a new character added to our set, and one of no small diversion, — Mr. Musgrave,[220] an Irish gentleman of fortune, and member of the Irish Parliament. He is tall, thin, and agreeable in his face and figure; is reckoned a good scholar, has travelled, and been very well educated. His manners are impetuous and abrupt; his language is high-flown and hyperbolical; his sentiments are romantic and tender; his heart is warm and generous; his head hot and wrong! And the whole of his conversation is a mixture the most uncommon, of knowledge and triteness, simplicity and fury, literature and folly!

Keep this character in your mind, and, contradictory as it seems, I will give you, from time to time, such specimens as shall remind you of each of these six epithets.

He was introduced into this house by Mr. Seward, with whom, and Mr. Graves of Worcester, he travelled into Italy: and some years ago he was extremely intimate here. But, before my acquaintance was made at Streatham, he had returned to Ireland; where, about a year since, he married Miss Cavendish. They are now, by mutual consent, parted. She is gone to a sister in France, and he is come to spend some time in England by way of diverting his chagrin.

Mrs. Thrale who, though open-eyed enough to his absurdities, thinks well of the goodness of his heart, has a real regard for him; and he quite adores her, and quite worships Dr. Johnson — frequently declaring (for what he once says, he says continually), that he would spill his blood for him, — or clean his shoes, — or go to the East Indies to do him any good! "I am never," says he, "afraid of him; none but a fool or a rogue has any need to be afraid of him. What a fine old lion (looking up at his picture)[221] he is! Oh! I love him, — I honour him, — I reverence him! I would black his shoes for him. I wish I could give him my night's sleep!"[222]

These are exclamations which he is making continually. Mrs. Thrale has extremely well said that he is a caricature of Mr. Boswell, who is a caricature, I must add, of all other of Dr. Johnson's admirers.

The next great favourite he has in the world to our Doctor, and the person whom he talks *next most* of, is Mr. Jessop, who was his school-master, and whose praise he is never tired of singing in terms the most vehement, — quoting his authority for every other thing he says, and lamenting our misfortune in not knowing him.

His third favourite topic, at present, is *The Life of Louis XV.* in 4 vols. 8vo, lately translated from the French;[223] and of this he is so extravagantly fond, that he talks of it as a man might talk of his mistress, provided he had so little wit as to talk of her at all.

Painting, music, all the fine arts in their turn, he also speaks of in raptures. He is himself very accomplished, plays the violin extremely well, is a very good linguist, and a very decent painter. But no subject in his hands fails to be ridiculous, as he is sure, by the abruptness of its introduction, the strange turn of his expressions, or the Hibernian twang of his pronunciation, to make everything he says, however usual or common, seem peculiar and absurd.

When he first came here, upon the present renewal of his acquaintance at Streatham, Mrs. Thrale sent a summons to her daughter and me to come downstairs. We went together; I had long been curious to see him, and was glad of the opportunity. The moment Mrs. Thrale introduced me to him, he began a warm *éloge* of my father, speaking so fast, so much, and so Irish, that I could hardly understand him.

That over, he began upon this book, entreating Mrs. Thrale and all of us to read it, assuring us nothing could give us equal pleasure, minutely relating all its principal incidents with vehement expressions of praise or abhorrence, according to the good or bad he mentioned; and telling us that he had devoted three days and nights to making an index to it himself!

Then he touched upon his dear schoolmaster, Mr. Jessop, and then opened upon Dr. Johnson, whom he calls "the old lion," and who lasted till we left him to dress.

When we met again at dinner, and were joined by Dr. Johnson, the incense he paid him, by his solemn manner of listening, by the earnest reverence with which he eyed him, and by a theatric start of admiration every time he spoke, joined to the Doctor's utter insensibility to all these tokens, made me find infinite difficulty in keeping my countenance during the whole meal. His talk, too, is incessant; no female, however famed, can possibly excel him for volubility.

He told us a thousand strange staring stories, of noble deeds of valour and tender proofs of constancy, interspersed with extraordinary, and indeed incredible accidents, and with jests, and jokes, and bon-mots, that I am sure must be in Joe Miller.[224] And in the midst of all this jargon he abruptly called out, "Pray, Mrs. Thrale, what is the Doctor's opinion of the American war?"[225]

Opinion of the American war at this time of day! We all laughed cruelly; yet he repeated his question to the Doctor, who, however, made no other answer but by laughing too. But he is never affronted with Dr. Johnson, let him do what he will; and he seldom ventures to speak to him till he has asked some other person present for advice how he will *take* such or such a question...

[*Diary*, ii, 26-30]

...We have had[226] some *extra* diversion from two queer letters. The first of these was to Dr. Johnson, dated from the Orkneys, and costing him 1*s.* 6*d.* The contents were, to beg the Doctor's advice and counsel upon a very embarrassing matter; the writer, who signs his name and place of abode, says he is a clergyman, and labours under a most peculiar misfortune, for which he can give no account; and which is, — that though he very often writes letters to his friends and others, he never gets any answers; he entreats, therefore, that Dr. Johnson will take this into consideration, and explain to him to what so strange a thing may be attributed.

He then gives his direction.

The other of these curious letters is to myself; it is written upon fine French-glazed and gilt paper.

> "Miss F. Burney,
>   "At Lady Thrale's,
>   "Streatham, Surrey.

"*Madam* — I lately have read the three elegant volumes of *Evelina*, which were penned by you; and am desired by my friends, which are very numerous, to entreat the favour of you to oblige the public with a fourth.[227]

"Now, if this desire of mine should meet with your approbation, and you will honour the public with another volume (for it will not be ill-bestowed time), it will greatly add to the happiness of, — Honoured madam, a sincere admirer of you and *Evelina*.

> "*Snow Hill.* "[228]

Now don't our two epistles vie well with each other for singular absurdity? Which of them shows least meaning, who can tell? This is the third queer anonymous letter I have been favoured with. The date is more curious than the contents; one would think the people on Snow Hill might think three volumes enough for what they are the better, and not desire a fourth to celebrate more Smiths and Branghtons...

[Diary, ii, 41-2]

...At dinner,[229] Dr. Johnson returned, and Mr. Musgrave came with him. I did not see them till dinner was upon the table; and then Dr. Johnson, more in earnest than in jest, reproached me with not coming to meet him, and afterwards with not speaking to him, which, by the way, across a large table, and before company, I could not do, were I to be reproached ever so solemnly. It is requisite to speak so loud in order to be heard by him, and everybody listens so attentively for his reply, that not all his kindness will ever, I believe, embolden me to discourse with him willingly except *tête-à-tête*, or only with his family or my own.

Mr. Crutchley, who has more odd spite in him than all the rest of the world put together, enjoyed this call upon me, at which Mr. Musgrave no less wondered! He seemed to think it an honour that raised me to the highest pinnacle of glory, and started, and lifted up his hands in profound admiration.

This, you may imagine, was no great inducement to me to talk more; and when in the evening we all met again in the library, Dr. Johnson still continuing his accusation, and vowing I cared nothing for him, to get rid of the matter, and the grinning of Mr. Crutchley, and the theatrical staring of Mr. Musgrave, I proposed to Miss Thrale, as soon as tea was over, a walk round the grounds.

The next morning, the instant I entered the library at breakfast-time, where nobody was yet assembled but Messrs. Musgrave and Crutchley, the former ran up to me the moment I opened the door with a large folio in his hand, calling out,

"See here, Miss Burney, you know what I said about the Racks – "

"The what, sir?" cried I, having forgot it all.

"Why, the Racks; and here you see is the very same account. I must show it to the Doctor presently; the old lion hardly believed it."

He then read to me I know not how much stuff, not a word of which could I understand, because Mr. Crutchley sat laughing slyly, and casting up his eyes exactly before me, though unseen by Mr. Musgrave.

As soon as I got away from him, and walked on to the other end of the room, Mr. Crutchley followed me, and said,

"You went to bed too soon last night; you should have stayed a little longer, and then you would have heard such a panegyric as never before was spoken."

"So I suppose," quoth I, not knowing what he drove at.

"Oh yes!" cried Mr. Musgrave, "Dr. Johnson pronounced such a panegyric upon Miss Burney as would quite have intoxicated anybody else; not *her*, indeed, for she can bear it, but nobody else could."

"Oh! such praise," said Mr. Crutchley, "never did I hear before. It kept *me* awake, even *me*, after eleven o'clock, when nothing else could, – poor drowsy wretch that I am!"

They then both ran on praising this praise (*à qui mieux mieux*), and trying which should distract me most with curiosity to hear it; but I know Mr. Crutchley holds *all* panegyric in such infinite contempt and ridicule, that I felt nothing but mortification in finding he had been an auditor to my dear Dr. Johnson's partiality.

"Woe to him," cried he at last, "of whom no one speaks ill! Woe, therefore, to *you* in this house, I am sure!"

"No, no," cried I, "*you*, I believe, will save me from *that* woe."

In the midst of this business entered Miss Thrale. Mr. Musgrave, instantly flying up to her with the folio, exclaimed, "See, Miss Thrale, here's all that about the origin of Racks, that – "

"Of *what*?" cried she. "Of *rats*?"

This set us all grinning; but Mr. Crutchley, who had pretty well recovered his spirits, would not rest a moment from plaguing me about this praise, and began immediately to tell Miss Thrale what an oration had been made the preceding evening.

The moment Mrs. Thrale came in, all this was again repeated, Mr. Musgrave almost blessing himself with admiration while he talked of it, and Mr. Crutchley keeping me in a perpetual fidget, by never suffering the subject to drop.

When they had both exhausted all they had to say in a general manner of this *éloge*, and Dr. Johnson's fondness for me, for a little while we were allowed to rest; but scarce had I time to even hope the matter would be dropped, when Mr. Crutchley said to Mr. Musgrave,

"Well, sir, but now we have paved the way, I think you might as well go on."

"Yes," said Miss Thrale, never backward in promoting mischief, "methinks you might now disclose some of the particulars."

"Ay, do," said Mr. Crutchley, "pray repeat what he said."

"Oh! it is not in my power," cried Mr. Musgrave; "I have not the Doctor's eloquence. However, as well as I can remember, I will do it. He said that her manners were extraordinarily pleasing, and her language remarkably elegant; that she had as much virtue of mind as knowledge of the world; that with all her skill in human nature, she was at the same time as pure a little creature — "

This phrase, most comfortably to me, helped us to a laugh, and carried off in something like a joke praise that almost carried *me* off, from very shame not better to deserve it.

"Go on, go on!" cried Mr. Crutchley; "you have not said half."

"I am sensible of that," said he, very solemnly; "but it really is not in my power to do him justice, else I would say on, for Miss Burney I know would not be intoxicated."

"No, no; more, more," cried that tiresome creature; "at it again."

"Indeed, sir; and upon my word I would if I could; but only himself can do the old lion justice."...

...We had half done breakfast before he came down; he then complained he had had a bad night and was not well.

"I could not sleep," said he, laughing; "no, not a wink, for thinking of Miss Burney; her cruelty destroys my rest."

"Mercy, sir!" cried Mrs. Thrale; "what, beginning already? — why, we shall all assassinate her. Late at night, and early at morn, — no wonder you can't sleep!"

"Oh! what would I give," cried he, "that Miss Burney would come and tell me stories all night long! — if she would but come and talk to me!"

"That would be delightful, indeed!" said I; "but when, then, should I sleep?"

"Oh, that's *your* care! I should be happy enough in keeping you awake."

"I wish, sir," cried Mr. Musgrave, with vehemence, "I could give you my own night's sleep!"

"I would have you," continued Dr. Johnson to me (taking no notice of this flight), "come and talk to me of *Mr. Smith*, and then tell me stories of old *Branghton*, and then of his son, and then of your sea-captain."[230]

"And pray, sir," cried Mrs. Thrale, "don't forget *Lady Louisa*, for I shall break my heart if you do."

"Ay," answered he, "and of *Lady Louisa*, and of *Evelina* herself as much as you please, but not of *Mr. Macartney*[231] – no, not a word of him!"

"I assure you, ma'am," said Mr. Musgrave, "the very person who first told me of that book was Mr. Jessop,[232] my schoolmaster. Think of that! – was it not striking? 'A daughter,' says he, 'of your friend Dr. Burney has written a book; and it does her much credit.' Think of that! (lifting up his hands to enforce his admiration); and he desired me to read it – he recommended it to me; – a man of the finest taste, – a man of great profundity, – an extraordinary scholar, – living in a remote part of Ireland, – a man I esteem, upon my word!"

"But, sir," cried Mrs. Thrale to Dr. Johnson, "why, these men tell such wonders of what you said last night! Why, you spoke quite an oration in favour of Miss Burney."

"Ay," said Mr. Crutchley, "the moment it was over I went to bed. I stayed to hear the panegyric; but I thought I could bear nothing after it, and made off."

"I would you were off now," cried I, "and in your phaeton in the midst of this rain!"

"Oh, sir!" cried Mr. Musgrave, "the Doctor went on with it again after you went; I had the honour to hear a great deal more."

"Why, this is very fine indeed!" said Mrs. Thrale; "why, Dr. Johnson, – why, what is all this?"

"These young fellows," answered he, "play me false; they take me in; they start the subject, and make me say something of that Fanny Burney, and then the rogues know that when I have once begun I shall not know when to leave off."

"We are glad, sir," said Mr. Crutchley, "to hear our own thoughts expressed so much better than we can express them ourselves."

I could only turn up my eyes at him.

"Just so," said Mrs. Thrale,

'What oft was thought, but ne'er so well express'd.'[233]

Here, much to my satisfaction, the conversation broke up...

[*Diary*, ii, 43-9]

...Dr. Johnson[234] has been very unwell indeed. Once I was quite frightened about him; but he continues his strange discipline – starving, mercury, opium; and though for a time half demolished by its severity, he always, in the end, rises superior both to the disease and the remedy, — which commonly is the most alarming of the two. His kindness for me, I think, if possible, still increased: he actually *bores* everybody so about me that the folks even complain of it. I must, however, acknowledge I feel but little pity for their fatigue...

[*Diary*, ii, 52]

Oct. 15, 1782.

...I am very sorry you[235] could not come to Streatham at the time Mrs. Thrale hoped to see you, for when shall we be likely to meet there again? You would have been much pleased, I am sure, by meeting with General Paoli,[236] who spent the day there, and was extremely communicative and agreeable. I had seen him in large companies, but was never made known to him before; nevertheless, he conversed with me as if well acquainted not only with myself, but my connections, — inquiring of me when I had last seen Mrs. Montagu? and calling Sir Joshua Reynolds, when he spoke of him, my friend. He is a very pleasing man, tall and genteel in his person, remarkably well bred, and very mild and soft in his manners.

I will try to give you a little specimen of his conversation, because I know you love to hear particulars of all out-of-the-way persons. His English is blundering, but not unpretty. Speaking of his first acquaintance with Mr. Boswell,[237]

"He came," he said, "to my country, and he fetched me some letter of recommending him; but I was of the belief he might be an impostor, and I supposed, in my minte, he was an espy; for I look away from him, and in a moment I look to him again, and I behold his tablets. Oh! he was to the work of writing down all I say! Indeed I was angry. But soon I discover he was no impostor and no espy; and I only find I was myself the monster he had come to discern. Oh, —— is a very good man; I love him indeed; so cheerful! so gay! so pleasant! but at the first, oh! I was indeed angry."

After this he told us a story of an expectation he had had of being robbed, and of the protection he found from a very large dog that he is very fond of.

"I walk out," he said, "in the night; I go towards the field; I behold a man — oh, ugly one! I proceed — he follow; I go on — he address me, 'You have one dog,' he says. 'Yes,' say I to him. 'Is a fierce dog?' he says; 'is he fiery?' 'Yes,' reply I, 'he can bite.' 'I would not attack in the night,' says he, 'a house to have such dog in it.' Then I conclude he was a breaker;[238] so I turn to him — oh, very rough! not gentle — and I say, very fierce, 'He shall destroy you, if you are ten!' "

Afterwards, speaking of the Irish giant,[239] who is now shown in town, he said,

"He is so large I am as a baby! I look at him–oh! I find myself so little as a child! Indeed, my indignation it rises when I see him hold up his hand so high. I am as nothing; and I find myself in the power of a man who fetches from me a half-a-crown."

This language, which is all spoke very pompously by him, sounds comical from himself, though I know not how it may read.

Adieu, my dear and kind daddy, and believe me your ever obliged and ever affectionate,

F. B.

Brighthelmstone,[240] *October 26.* – My journey was incidentless; but the moment I came into Brighthelmstone I was met by Mrs. Thrale, who had most eagerly been waiting for me a long while, and therefore I dismounted, and walked home with her. It would be very superfluous to tell you how she received me, for you cannot but know, from her impatient letters, what I had reason to expect of kindness and welcome.[241]

I was too much tired to choose appearing at dinner, and therefore eat my eat upstairs, and was then decorated a little, and came forth to tea.

Mr. Harry Cotton[242] and Mr. Swinerton[243] were both here. Mrs. Thrale said they almost lived with her, and therefore were not to be avoided, but declared she had refused a flaming party of blues, for fear I should think, if I met them just after my journey, she was playing Mrs. Harrel.[244]

Dr. Johnson received me too with his usual goodness, and with a salute so loud, that the two young beaus, Cotton and Swinerton, have never done laughing about it.

Mrs. Thrale spent two or three hours in my room, talking over all her affairs, and then we wished each other *bon repos*, and – retired. *Grandissima* conclusion.

Oh, but let me not forget that a fine note came from Mr. Pepys, who is here with his family, saying he was *pressé de vivre*, and entreating to see Mrs. and Miss T., Dr. Johnson, and Cecilia, at his house the next day. I hate mightily this method of naming me from my heroines, of whose honour I think I am more jealous than of my own.

Oct. 27. – The Pepyses came to visit me in form, but I was dressing; in the evening, however, Mrs. and Miss T. took me to them. Dr. Johnson would not go; he told me it was my day, and I should be crowned, for Mr. Pepys was wild about *Cecilia*.

"However," he added, "do not hear too much of it; but when he has talked about it for an hour or so, tell him to have done. There is no other way."

A mighty easy way, this! however,'tis what he literally practises for himself...

[Diary, ii, 100-3]

...At dinner[245] we had Dr. Delap[246] and Mr. Selwyn,[247] who accompanied us in the evening to a ball; as did also Dr. Johnson, to the universal amazement of all who saw him there; — but he said he had found it so dull being quite alone the preceding evening, that he determined upon going with us; "for," he said, "it cannot be worse than being alone."[248]

Strange that he should think so! I am sure I am not of his mind...

...Dr. Johnson was joined by a friend of his own, Mr. Metcalf,[249] and did tolerably well...

[Diary, ii, 105-6]

...Poor Mr. Pepys had, however, real cause to bemoan my escape;[250] for the little set was broken up by my retreat, and he joined Dr. Johnson, with whom he entered into an argument upon some lines of Gray, and upon Pope's definition of wit, in which he was so roughly confuted, and so severely ridiculed, that he was hurt and piqued beyond all power of disguise, and, in the midst of this discourse, suddenly turned from him, and, wishing Mrs. Thrale good-night, very abruptly withdrew.

Dr. Johnson was certainly right with respect to the argument and to reason; but his opposition was so warm, and his wit so satirical and exulting, that I was really quite grieved to see how unamiable he appeared, and how greatly he made himself dreaded by all, and by many abhorred. What pity that he will not curb the vehemence of his love of victory and superiority![251]

The sum of the dispute was this. Wit being talked of, Mr. Pepys repeated, —

> True wit is Nature to advantage dress'd,
> What oft was thought, but ne'er so well express'd.[252]

"That, sir," cried Dr. Johnson, "is a definition both false and foolish. Let wit be dressed how it will, it will equally be wit, and neither the more nor the less for any advantage dress can give it."

Mr. P. — But, sir, may not wit be so ill expressed, and so obscure, by a bad speaker, as to be lost?

Dr. J. — The fault, then, sir, must be with the hearer. If a man cannot distinguish wit from words, he little deserves to hear it.

Mr. P. — But, sir, what Pope means —

Dr. J. — Sir, what Pope means, if he means what he says, is both false and foolish. In the first place, "what oft was thought," is all the worse for being often thought, because to be wit, it ought to be newly thought.

Mr. P. — But, sir, 'tis the expression makes it new.

Dr. J. — How can the expression make it new? It may make it clear, or may make it elegant; but how new? You are confounding words with things.

Mr. P. — But, sir, if one man says a thing very ill, may not another man say it so much better that——

Dr. J. — That other man, sir, deserves but small praise for the amendment; he is but the tailor to the first man's thoughts.

Mr. P. — True, sir, he may be but the tailor; but then the difference is as great as between a man in a gold lace suit and a man in a blanket.

Dr. J. — Just so, sir, I thank you for that: the difference is precisely such, since it consists neither in the gold lace suit nor the blanket, but in the man by whom they are worn.

This was the summary; the various contemptuous sarcasms intermixed would fill, and very unpleasantly, a quire...

[*Diary*, ii, 107-9]

...*Thursday, Oct. 31.* — A note came this morning to invite us all, except Dr. Johnson, to Lady Rothes's.[253] Dr. Johnson has tortured poor Mr. Pepys so much that I fancy her ladyship omitted him in compliment to her brother-in-law...

[*Diary*, ii, 112]

...*Saturday, Nov. 2*, we went to Lady Shelley's.[254] Dr. Johnson, again, excepted in the invitation. He is almost constantly omitted, either from too much respect or too much fear. I am sorry for it, as he hates being alone, and as, though he scolds the others, he is well enough satisfied himself; and, having given vent to all his own occasional anger or ill-humour, he is ready to begin again, and is never aware that those who have so been "downed" by him, never can much covet so triumphant a visitor. In contests of wit, the victor is as ill off in future consequences as the vanquished in present ridicule.

Monday, Nov. 4. — This was a grand and busy day. Mr. Swinerton has been some time arranging a meeting for all our house, with Lady De Ferrars.[255] ...

...I happened to be standing by Dr. Johnson when all the ladies came in; but, as I dread him before strangers, from the staring attention he attracts both for himself and all with whom he talks, I endeavoured to change my ground. However, he kept prating a sort of comical nonsense that detained me some minutes whether I would or not; but when we were all taking places at the breakfast-table I made another effort to escape. It proved vain; he drew his chair next to mine, and went rattling on in a humorous sort of comparison he was drawing of himself to me, — not one word of which could I enjoy, or can I remember, from the hurry I was in to get out of his way. In short, I felt so awkward from being thus marked out, that I was reduced to whisper a request to Mr. Swinerton to put a chair between us, for which I presently made a space: for I have often known him stop all conversation with me, when he has ceased to have me for his next neighbour. Mr. Swinerton, who is an extremely good-natured young man, and so intimate here that I make no scruple with him, instantly complied, and placed himself between us.

But no sooner was this done, than Dr. Johnson, half seriously, and very loudly, took him to task.

"How now, sir! what do you mean by this? Would you separate me from Miss Burney?"

Mr. Swinerton, a little startled, began some apologies, and Mrs. Thrale winked at him to give up the place; but he was willing to oblige me, though he grew more and more frightened every minute, and coloured violently as the Doctor continued his remonstrance, which he did with rather unmerciful raillery, upon his taking advantage of being in his own house to thus supplant him, and *crow*; but when he had borne it for about ten minutes, his face became so hot with the fear of hearing something worse, that he ran from the field, and took a chair between Lady De Ferrars and Mrs. Thrale.

I think I shall take warning by this failure, to trust only to my own expedients for avoiding his public notice in future. However it stopped here; for Lord De Ferrars came in, and took the disputed place without knowing of the contest, and all was quiet.

All that passed afterwards was too general and too common to be recollected...

..."Ay," cried Dr. Johnson, "some people want to make out some credit to me from the little rogue's book. I was told by a gentleman this morning, that it was a very fine book, if it was all her own. 'It is all her own,' said I, 'for me, I am sure, for I never saw one word of it before it was printed.'

This gentleman I have good reason to believe is Mr. Metcalf...He is much with Dr. Johnson, but seems to have taken an unaccountable dislike to Mrs. Thrale, to whom he never speaks. I have seen him but once or twice myself; and as he is dry, and I am shy, very little has passed between us...

...While we were debating this matter,[256] a gentleman suddenly said to me, – "Did you walk far this morning, Miss Burney?" And, looking at him, I saw Mr. Metcalf, whose graciousness rather surprised me, for he only made to Mrs. Thrale a cold and distant bow, and it seems he declares, aloud and around, his aversion to literary ladies. That he can endure, and even seek me, is, I presume, only from the general perverseness of mankind, because he sees I have always turned from him; not, however, from disliking him, for he is a shrewd, sensible, keen, and very clever man; but merely from a dryness on his own side that has excited retaliation.

"Yes," I answered, "we walked a good way."

"Dr. Johnson," said he, "told me in the morning you were no walker; but I informed him that I had had the pleasure of seeing you upon the Newmarket Hill."

"Oh, he does not know," cried I, "whether I am a walker or not – he does not see me walk, because he never walks himself."

"He has asked me," said he, "to go with him to Chichester, to see the cathedral,[257] and I told him I would certainly go if he pleased; but why, I cannot imagine, for how shall a blind man see a cathedral?"

"I believe," quoth I, "his blindness is as much the effect of absence as of infirmity, for he sees wonderfully at times."

"Why, he has assured me he cannot see the colour of any man's eyes, and does not know what eyes any of his acquaintances have."

"I am sure, however," cried I, "he can see the colour of a lady's top-knot, for he very often finds fault with it."

"Is that possible?"

"Yes, indeed; and I was much astonished at it at first when I knew him, for I had concluded that the utmost of his sight would only reach to tell him whether he saw a cap or a wig."

Here he was called away by some gentleman...

[Diary, ii, 113-19]

Thursday.[258] – Mr. Metcalf called upon Dr. Johnson, and took him out an airing. Mr. Hamilton[259] is gone, and Mr. Metcalf is now the only person out of this house that voluntarily communicates with the Doctor. He has been in a terrible severe humour of late, and has really frightened all the people, till they almost ran from him. To me only I think he is now kind, for Mrs. Thrale fares worse than anybody. 'Tis very strange and very melancholy that he will not a little more accommodate his manners and language to those of other people. He likes Mr. Metcalf, however, and so do I, for he is very clever and entertaining when he pleases. Capt. Phillips[260] will remember that was not the case when we saw him at Sir Joshua's. He has, however, all the *de quoi*.

Poor Dr. Delap confessed to us that the reason he now came so seldom, though he formerly almost lived with us when at this place, was his being too unwell to cope with Dr. Johnson. And the other day Mr. Selwyn having refused an invitation from Mr. Hamilton to meet the Doctor, because he preferred being here upon a day when he was out, suddenly rose at the time he was expected to return, and said he must run away, "for fear the Doctor should call him to account."...

[Diary, ii, 122]

...We spent this evening[261] at Lady De Ferrars, where Dr. Johnson accompanied us, for the first time he has been invited of our parties since my arrival...

...*Monday* and *Tuesday*.[262] – I have no time, except to tell you a comical tale which Mrs. Thrale ran to acquaint me with. She had been calling upon Mr. Scrase, an old and dear friend, who is confined with the gout; and while she was inquiring about him of his nurse and housekeeper, the woman said,

"Ah, madam, how happy are you to have Minerva in the house with you!"

"Oh," cried Mrs. Thrale, "you mean my dear Miss Burney, that wrote *Cecilia*. So you have read it; and what part did you like?"

"Oh, madam, I liked it all better than anything I ever saw in my life; but most of all I liked that good old gentleman, Mr. Albany,[263] that goes about telling people their duty, without so much as thinking of their fine clothes."

When Mrs. Thrale told us this at dinner, Dr. Johnson said,

"I am all of the old housekeeper's mind; Mr. Albany I have always stood up for; he is one of my first favourites. Very fine indeed are the things he says."

My dear Dr. Johnson! – what condescension is this! He fully, also, enters into all my meaning in the high-flown language of Albany, from his partial insanity and unappeasable remorse.

So here concludes Brighthelmstone for 1782...

[*Diary*, ii, 127-8]

...*Dec. 8.* – Now for Miss Monckton's[264] assembly...

...I was presently separated from Mrs. Thrale, and entirely surrounded by strangers, all dressed superbly, and all looking saucily; and as nobody's names were spoken, I had no chance to discover any acquaintances. Mr. Metcalf, indeed, came and spoke to me the instant I came in, and I should have been very happy to have had him for my neighbour; but he was engaged in attending to Dr. Johnson, who was standing near the fire, and environed with listeners.

Some new people now coming in, and placing themselves in a regular way, Miss Monckton exclaimed, – "My whole care is to prevent a circle"; and hastily rising, she pulled about the chairs, and planted the people in groups, with as dexterous a disorder as you would desire to see...

...Then came in Sir Joshua Reynolds, and he soon drew a chair near mine, and from that time I was never without some friend at my elbow.

"Have you seen," he said, "Mrs. Montagu lately?"

"No, not very lately."

"But within these few months?"

"No, not since last year."

"Oh, you must see her, then. You ought to see and to hear her — 'twill be worth your while. Have you heard of the fine long letter she has written?"

"Yes, but I have not met with it."

"I have."

"And who is it to?"

"The old Duchess of Portland.[265] She desired Mrs. Montagu's opinion of *Cecilia*, and she has written it at full length. I was in a party at Her Grace's, and heard of nothing but you. She is so delighted, and so sensibly, so rationally, that I only wish you could have heard her. And old Mrs. Delany[266] had been forced to begin it, though she had said she should never read any more; however, when we met, she was reading it already for the third time."

Pray tell my daddy[267] to rejoice for me in this conquest of the Duchess, his old friend, and Mrs. Delany, his sister's.

Sir Joshua is extremely kind; he is always picking up some anecdote of this sort for me; yet, most delicately, never lets me hear his own praises but through others. He looks vastly well, and as if he had never been ill.[268]

After this Mrs. Burke saw me, and, with much civility and softness of manner, came and talked with me, while her husband, without seeing me, went behind my chair to speak to Mrs. Hampden.

Miss Monckton, returning to me, then said,

"Miss Burney, I had the pleasure yesterday of seeing Mrs. Greville."[269]

I suppose she concluded I was very intimate with her.

"I have not seen her," said I, "many years."

"I know, however," cried she, looking surprised, "she is your godmother."

"But she does not do her duty and answer for me, for I never see her."

"Oh, you have answered very well for yourself! But I know by that your name is Fanny."

She then tripped to somebody else, and Mr. Burke[270] very quietly came from Mrs. Hampden, and sat down in the vacant place at my side. I could then wait no longer, for I found he was more near-sighted than myself; I, therefore, turned towards him and bowed: he seemed quite amazed, and really made me ashamed, however delighted, by the expressive civility and distinction with which he instantly rose to return my bow, and stood the whole time he was making his compliments upon seeing me, and calling himself the blindest of men for not finding me out sooner. And Mrs. Burke, who was seated near me, said, loud enough for me to hear her,

"See, see! what a flirtation Mr. Burke is beginning with Miss Burney! and before my face too!"

These ceremonies over, he sate down by me, and began a conversation which you, my dearest Susy, would be glad to hear, for my sake, word for word; but which I really could not listen to with sufficient ease, from shame at his warm eulogiums, to remember with any accuracy. The general substance, however, take as I recollect it.

After many most eloquent compliments upon the book, too delicate either to shock or sicken the nicest ear, he very emphatically congratulated me upon its most universal success; said "he was now too late to speak of it, since he could only echo the voice of the whole nation"; and added, with a laugh, "I had hoped to have made some merit of my enthusiasm; but the moment I went about to hear what others say, I found myself merely one in a multitude."

He then told me that, notwithstanding his admiration, he was the man who had dared to find some faults with so favourite and fashionable a work. I entreated him to tell me what they were, and assured him nothing would make me so happy as to correct them under his direction. He then enumerated them...[271]

..."But," said he, when he had finished his comments, "what excuse must I give for this presumption? I have none in the world to offer but the real, the high esteem I feel for you; and I must at the same time acknowledge it is all your own doing that I am able to find fault; for it is your general perfection in writing that has taught me to criticise where it is not quite uniform."

Here's an orator, dear Susy!

Then, looking very archly at me, and around him, he said,

"Are you sitting here for characters? Nothing, by the way, struck me more in reading your book than the admirable skill with which your ingenious characters make themselves known by their own words."[272]

He then went on to tell me that I had done the most wonderful of wonders in pleasing the old wits, particularly the Duchess of Portland and Mrs. Delany, who resisted reading the book till they were teased into it, and, since they began, could do nothing else; and he failed not to point out, with his utmost eloquence, the difficulty of giving satisfaction to those who piqued themselves upon being past receiving it.

"But," said he, "I have one other fault to find, and a far more material one than I have mentioned."

"I am the more obliged to you. What is it?"

"The disposal of this book. I have much advice to offer to you upon that subject. Why did not you send for your own friend out of the city? he would have taken care you should not part with it so much below par."[273]

He meant Mr. Briggs.[274]

Sir Joshua Reynolds now joined us.

"Are you telling her," said he, "of our conversation with the old wits? I am glad you hear it from Mr. Burke, Miss Burney, for he can tell it so much better than I can, and remember their very words."

"Nothing else would they talk of for three whole hours," said he, "and we were there at the third reading of the bill."

"I believe I was in good hands," said I, "if they talked of it to you?"

"Why, yes," answered Sir Joshua, laughing, "we joined in from time to time. Gibbon says he read the whole five volumes in a day."

"'Tis impossible," cried Mr. Burke, "it cost me three days; and you know I never parted with it from the time I first opened it."

Here are laurels, Susy! My dear daddy and Kitty, are you not doubly glad you so kindly hurried me upstairs to write when at Chessington?[275]

Mr. Burke then went to some other party, and Mr. Swinerton took his place, with whom I had a dawdling conversation upon dawdling subjects; and I was not a little enlivened, upon his quitting the chair, to have it filled by Mr. Metcalfe, who, with much satire, but much entertainment, kept chattering with me till Dr. Johnson found me out, and brought a chair opposite to me.

Do you laugh, my Susan, or cry at your F. B.'s honours?

"So," said he to Mr. Metcalfe, "it is you, is it, that are engrossing her thus?"

"He's jealous," said Mr. Metcalfe drily.

"How these people talk of Mrs. Siddons!"[276] said the Doctor. "I came hither in full expectation of hearing no name but the name I love and pant to hear, — when from one corner to another they are talking of that jade Mrs. Siddons! till, at last wearied out, I went yonder into a corner, and repeated to myself Burney! Burney! Burney! Burney!"

"Ay, sir," said Mr. Metcalfe, "you should have carved it upon the trees."

"Sir, had there been any trees, so I should; but, being none, I was content to carve it upon my heart."...

...Miss Monckton now came to us again, and I congratulated her upon her power in making Dr. Johnson sit in a group; upon which she immediately said to him,

"Sir, Miss Burney says you like best to sit in a circle!"[277]

"Does she?" said he, laughing. "Ay, never mind what she says. Don't you know she is a writer of romances?"

"Yes, that I do, indeed!" said Miss Monckton, and every one joined in a laugh that put me horribly out of countenance.

"She may write romances and speak truth," said my dear Sir Joshua, who, as well as young Burke, and Mr. Metcalfe, and two strangers, joined now in our little party.

"But, indeed, Dr. Johnson," said Miss Monckton, "you *must* see Mrs. Siddons. Won't you see her in some fine part?"

"Why, if I *must*, madam, I have no choice."[278]

"She says, sir, she shall be very much afraid of you."

"Madam, that cannot be true."

"Not true," cried Miss Monckton, staring, "yes it is."

"It *cannot* be, madam."

"But she said so to me; I heard her say it myself."

"Madam, it is not *possible*! remember, therefore, in future, that even fiction should be supported by probability."

Miss Monckton looked all amazement, but insisted upon the truth of what she had said.

"I do not believe, madam," said he warmly, "she knows my name."

"Oh, that is rating her too low," said a gentleman stranger.

"By not knowing my name," continued he, "I do not mean so literally; but that, when she sees it abused in a newspaper, she may possibly recollect that she has seen it abused in a newspaper before."

"Well, sir," said Miss Monckton, "but you must see her for all this."

"Well, madam, if you desire it, I will go. See her I shall not, nor hear her; but I'll go, and that will do. The last time I was at a play, I was ordered there by Mrs. Abington,[279] or Mrs. Somebody, I do not well remember who, but I placed myself in the middle of the first row of the front boxes, to show that when I was called I came."

[The talk upon this matter went on very long, and with great spirit; but I have time for no more of it. I felt myself extremely awkward about going away, not choosing, as it was my first visit, to take French leave, and hardly knowing how to lead the way alone among so many strangers.

At last, and with the last, I made my attempt. A large party of ladies arose at the same time, and I tripped after them; Miss Monckton, however, made me come back, for she said I must else wait in the other room till those ladies' carriages drove away.

When I returned, Sir Joshua came and desired he might convey me home; I declined the offer, and he pressed it a good deal, drolly saying,

"Why, I am old enough, a'n't I?"

And when he found me stout, he said to Dr. Johnson,

"Sir, is not this very hard? Nobody thinks me very young, yet Miss Burney won't give me the privilege of age in letting me see her home? She says I a'n't old enough."

I had never said any such thing.

"Ay, sir," said the doctor, "did I not tell you she was a writer of romances?"

Again I tried to run away, but the door stuck, and Miss Monckton prevented me, and begged I would stay a little longer. She then went and whispered something to her mother, and I had a notion from her manner, she wanted to keep me to supper, which I did not choose, and, therefore, when her back was turned, I prevailed upon young Burke to open the door for me, and out I went. Miss Monckton ran after me, but I would not come back. I was, however, and I am, much obliged by her uncommon civility and attentions to me. She is far better at her own house than elsewhere.]...

[*Diary*, ii, 132-44]

...Now, to return to Tuesday,[280] one of my out-days.

I went in the evening to call on Mrs. Thrale, and tore myself away from her to go to Bolt Court to see Dr. Johnson, who is very unwell. He received me with great kindness, and bade me come oftener, which I will try to contrive. He told me he heard of nothing but me, call upon him who would; and, though he pretended to growl, he was evidently delighted for me. His usual set, Mrs. Williams and Mrs. De Mullins, were with him; and some queer man of a parson who, after grinning at me some time, said,

"Pray, Mrs. De Mullins, is the fifth volume of *Cecilia* at home yet? Dr. Johnson made me read it, ma'am."

"Sir, he did it much honour —"

"*Made* you, sir?" said the Doctor; "you give an ill account of your own taste or understanding, if you wanted any *making* to read such a book as *Cecilia*."

"Oh, sir, I don't mean that; for I am sure I left everything in the world to go on with it."

A shilling was now wanted for some purpose or other, and none of them happened to have one; I begged that I might lend one.

"Ay, do," said the Doctor, "I will borrow of you;[281] authors are like privateers, always fair game for one another."

"True, sir," said the parson, "one author is always robbing another."

"I don't know that, sir," cried the Doctor; "there sits an author who, to my knowledge, has robbed nobody. I have never once caught her at a theft. The rogue keeps her resources to herself!"...

[*Diary*, ii, 156-7]

...*Friday*.[282] — I dined with Mrs. Thrale and Dr. Johnson, who was very comic and good-humoured. Susan Thrale had just had her hair turned up, and powdered, and has taken to the womanly robe. Dr. Johnson sportively gave her instructions how to increase her consequence, and to "take upon her" properly.

"Begin," said he, "Miss Susy, with something grand — something to surprise mankind! Let your first essay in life be a warm censure of *Cecilia*. You can no way make yourself more conspicuous. Tell the world how ill it was conceived, and how ill executed. Tell them how little there is in it of human nature, and how well your knowledge of the world enables you to judge of the failings in that book. Find fault without fear; and if you are at a loss for any to find, invent whatever comes into your mind, for you may say what you please, with little fear of detection, since of those who praise *Cecilia* not half have read it, and of those who have read it, not half remember it. Go to work, therefore, boldly; and particularly mark that the character of Albany is extremely unnatural, to your own knowledge, since you never met with such a man at Mrs. Cummyn's School."[283]

This stopped his exhortation, for we laughed so violently at this happy criticism that he could not recover the thread of his harangue.

Mrs. Thrale, who was to have gone with me to Mrs. Ord's, gave up her visit in order to stay with Dr. Johnson; Miss Thrale, therefore, and I went together...

[*Diary*, ii, 159-60]

...*Friday, 4th Jan.* — We had an invited party at home, both for dinner and the evening...

...Dr. Johnson came so very late, that we had all given him up: he was, however, very ill, and only from an extreme of kindness did he come at all. When I went up to him, to tell how sorry I was to find him so unwell, — "Ah!" he cried, taking my hand and kissing it, "who shall ail anything when 'Cecilia' is so near? Yet you do not think how poorly I am!"

This was quite melancholy, and all dinner-time he hardly opened his mouth but to repeat to me, — "Ah! you little know how ill I am." He was excessively kind to me, in spite of all his pain, and indeed I was so sorry for him, that I could talk no more than himself. All our comfort was from Mr. Seward, who enlivened us as much as he possibly could by his puns and his sport. But poor Dr. Johnson was so ill, that after dinner he went home —

[*Diary*, ii, 171-2]

...I made a visit to poor Dr. Johnson[284] to inquire after his health. I found him better, yet extremely far from well. One thing, however, gave me infinite satisfaction. He was so good as to ask me after Charles,[285] and said, "I shall be glad to see him; pray tell him to call upon me." I thanked him very much, and said how proud he would be of such a permission.

"I should be glad," said he, still more kindly, "to see him, if he were not your brother; but were he a dog, a cat, a rat, a frog, and belonged to you, I must needs be glad to see him!"

Mr. Seward has sent me a proof plate, upon silver paper, of an extremely fine impression of this dear Doctor, a mezzotinto, by Doughty,[286] from Sir Joshua's picture, and a very pretty note to beg my acceptance of it. I am much obliged to him, and very glad to have it...

[*Diary*, ii, 177]

...Thursday, June 19. — We heard to-day that Dr. Johnson had been taken ill,[287] in a way that gave a dreadful shock to himself, and a most anxious alarm to his friends. Mr. Seward brought the news here, and my father and I instantly went to his house. He had earnestly desired me, when we lived so much together at Streatham, to see him frequently if he should be ill. He saw my father, but he had medical people with him, and could not admit me upstairs, but he sent me down a most kind message, that he thanked me for calling, and when he was better should hope to see me often. I had the satisfaction to hear from Mrs. Williams that the physicians had pronounced him to be in no danger, and expected a speedy recovery.

The stroke was confined to his tongue. Mrs. Williams told me a most striking and touching circumstance that attended the attack. It was at about four o'clock in the morning: he found himself with a paralytic affection; he rose, and composed in his own mind a Latin prayer to the Almighty, "that whatever were the sufferings for which he must prepare himself, it would please Him, through the grace and mediation of our blessed Saviour, to spare his intellects, and let them all fall upon his body." When he had composed this, internally, he endeavoured to speak it aloud, but found his voice was gone...

[*Diary*, ii, 213-14]

...Wednesday, July 1. — I was again at Mrs. Vesey's where again I met Mr. Walpole, Mr. Pepys, Miss Elliott, Mr. Burke, his wife and son, Sir Joshua Reynolds, and some others...

...I had the satisfaction to hear from Sir Joshua that Dr. Johnson had dined with him at the Club. I look upon him, therefore, now, as quite recovered. I called the next morning to congratulate him, and found him very gay and very good-humoured...

[*Diary*, ii, 215]

...Thursday, Feb. 23[288]...He [Mr. Cambridge[289]] began talking of Dr. Johnson, and asking after his present health.

"He is very much recovered," I answered, "and out of town, at Mr. Langton's. And there I hope he will entertain him with enough of Greek."

"Yes," said Mr. Cambridge, "and make his son repeat the Hebrew alphabet to him."[290]

"He means," said I, "to go, when he returns, to Mr. Bowles, in Wiltshire.[291] I told him I had heard that Mr. Bowles was very much delighted with the expectation of seeing him, and he answered me, — 'He is so delighted, that it is shocking! — it is really shocking to see how high are his expectations.' I asked him why; and he said, — 'Why, if any man is expected to take a leap of twenty yards, and does actually take one of ten, everybody will be disappointed, though ten yards may be more than any other man ever leaped!' "...

[Diary, ii, 204]

...Well[292] – I am much disappointed, & very much terrified at the idea of speaking to Mr. C.[293] – What end upon Earth can be answered by letting poor Dr. Johnson into such a secret? – Fury, rage, *Madness*, almost, will be all that can follow. If you *can* prevent this measure, indeed I think you had far better. This dear soul is not their *Ward*; they cannot prevent her marrying, though they may, with added dishonour & hazard, *hurry* her into it. Any thing will be better than this turbulent measure, which *cannot* end in doing good.

I see, my dear Miss Thrale, you have far more affection for your dear unhappy Mother than she gives you credit for; & I see it with added esteem & regard for yourself. When you say you "sometimes think her peace of Mind should be purchased at almost any rate," – you touch me more than I can express. Your account of her Health, too, & of your fears about it, – O how it grieves me! – I would her Eyes could at least be opened to *your* behaviour in this business, – but there is a *film* before them, & she sees nothing. May it *soon*, or *never* be removed! I often think with dread of what her feelings will be when, all opposition being conquered, she considers what she has done! – And this thought weighs yet more powerfully than any other against *our* leading to an action that will so ill bear retrospection. I say *our*, my dear Miss Thrale, for who in the World but yourself can be so deeply interested in her conduct or her happiness as I am? – not even your sisters for *her* sake, for they are too young to see any evils but their *own* in this unhappy business & they did not, as we did, know her in her better Day...

[Queeney, pp. 72-3]

...*Thursday, Oct, 29.* – This morning, at breakfast, Mr. Hoole[294] called. I wanted to call upon Dr. Johnson, and it is so disagreeable to me to go to him alone, now poor Mrs. Williams is dead,[295] on account of the quantity of men always visiting him,[296] that I most gladly accepted, almost asked, his 'squireship.

We went together. The dear Doctor received me with open arms.

"Ah, dearest of all dear ladies!" he cried, and made me sit in his best chair.

He had not breakfasted.

"Do you forgive my coming so soon?" said I.

"I cannot forgive your not coming sooner," he answered.

I asked if I should make his breakfast, which I have done since we left Streatham; he readily consented.

"But, sir," quoth I, "I am in the wrong chair." For I was away from the table.

"It is so difficult," said he, "for anything to be wrong that belongs to you, that it can only be I am in the wrong chair, to keep you from the right one."

And then we changed.

You will see by this how good were his spirits and his health.

I stayed with him two hours, and could hardly get away; he wanted me to dine with him, and said he would send home to excuse me; but I could not possibly do that. Yet I left him with real regret.

Nov. 15th.[297] – I have been interrupted, & have now something indeed to communicate, – my dear Miss Thrale, Dr. J. *knows* of this terrible affair! – I have seen Mr. Seward, – it is he who has told me this, though he has not told me by what means he gained the intelligence. He does not, however, know its *present* state, but concludes it is all over. O would it were! – The dread this news has given me of his Sight is inexpressible. I am sure I shall feel & look as if a Culprit myself when I appear before him: which must be soon, as I have been out of Town, & not called upon him, this fortnight. In what way he will take it, I know not, – Heaven forbid he should examine me upon it! – Is it not terrible that I should now be *ashamed* of being the chosen friend of one in whose friendship I so lately gloried? – & you my dear Miss Thrale, – how truly do I compassionate you! – Mr. Seward says we *are* all to pay for our greatest delight by the greatest suffering.

I dare not tell Mrs. T. of this discovery, – she is so warm, so unguarded, so exquisitely susceptible, that I fear her knowing it. Mr. Seward urges me vehemently to go to Bath, – but what can I do there? I have *no* weight in fact, though I seem to have the greatest. Dear, lost, infatuated Soul! – she calls upon me for-ever; & yet never listens to me when called. But come I will, the moment it is in my power, though with no view but to let her open her loaded bosom into my unwilling Ears. All you say of her Health makes me tremble, & those emotions you so often feel to end all are not more natural than humane. – If I did not believe she would herself repent hereafter, – but I am *sure* she would. She must come to her senses some time; for it can never be, however she may flatter herself, that the whole World is mad, & she alone reasonable.

[*Queeney*, pp. 75-6]

Wednesday, Nov. 19. – I received a letter from Dr. Johnson,[298] which I have not by me, but will try to recollect.

"TO MISS BURNEY"

"*Madam* – You have now been at home this long time, and yet I have neither seen nor heard from you. Have we quarrelled?

"I have met with a volume of the *Philosophical Transactions*, which I imagine to belong to Dr. Burney.[299] Miss Charlotte[300] will please to examine.

"Pray send me a direction where Mrs. Chapone[301] lives; and pray, some time, let me have the honour of telling you how much I am, madam, your most humble servant,   "SAM. JOHNSON."[302]

Now if ever you read anything more dry, tell me. I was shocked to see him undoubtedly angry, but took courage, and resolved to make a serious defence; therefore thus I answered,

"TO DR. JOHNSON"

"*Dear Sir*— May I not say dear? for quarrelled I am sure we have not. The bad weather alone has kept me from waiting upon you; but now you have condescended to give me a summons, no lion shall stand in the way of my making your tea this afternoon, unless I receive a prohibition from yourself, and then I must submit; for what, as you said of a certain great lady, signifies the barking of a lap-dog, if once the lion puts out his paw?[303]

"The book was very right. Mrs. Chapone lives at either No. 7 or 8 in Dean Street, Soho.

"I beg you, sir, to forgive a delay for which I can only 'tax the elements with unkindness,'[304] and to receive, with your usual goodness and indulgence, your ever most obliged and most faithful humble servant,

"F. BURNEY.

"St.Martin's Street, Nov. 19, 1783."

My dear father spared me the coach, and to Bolt Court, therefore, I went, and with open arms was I received. Nobody was there but Charles[301] and Mr. Sastres,[306] and Dr. Johnson was, if possible, more instructive, entertaining, good-humoured, and exquisitely fertile, than ever. He thanked me repeatedly for coming, and was so kind I could hardly ever leave him...

[*Diary*, ii, 226-8]

...Just then[307] my father came in: and then Mr. G. C.[308] came, and took the chair half beside me.

I told him of some new members for Dr. Johnson's club.[309]

"I think," said he, "it sounds more like some club that one reads of in the *Spectator*,[310] than like a real club in these times; for the forfeits of a whole year will not amount to those of a single night in other clubs. Does Pepys belong to it?"

"Oh no! he is quite of another party! He is head man on the side of the defenders of Lord Lyttelton. Besides, he has had enough of Dr.

Johnson; for they had a grand battle upon the 'Life of Lyttelton', at Streatham."[311]

"And had they really a serious quarrel? I never imagined it had amounted to that."

"Oh yes, serious enough, I assure you. I never saw Dr. Johnson really in a passion but then: and dreadful, indeed, it was to see. I wished myself away a thousand times. It was a frightful scene. He so red, poor Mr. Pepys so pale!"

"But how did it begin? What did he say?"

"Oh, Dr. Johnson came to the point without much ceremony. He called out aloud, before a large company, at dinner, 'What have you to say, sir, to me, or of me? Come forth, man! I hear you object to my 'Life of Lord Lyttelton'. What are your objections? If you have anything to say, let's hear it. Come forth, man, when I call you!' "

"What a call, indeed! Why then, he fairly bullied him into a quarrel!"

"Yes. And I was the more sorry, because Mr. Pepys had begged of me, before they met, not to let Lord Lyttelton be mentioned. Now I had no more power to prevent it than this macaroon cake in my hand."

"It was behaving ill to Mrs. Thrale, certainly, to quarrel in her house."

"Yes; but he never repeated it; though he wished of all things to have gone through just such another scene with Mrs. Montagu,[312] and to refrain was an act of heroic forbearance."

"Why, I rather wonder he did not; for she was the head of the set of Lytteltonians."

"Oh, he knows that; he calls Mr. Pepys only her prime minister."

"And what does he call her?"

" 'Queen,' to be sure; 'Queen of the Blues!' She came to Streatham one morning, and I saw he was dying to attack her. But he had made a promise to Mrs. Thrale to have no more quarrels in her house, and so he forced himself to forbear. Indeed he was very much concerned, when it was over, for what had passed; and very candid and generous in acknowledging it. He is too noble to adhere to wrong."

"And how did Mrs. Montagu herself behave?"

"Very stately, indeed, at first. She turned from him stiffly, and with a most distant air, and without even courtesying to him, and with a firm intention to keep to what she had publicly declared – that she would never speak to him more! However, he went up to her himself, longing to begin! and very roughly said, – 'Well, madam, what's become of your fine new house? I hear no more of it.' "

"But how did she bear this?"

"Why, she was obliged to answer him; and she soon grew so frightened – as everybody does – that she was as civil as ever."

He laughed heartily at this account. But I told him Dr. Johnson was now much softened. He had acquainted me, when I saw him last, that he had written to her upon the death of Mrs. Williams,[313] because she had allowed her something yearly, which now ceased.

"And I had a very kind answer from her," said he.

"Well then, sir," cried I, "I hope peace now will be again proclaimed."

"Why, I am now," said he, "come to that time when I wish all bitterness and animosity to be at an end. I have never done her any serious harm — nor would I; though I could give her a bite! — but she must provoke me much first. In volatile talk, indeed, I may have spoken of her not much to her mind; for in the tumult of conversation malice is apt to grow sprightly; and there, I hope, I am not yet decrepid!"

He quite laughed aloud at this characteristic speech.

I most readily assured the Doctor that I had never yet seen him limp!

[*Diary*, ii, 234-7]

... *Tuesday*.[314] — I spent the afternoon with Dr. Johnson, who indeed is very ill,[315] and whom I could hardly tell how to leave. But he is rather better since, though still in a most alarming way. Indeed, I am very much afraid for him! He was very, very kind! — Oh, what a cruel, heavy loss will he be!

[*Diary*, ii, 237-8]

... *Tuesday, Dec. 30.* — I went to Dr. Johnson, and spent the evening with him. He was very indifferent, indeed. There were some very disagreeable people with him; and he once affected me very much, by turning suddenly to me, and grasping my hand, and saying,

"The blister I have tried for my breath[316] has betrayed some very bad tokens; but I will not terrify myself by talking of them: ah, *priez Dieu pour moi!*"

You may believe I promised that I would! — Good and excellent as he is, how can he so fear death?[317] — Alas, my Susy, how awful is that idea! — He was quite touchingly affectionate to me. How earnestly I hope for his recovery!

Tuesday, Jan. 6. — I spent the afternoon with Dr. Johnson, and had the great satisfaction of finding him better...

[*Diary*, ii, 239-40]

... I assure you[318] I sometimes feel an indignation at the thought of this graceless & unfeeling return in a Man for whom she sacrifices all that ought to be dear, valuable, or right, that subsides into nothing but *shame & regret* that she can add to so many improperties a *wilful* blindness to an indifference which ought not only to cure, but disgust her. I thought, indeed, — amiable, accomplished, attractive & excellent as she is, she might have chose her Mate among all mankind, so she fixed not on one too Young, — but it is not so, — this man is as little worthy of her by a *sense* of her worth, as he is by partaking it. How universal is the disgrace which the fall of one so exalted spreads around her! — so invulnerable as I thought her! — but I don't know why I write all this, only that I am full of nothing else, for indeed, now the fatal time approaches, the long & wilful separation of a Friend so long, so truly loved, harrasses me more than can easily be conceived. May she but be happy in it herself! — I pray not more for that than I doubt it. — What Woman, again, shall chuse for herself? — No, no, we seem, at last, destined to be elected, not to elect, — the two Disciples of Dr. Collier,[319] 'wo Women, in their different ways, of the rarest attractions, have suffered nothing but disgrace from making the experiment. S.S.[320] is still kept in the humblest *suspence*, & submits to it with *joy*, because it is not *despondency*.

Dr. Johnson is amazingly recovered: but he never speaks to me of Mrs. Thrale but in a common way. What he knows of the matter I have not any means of discovering: & unable as I am to vindicate the Person who will be attacked, or to bear with hearing her abused in silence, I can only rejoice in his ignorance, or his forbearance, whichever it is occasions his quietness.

[*Queeney*, pp. 93-4]

...*Monday, April 19.* — I went in the evening to see dear Dr. Johnson. He received me with open arms, scolded me with the most flattering expressions for my absence, but would not let me come away without making me promise to dine with him next day, on a salmon from Mrs. Thrale.[321] This I did not dare refuse, as he was urgent, and I had played truant so long; but, to be sure, I had rather have dined first, on account of poor Blacky.[322] He is amazingly recovered, and perfectly good-humoured and comfortable, and smilingly alive to idle chat.

At Dr. Johnson's we had Mr. and Mrs. Hoole and their son, and Mrs. Hall,[323] a very good Methodist, and sister of John Wesley. The day was tolerable, but Dr. Johnson is never his best when there is nobody to draw him out;[324] but he was much pleased with my coming, and very kind indeed...

[*Diary*, ii, 252-3]

...*Norbury Park,*[325] *Sunday, Nov. 28.* — Last Thursday, Nov. 25, my father set me down at Bolt Court, while he went on upon business. I was anxious to again see poor Dr. Johnson, who has had terrible health since his return from Lichfield.[326] He let me in, though very ill. He was alone, which I much rejoiced at; for I had a longer and more satisfactory conversation with him than I have had for many months. He was in rather better spirits, too, than I have lately seen him; but he told me he was going to try what sleeping out of town might do for him.

"I remember," said he, "that my wife, when she was near her end,[327] poor woman, was also advised to sleep out of town; and when she was carried to the lodgings that had been prepared for her, she complained that the staircase was in very bad condition – for the plaster was beaten off the walls in many places. 'Oh,' said the man of the house, 'that's nothing but by the knocks against it of the coffins of the poor souls that have died in the lodgings!' "

He laughed, though not without apparent secret anguish, in telling me this. I felt extremely shocked, but, willing to confine my words at least to the literal story, I only exclaimed against the unfeeling absurdity of such a confession.

"Such a confession," cried he, "to a person then coming to try his lodging for her health, contains, indeed, more absurdity than we can well lay our account for."

I had seen Miss T.[328] the day before.

"So," said he, "did I."

I then said, "Do you ever, sir, hear from her mother?"

"No," cried he, "nor write to her. I drive her quite from my mind. If I meet with one of her letters, I burn it instantly. I have burnt all I can find. I never speak of her, and I desire never to hear of her more. I drive her, as I said, wholly from my mind."

Yet, wholly to change this discourse, I gave him a history of the Bristol milk-woman[329] and told him the tales I had heard of her writing so wonderfully, though she had read nothing but Young and Milton; "though those," I continued, "could never possibly, I should think, be the first authors with anybody. Would children understand them? and grown people who have not read are children in literature."

"Doubtless," said he; "but there is nothing so little comprehended among mankind as what is genius. They give to it all, when it can be but a part. Genius is nothing more than knowing the use of tools; but there must be tools for it to use: a man who has spent all his life in this room will give a very poor account of what is contained in the next."

"Certainly, sir; yet there is such a thing as invention? Shakspeare could never have seen a Caliban."

"No; but he had seen a man; and knew, therefore, how to vary him to a monster. A man who would draw a monstrous cow, must first know what a cow commonly is; or how can he tell that to give her an an ass's head or an elephant's tusk will make her monstrous? Suppose you show me a man who is a very expert carpenter; another will say he was born to be a carpenter – but what if he had never seen any wood? Let two men, one with genius, the other with none, look at an overturned waggon: – he who has no genius, will think of the waggon only as he sees it, overturned, and walk on; he who has genius, will paint it to himself before it was overturned, – standing still, and moving on, and heavy loaded, and empty; but both must see the waggon, to think of it at all."

How just and true all this, my dear Susy! He then animated, and talked on, upon this milk-woman, upon a once as famous shoemaker,[330] and upon our immortal Shakspeare, with as much fire, spirit, wit, and truth of criticism and judgment, as ever yet I have heard him. How delightfully bright are his faculties, though the poor and infirm machine that contains them seems alarmingly giving way.

Yet, all brilliant as he was, I saw him growing worse, and offered to go, which, for the first time I ever remember, he did not oppose; but, most kindly pressing both my hands,

"Be not," he said, in a voice of even tenderness, "be not long in coming again for my letting you go now."

I assured him I would be the sooner, and was running off, but he called me back, in a solemn voice, and, in a manner the most energetic, said,

"Remember me in your prayers!"

I longed to ask him to remember me, but did not dare. I gave him my promise, and, very heavily indeed, I left him. Great, good, and excellent that he is, how short a time will he be our boast! Ah, my dear Susy, I see he is going! This winter will never conduct him to a more genial season here! Elsewhere, who shall hope a fairer? I wish I had bid him pray for me; but it seemed to me presumptuous, though this repetition of so kind a condescension might, I think, have encouraged me...

[*Diary*, ii, 270-3]

...*St. Martin's Street, Wednesday, Dec. 10.* – I went in the evening to poor Dr. Johnson. Frank[331] told me he was very ill, but let me in. He would have taken me upstairs, but I would not see him without his direct permission. I desired Frank to tell him I called to pay my respects to him, but not to disturb him if he was not well enough to see me. Mr. Strahan,[332] a clergyman, he said, was with him alone.

In a few minutes, this Mr. Strahan came to me himself. He told me Dr. Johnson was very ill, very much obliged to me for coming, but so weak and bad he hoped I would excuse his not seeing me...

...Dear, dear, and much-reverenced Dr. Johnson! how ill or how low must he be, to decline seeing a creature he has so constantly, so fondly, called about him! If I do not see him again I shall be truly afflicted. And I fear, I almost know, I cannot!...

...At night my father brought us the most dismal tidings of dear Dr. Johnson. Dr. Warren had seen him, and told him to take what opium he pleased![333] He had thanked and taken leave of all his physicians. Alas! – I shall lose him, and he will take no leave of me! My father was deeply depressed; he has himself tried in vain for admission this week. Yet some people see him – the Hooles, Mr. Sastres, Mr. Langton; – but then they must be in the house, watching for one moment, whole hours. I hear from every one he is now perfectly resigned to his approaching fate, and no longer in terror of death. I am thankfully happy in hearing that he speaks himself now of the change his mind has undergone, from its dark horror, and says – "He feels the irradiation of hope!" Good, and pious, and excellent Christian – who shall feel it if not he?...

[Diary, ii, 278-9]

... Thursday morning.[334] – I am told by Mr. Hoole, that he inquired of Dr. Brocklesby[335] if he thought it likely he might live six weeks? and the Doctor's hesitation saying – No – he has been more deeply depressed than ever. Fearing death as he does, no one can wonder. Why he should fear it, all may wonder.

He sent me down yesterday, by a clergyman who was with him,[336] the kindest of messages, and I hardly know whether I ought to go to him again or not; though I know still less why I say so, for go again I both must and shall. One thing, his extreme dejection of mind considered, has both surprised and pleased me; he has now constantly an amanuensis with him, and dictates to him such compositions, particularly Latin and Greek, as he has formerly made, but repeated to his friends without ever committing to paper.[337] This, I hope, will not only gratify his survivors, but serve to divert him.

The good Mr. Hoole and equally good Mr. Sastres attend him, rather as nurses than friends, for they sit whole hours by him, without even speaking to him. He will not, it seems, be talked to – at least very rarely. At times, indeed, he reanimates; but it is soon over, and he says of himself, "I am now like Macbeth, – question enrages me."[338]

My father saw him once while I was away, and carried Mr. Burke with him,[339] who was desirous of paying his respects to him once more in person. He rallied a little while they were there; and Mr. Burke, when they left him, said to my father – "His work is almost done; and well has he done it!"

[Diary, ii, 276-7]

Dec. 11. – We had a party to dinner, by long appointment, for which, indeed, none of us were well disposed, the apprehension of hearing news only of death being hard upon us all. The party was, Dr. Rose, Dr. Gillies, Dr. Garthshore, and Charles.[340]

The day could not be well – but mark the night.

My father, in the morning, saw this first of men! I had not his account till bedtime; he feared overexciting me. He would not, he said, but have seen him for worlds! He happened to be better, and admitted him. He

was up, and very composed. He took his hand very kindly, asked after all
his family, and then, in particular, how Fanny did?

"I hope," he said, "Fanny did not take it amiss that I did not see her?
I was very bad!"

Amiss! – what a word! Oh that I had been present to have answered
it! My father stayed, I suppose, half an hour, and then was coming away.
He again took his hand, and encouraged him to come again to him; and
when he was taking leave, said – "Tell Fanny to pray for me!"

Ah! dear Dr. Johnson! might I but have *your* prayers! After which,
still grasping his hand, he made a prayer himself, – the most fervent,
pious, humble, eloquent, and touching, my father says, that ever was
composed. Oh, would I had heard it! He ended it with Amen! in which
my father joined, and was echoed by all present. And again, when my
father was leaving him, he brightened up, something of his arch look
returned, and he said – "I think I shall throw the ball at Fanny yet!"[341]

Little more passed ere my father came away, decided, most tenderly,
not to tell me this till our party was gone.

This most earnestly increased my desire to see him; this kind and
frequent mention of me melted me into double sorrow and regret. I would
give the world I had but gone to him that day! It was, however, impossible,
and the day was over before I knew he had said what I look upon as a call
to me. This morning, after church time, I went. Frank said he was very ill,
and saw nobody; I told him I had understood by my father the day before
that he meant to see me. He then let me in. I went into his room upstairs;
he was in his bedroom. I saw it crowded, and ran hastily down. Frank told
me his master had refused seeing even Mr. Langton. I told him merely to
say I had called, but by no means to press my admission. His own feelings
were all that should be consulted; his tenderness, I knew, would be equal,
whether he was able to see me or not.

I went into the parlour, preferring being alone in the cold, to any
company with a fire. Here I waited long, here and upon the stairs, which
I ascended and descended to meet again with Frank, and make inquiries;
but I met him not. At last, upon Dr. Johnson's ringing his bell, I saw Frank
enter his room, and Mr. Langton follow. "Who's that?" I heard him say;
they answered, "Mr. Langton," and I found he did not return.

Soon after, all the rest went away but a Mrs. Davis, a good sort of
woman,[342] whom this truly charitable soul had sent for to take a dinner at
his house. I then went and waited with her by the fire: it was, however,
between three and four o'clock before I got any answer. Mr. Langton then
came himself. He could not look at me, and I turned away from him. Mrs.
Davis asked how the Doctor was? "Going on to death very fast!" was his
mournful answer. "Has he taken," she said, "anything?" "Nothing at all!
We carried him some bread and milk – he refused it, and said – '*The less*

the better.' " She asked more questions, by which I found his faculties were perfect, his mind composed, and his dissolution was quick drawing on.

I could not immediately go on, and it is now long since I have written at all; but I will go back to this afflicting theme, which I can now better bear.

Mr. Langton was, I believe, a quarter of an hour in the room before I suspected he meant to speak to me, never looking near me. At last he said,

"This poor man, I understand, ma'am, desired yesterday to see you."

"My understanding that, sir, brought me today."

"Poor man! it is pity he did not know himself better, and that you should have had this trouble."

"Trouble!" cried I; "I would come a hundred times to see him the hundredth and first!"

"He hopes, now, you will excuse him; he is very sorry not to see you; but he desired me to come and speak to you myself, and tell you he hopes you will excuse him, he feels himself too weak for such an interview."

I hastily got up, left him my most affectionate respects, and every good wish I could half utter, and ran back to the coach. Ah, my Susy! I have never been to Bolt Court since!

Dec. 20. — This day was the ever-honoured, ever-lamented Dr. Johnson committed to the earth. Oh, how sad a day to me! My father attended, and so did Charles. I could not keep my eyes dry all day; nor can I now, in the recollecting it; but let me pass over what to mourn is now so vain!...

[*Diary*, ii, 279-82]

...I long to know[343] what you think of our dear Dr. Johnson's meditations,[344] and if you do not, in the midst of what you will wish unpublished, see stronger than ever the purity of his principles and character, and only lament that effusions should be given to the world that are too artless to be suited to it...

[*Diary*, ii, 298]

Tuesday Dec. 20.[345] — 1st summons; 2ndly, entrée.

"Miss Burney, have you heard that Boswell is going to publish a life of your friend Dr. Johnson?"[346]

"No, ma'am."

"I tell you as I heard. I don't know for the truth of it, and I can't tell what he will do. He is so extraordinary a man, that perhaps he will devise something extraordinary."...

[*Diary*, ii, 345]

...*Feb. 26.*–He[347] had lately, he told me, had much conversation concerning me with Mr. Boswell. I feel sorry to be named or remembered by that biographical, anecdotical memorandummer, till his book of poor Dr. Johnson's life is finished and published. What an anecdote, however, did he tell me of that most extraordinary character! He is now an actual admirer and follower of Mrs. Rudd![348]–and avows it, and praises her extraordinary attractions aloud!

The King came into the room during coffee, and talked over Sir John Hawkins's *Life of Dr. Johnson*[349] and with great candour and openness. I have not yet read it...

[*Diary*, iii, 219-20]

...Once before, when I lived in the world,[350] I had met with Dr. Beattie,[351] but he then spoke very little, the company being large; and for myself, I spoke not at all. Our personal knowledge of each other therefore sunk not very deep. It was at the house of Miss Reynolds. My ever-honoured Dr. Johnson was there, and my poor Mrs. Thrale, her daughter, Mrs. Ord, Mrs. Horneck, Mrs. Gwynn, the Bishop of Dromore,[352] and Mrs. Percy, and Mr. Boswell, and Mr. Seward, with some others.

Many things I do recollect of that evening, particularly one laughable circumstance. I was coming away at night, without having been seen by Dr. Johnson, but knowing he would reproach me afterwards, I begged my father to tell him I wished him good-night. He instantly called me up to him, took both my hands, which he extended as far asunder as they would go, and just as I was unfortunately curtseying to be gone, he let them loose and dropped both his own on the two sides of my hoop, with so ponderous a weight, that I could not for some time rise from the inclined posture into which I had put myself, and in which, though quite unconscious of what he was about, he seemed forcibly holding me...

[*Diary*, iii, 281-2]

...*Wednesday, January 9.* – To-day Mrs. Schwellenberg[353] did me a real favour, and with real good-nature; for she sent me the letters of my poor lost friends, Dr. Johnson and Mrs. Thrale,[354] which she knew me to be almost pining to procure. The book belongs to the Bishop of Carlisle, who lent it to Mr. Turbulent, from whom it was again lent to the Queen, and so passed on to Mrs. Schwellenberg. It is still unpublished.

With what a sadness have I been reading! what scenes has it revived!–what regrets renewed! These letters have not been more improperly published in the whole, than they are injudiciously displayed in their several parts. She has given all–every word–and thinks that, perhaps, a justice to Dr. Johnson, which, in fact, is the greatest injury to his memory.[355]

The few she has selected of her own do her, indeed, much credit: she has discarded all that were trivial and merely local, and given only such as contain something instructive, amusing, or ingenious.

About four of the letters, however, of my ever-revered Dr. Johnson are truly worthy his exalted powers: one is upon Death,[356] in considering its approach as we are surrounded, or not, by mourners; another, upon the sudden and premature loss of poor Mrs. Thrale's darling and only son.[357]

Our name once occurs: how I started at its sight! – 'Tis to mention the party that planned the first visit to our house:[358] Miss Owen, Mr. Seward, Mrs. and Miss Thrale, and Dr. Johnson. How well shall we ever, my Susan, remember that morning!...

[*Diary*, iii, 365-6]

...He loved Dr. Johnson,[359] – and Dr. Johnson returned his affection. Their political principles and connections were opposite, but Mr. Wyndham respected his venerable friend too highly to discuss any points that could offend him; and showed for him so true a regard, that, during all his late illnesses, for the latter part of his life, his carriage and himself were alike at his service, to air, visit, or go out, whenever he was disposed to accept them.

Nor was this all; one tender proof he gave of warm and generous regard, that I can never forget, and that rose instantly to my mind when I heard his name, and gave him a welcome in my eyes when they met his face: it is this: Dr. Johnson, in his last visit to Lichfield, was taken ill, and waited to recover strength for travelling back to town in his usual vehicle, a stage-coach; – as soon as this reached the ears of Mr. Wyndham, he set off for Lichfield in his own carriage, to offer to bring him back to town in it, and at his own time.

For a young man of fashion, such a trait towards an old, however dignified philosopher, must surely be a mark indisputable of an elevated mind and character; and still the more strongly it marked a noble way of thinking, as it was done in favour of a person in open opposition to all his own party, and declared prejudices...

[*Diary*, iii, 420]

...I reminded him of the airings, in which he gave his time with his carriage for the benefit of Dr. Johnson's health. "What an advantage!" he cried, "was all that to myself! I had not merely an admiration, but a tenderness for him, – the more I knew him, the stronger it became. We never disagreed; even in politics I found it rather words than things in which we differed."

"And if you could so love him," cried I, "knowing him only in a general way, what would you have felt for him had you known him at Streatham?"

I then gave him a little history of his manners and way of life there, — his good humour, his sport, his kindness, his sociability, and all the many excellent qualities that, in the world at large, were by so many means obscured.

He was extremely interested in all I told him, and regrettingly said he had only known him in his worst days, when his health was upon its decline, and infirmities were crowding fast upon him.

"Had he lived longer," he cried, "I am satisfied I should have taken him to my heart! have looked up to him, applied to him, advised with him in the most essential occurrences of my life? I am sure too, — though it is a proud assertion, — he would have liked me, also, better, had we mingled more. I felt a mixed fondness and reverence growing so strong upon me, that I am satisfied the closest union would have followed his longer life."

I then mentioned how kindly he had taken his visit to him at Lichfield during a severe illness. "And he left you," I said, "a book?"[360]

"Yes," he answered, "and he gave me one, also, just before he died. 'You will look into this sometimes,' he said, 'and not refuse to remember whence you had it.' "

And then he added he had heard him speak of me, — and with so much kindness, that I was forced not to press a recapitulation: yet now I wish I had heard it.

Just before we broke up, "There is nothing," he cried, with energy, "for which I look back upon myself with severer discipline than the time I have thrown away in other pursuits, that might else have been devoted to that wonderful man!"...

[*Diary*, iii, 476-8]

...And now for a scene a little surprising.[361]

The beautiful chapel of St. George, repaired and finished by the best artists at an immense expense, which was now opened after a very long shutting up for its preparations, brought innumerable strangers to Windsor, and, among others, Mr. Boswell.

This I heard, in my way to the chapel, from Mr. Turbulent,[362] who overtook me, and mentioned having met Mr. Boswell at the Bishop of Carlisle's the evening before. He proposed bringing him to call upon me; but this I declined, certain how little satisfaction would be given here by the entrance of a man so famous for compiling anecdotes. But yet I really wished to see him again, for old acquaintance' sake, and unavoidable amusement from his oddity and good humour, as well as respect for the object of his constant admiration, my revered Dr. Johnson. I therefore told Mr. Turbulent I should be extremely glad to speak with him after the service was over.

Accordingly, at the gate of the choir, Mr. Turbulent brought him to me. We saluted with mutual glee: his comic-serious face and manner have lost nothing of their wonted singularity; nor yet have his mind and language, as you will soon confess.

"I am extremely glad to see you indeed," he cried, "but very sorry to see you here. My dear ma'am, why do you stay? — it won't do, ma'am! you must resign![363] — we can put up with it no longer. I told my good host the Bishop so last night; we are all grown quite outrageous!"

Whether I laughed the most, or stared the most, I am at a loss to say; but I hurried away from the cathedral, not to have such treasonable declarations overheard, for we were surrounded by a multitude.

He accompanied me, however, not losing one moment in continuing his exhortations: "If you do not quit, ma'am, very soon, some violent measures, I assure you, will be taken. We shall address Dr. Burney in a body; I am ready to make the harangue myself. We shall fall upon him all at once."

I stopped him to inquire about Sir Joshua;[364] he said he saw him very often, and that his spirits were very good. I asked about Mr. Burke's book.[365] "Oh," cried he, "it will come out next week: 'tis the first book in the world, except my own, and that's coming out also very soon; only I want your help."

"My help?"

"Yes, madam; you must give me some of your choice little notes of the Doctor's; we have seen him long enough upon stilts; I want to show him in a new light. Grave Sam, and great Sam, and solemn Sam, and learned Sam, — all these he has appeared over and over. Now I want to entwine a wreath of the graces across his brow; I want to show him as gay Sam, agreeable Sam, pleasant Sam; so you must help me with some of his beautiful billets to yourself."

I evaded this by declaring I had not any stores at hand. He proposed a thousand curious expedients to get at them, but I was invincible.

Then I was hurrying on, lest I should be too late. He followed eagerly, and again exclaimed, "But, ma'am, as I tell you, this won't do — you must resign off-hand! Why, I would farm you out myself for double, treble the money! I wish I had the regulation of such a farm, — yet I am no farmer-general. But I should like to farm you, and so I will tell Dr. Burney. I mean to address him; I have a speech ready for the first opportunity."

He then told me his *Life of Dr. Johnson* was nearly printed,[366] and took a proof-sheet out of his pocket to show me; with crowds passing and repassing, knowing me well, and staring well at him: for we were now at the iron rails of the Queen's Lodge.

I stopped; I could not ask him in: I saw he expected it, and was reduced to apologise, and tell him I must attend the Queen immediately.

He uttered again stronger and stronger exhortations for my retreat, accompanied by expressions which I was obliged to check in their bud. But finding he had no chance for entering, he stopped me again at the gate, and said he would read me a page of his work.

There was no refusing this; and he began, with a letter of Dr. Johnson's to himself. He read it in strong imitation of the Doctor's manner, very well, and not caricature.[367] But Mrs. Schwellenberg was at her window, a crowd was gathering to stand round the rails, and the King and Queen and Royal Family now approached from the Terrace. I made a rather quick apology, and, with a step as quick as my now weakened limbs have left in my power, I hurried to my apartment.

You may suppose I had inquiries enough, from all around, of "Who was the gentleman I was talking to at the rails?" And an injunction rather frank not to admit him beyond those limits.

However, I saw him again the next morning, in coming from early prayers, and he again renewed his remonstrances, and his petition for my letters of Dr. Johnson.

I cannot consent to print private letters, even of a man so justly celebrated, when addressed to myself: no, I shall hold sacred those revered and but too scarce testimonies of the high honour his kindness conferred upon me. One letter I have from him that is a masterpiece of elegance and kindness united. 'Twas his last.[368] ...

[*Diary*, iv, 430-3]

...*June 5.* – Mr. Turbulent at this time outstayed the tea-party one evening, not for his former rhodomontading,[369] but to seriously and earnestly advise me to resign. My situation, he said, was evidently death to me.

He was eager to inquire of me who was Mrs. Lenox? He had been reading, like all the rest of the world, Boswell's *Life of Dr. Johnson*, and the preference there expressed of Mrs. Lenox to all other females[370] had filled him with astonishment, as he had never even heard her name.

These occasional sallies of Dr. Johnson, uttered from local causes and circumstances, but all retailed verbatim by Mr. Boswell, are filling all sort of readers with amaze, except the small party to whom Dr. Johnson was known, and who, by acquaintance with the power of the moment over his unguarded conversation, know how little of his solid opinion was to be gathered from his accidental assertions.

The King, who was now also reading this work, applied to me for explanations without end. Every night at this period he entered the

Queen's dressing room, and delayed Her Majesty's proceedings by a length of discourse with me upon this subject. All that flowed from himself was constantly full of the goodness and benevolence of his character; and I was never so happy as in the opportunity thus graciously given me of vindicating, in instances almost innumerable, the serious principles and various excellences of Dr. Johnson from the clouds so frequently involving and darkening them, in narrations so little calculated for any readers who were strangers to his intrinsic worth, and therefore worked upon and struck by what was faulty in his temper and manners.

I regretted not having strength to read this work to Her Majesty myself. It was an honour I should else have certainly received; for so much wanted clearing! so little was understood! However, the Queen frequently condescended to read over passages and anecdotes which perplexed or offended her; and there were none I had not a fair power to soften or to justify. Dear and excellent Dr. Johnson! I have never forgot nor neglected his injunction given me when he was ill – to stand by him and support him, and not hear him abused when he was no more, and could not defend himself! but little – little did I think it would ever fall to my lot to vindicate him to his King and Queen...

[*Diary*, iv, 476-8]

...This day[371] had been long engaged for breakfasting with Mrs. Dickenson and dining with Mrs. Ord.

The breakfast guests were Mr. Langton, Mr. Foote, Mr. Dickenson, jun., a cousin, and a very agreeable and pleasing man; Lady Herries, Miss Dickenson, another cousin, and Mr. Boswell.

This last was the object of the morning. I felt a strong sensation of that displeasure which his loquacious communications of every weakness and infirmity of the first and greatest good man of these times have awakened in me, at his first sight; and, though his address to me was courteous in the extreme, and he made a point of sitting next me, I felt an indignant disposition to a nearly forbidding reserve and silence. How many starts of passion and prejudice has he blackened into record, that else might have sunk, for ever forgotten, under the preponderance of weightier virtues and excellences!

Angry, however, as I have long been with him, he soon insensibly conquered, though he did not soften me: there is so little of ill design or ill nature in him, he is so open and forgiving for all that is said in return that he soon forced me to consider him in a less serious light, and change my resentment against his treachery into something like commiseration of his levity; and before we parted, we became good friends. There is no resisting great good-humour, be what will in the opposite scale.

He entertained us all as if hired for that purpose, telling stories of Dr. Johnson, and acting them with incessant buffoonery. I told him frankly that, if he turned him into ridicule by caricature, I should fly the premises: he assured me he would not, and indeed, his imitations, though comic to excess, were so far from caricature that he omitted a thousand gesticulations which I distinctly remember.

Mr. Langton told some stories himself[372] in imitation of Dr. Johnson; but they became him less than Mr. Boswell, and only reminded of what Dr. Johnson himself once said to me – "Every man has, some time in his life, an ambition to be a wag." If Mr. Langton had repeated anything from his truly great friend quietly, it would far better have accorded with his own serious and respectable character.

[*Diary*, v, 83-4]

A few months after the Streathamite morning visit to St. Martin's-street that has been narrated,[373] an evening party was arranged by Dr. Burney, for bringing thither again Dr. Johnson and Mrs. Thrale, at the desire of Mr. and Mrs. Greville and Mrs. Crewe;[374] who wished, under the quiet roof of Dr. Burney, to make acquaintance with these celebrated personages...

...The party consisted of Dr. Johnson, Mr. and Mrs. Greville, Mrs. Crewe, Mr., Mrs., and Miss Thrale; Signor Piozzi, Mr. Charles Burney, the Doctor, his wife and four of his daughters.

Mr. Greville, in manner, mien, and high personal presentation, was still the superb Mr. Greville of other days;...

...the first step taken by Dr. Burney for social conciliation, which was calling for a cantata from Signor Piozzi, turned out, on the contrary, the herald to general discomfiture; for it cast a damp of delay upon the mental gladiators, that dimmed the brightness of the spirit with which, it is probable, they had meant to vanquish each the other.

Piozzi, a first-rate singer, whose voice was deliciously sweet, and whose expression was perfect, sung in his very best manner, from his desire to do honour to *il Capo di Casa*[375]; but *il Capo di Casa* and his family alone did justice to his strains: neither the Grevilles nor the Thrales heeded music beyond what belonged to it as fashion: the expectations of the Grevilles were all occupied by Dr. Johnson...

...Mr. Greville, who had been curious to see, and who intended to examine this leviathan of literature, as Dr. Johnson was called in the current pamphlets of the day,[376] considered it to be his proper post to open the campaign of the *conversatione*. But he had heard so much, from his friend Topham Beauclerk, whose highest honour was classing himself as one of the friends of Dr. Johnson,...that he was cautious how to encounter so tremendous a literary athletic. He thought it, therefore, most consonant to his dignity to leave his own character as an author in the back ground; and to take the field with the aristocratic armour of pedigree and distinction. Aloof, therefore, he kept from all; and assuming his most supercilious air of distant superiority, planted himself, immovable as a noble statue, upon the hearth, as if a stranger to the whole set.

Mrs. Greville would willingly have entered the lists herself, but that she naturally concluded Dr. Johnson would make the advances.

And Mrs. Crewe, to whom all this seemed odd and unaccountable, but to whom, also, from her love of any thing unusual, it was secretly amusing, sat perfectly passive in silent observance.

Dr. Johnson, himself, had come with the full intention of passing two or three hours, with well chosen companions, in social elegance. His own expectations, indeed, were small – for what could meet their expansion? his wish, however, to try all sorts and conditions of persons, as far as belonged to their intellect, was unqualified and unlimited; and gave to him nearly as much desire to see others, as his great fame gave to others to see his eminent self. But his signal peculiarity in regard to society, could not be surmised by strangers; and was as yet unknown even to Dr. Burney. This was that, notwithstanding the superior powers with which he followed up every given subject, he scarcely ever began one himself;[377]... though the masterly manner in which, as soon as any topic was started, he seized it in all its bearings, had so much the air of belonging to the leader of the discourse, that this singularity was unnoticed and unsuspected, save by the experienced observation of long years of acquaintance.

Not, therefore, being summoned to hold forth, he remained silent; composedly at first, and afterwards abstractedly.

Dr. Burney now began to feel considerably embarrassed; though still he cherished hopes of ultimate relief from some auspicious circumstance ... Vainly, however, he sought to elicit some observations that might lead to disserting discourse; all his attempts received only quiet, acquiescent replies, "signifying nothing." Every one was awaiting some spontaneous opening from Dr. Johnson.

Mrs. Thrale, of the whole coterie, was alone at her ease. She feared not Dr. Johnson; for fear made no part of her composition...She grew tired of the music, and yet more tired of remaining...a mere cipher in the company...Her spirits rose rebelliously above her control; and, in a fit of utter recklessness of what might be thought of her by her fine new acquaintance, she suddenly, but softly, arose, and stealing on tip-toe behind Signor Piozzi; who was accompanying himself on the piano forte to an animated *arria parlante*, with his back to the company, and his face to the wall; she ludicrously began imitating him by squaring her elbows, elevating them with ecstatic shrugs of the shoulders, and casting up her eyes, while languishingly reclining her head; as if she were not less enthusiastically, though somewhat more suddenly, struck with the transports of harmony than himself.

This grotesque ebullition of ungovernable gaiety was not perceived by Dr. Johnson, who faced the fire, with his back to the performer and the instrument. But the amusement which such an unlooked for exhibition caused to the party, was momentary; for Dr. Burney, shocked lest the poor Signor should observe, and be hurt by this mimicry, glided gently round to Mrs. Thrale, and, with something between pleasantry and severity, whispered to her, "Because, Madam, you have no ear yourself for music, will you destroy the attention of all who, in that one point, are otherwise gifted?"

It was now that shone the brightest attribute of Mrs. Thrale, sweetness of temper. She took this rebuke with a candour, and a sense of its justice the most amiable: she nodded her approbation of the admonition; and, returning to her chair, quietly sat down, as she afterwards said, like a pretty little miss, for the remainder of one of the most humdrum evenings that she had ever passed.

Strange, indeed, strange and most strange, the event considered, was this opening intercourse between Mrs. Thrale and Signor Piozzi. Little could she imagine that the person whom she was thus called away from holding up to ridicule, would become, but a few years afterwards, the idol of her fancy and the lord of her destiny!...

...The most innocent person of all that went forward was the laurelled chief of the little association, Dr. Johnson; who, though his love for Dr. Burney made it a pleasure to him to have been included in the invitation, marvelled, probably, by this time, since uncalled upon to distinguish himself, why he had been bidden to the meeting. But, as the evening advanced, he wrapt himself up in his own thoughts, in a manner it was frequently less difficult to him to do than to let alone, and became completely absorbed in silent rumination: sustaining, nevertheless, a grave and composed demeanour, with an air by no means wanting in dignity any more than in urbanity.

Very unexpectedly, however, ere the evening closed, he shewed himself alive to what surrounded him, by one of those singular starts of vision, that made him seem at times, – though purblind to things in common, and to things inanimate, – gifted with an eye of instinct for espying any action or position that he thought merited reprehension: for, all at once, looking fixedly on Mr. Greville, who, without much self-denial, the night being very cold, pertinaciously kept his station before the chimney-piece, he exclaimed: "If it were not for depriving the ladies of the fire, – I should like to stand upon the hearth myself!"

A smile gleamed upon every face at this pointed speech. Mr. Greville tried to smile himself, though faintly and scoffingly. He tried, also, to hold to his post, as if determined to disregard so cavalier a liberty: but the sight of every eye around him cast down, and every visage struggling vainly to appear serious, disconcerted him; and though, for two or three minutes, he disdained to move, the awkwardness of a general pause impelled him, ere long, to glide back to his chair; but he rang the bell with force as he passed it, to order his carriage.

It is probable that Dr. Johnson had observed the high air and mien of Mr. Greville, and had purposely brought forth that remark to disenchant him from his self-consequence.

The party then broke up...

[*Memoirs*, ii, 101-13]

...While this charming work[378] was in its progress, when only the Thrale family and its nearly adopted guests, the two Burneys, were assembled, Dr. Johnson, would frequently produce one of its proof sheets to embellish the breakfast table, which was always in the library; and was, certainly, the most sprightly and agreeable meeting of the day; for then, as no strangers were present to stimulate exertion, or provoke rivalry, argument was not urged on by the mere spirit of victory; it was instigated only by such truisms as could best bring forth that conflict of *pros* and *cons* which elucidates opposing opinions. Wit was not flashed with the keen sting of satire; yet it elicited not less gaiety from sparkling with an unwounding brilliancy, which brightened without inflaming, every eye, and charmed without tingling, every ear.

These proof sheets Mrs. Thrale was permitted to read aloud; and the discussions to which they led were in the highest degree entertaining. Dr. Burney wistfully desired to possess one of them; but left to his daughter the risk of the petition. A hint, however, proved sufficient, and was understood not alone with compliance, but vivacity. Boswell, Dr. Johnson said, had engaged Frank Barber, his negro servant, to collect and preserve all the proof sheets;[379] but though it had not been without the knowledge, it was without the order or the interference of their author: to the present solicitor, therefore, willingly and without scruple, he now offered an entire life; adding, with a benignant smile, "Choose your poet!"

Without scruple, also, was the acceptance; and, without hesitation, the choice was Pope. And that not merely because, next to Shakespeare himself, Pope draws human characters the most veridically, perhaps, of any poetic delineator; but for yet another reason. Dr. Johnson composed with so ready an accuracy, that he sent his copy to the press unread;[380] reserving all his corrections for the proof sheets: and, consequently, as not even Dr. Johnson could read twice without ameliorating some passages, his proof sheets were at times liberally marked with changes; and, as the Museum copy of Pope's Translation of the Iliad, from which Dr. Johnson has given many examples, contains abundant emendations by Pope, the Memorialist[381] secured at once, on the same page, the marginal alterations of that great author, and of his great biographer.

When the book was published, Dr. Johnson brought to Streatham a complete set, handsomely bound, of the Works of the Poets, as well as his own Prefaces, to present to Mr. and Mrs. Thrale. And then, telling this Memorialist that to the King, and to the chiefs of Streatham alone he could offer so large a tribute, he most kindly placed before her a bound copy of his own part of the work; in the title page of which he gratified her earnest request by writing her name, and "From the Author."

After which, at her particular solicitation, he gave her a small engraving of his portrait from the picture of Sir Joshua Reynolds.[382] And while, some time afterwards, she was examining it at a distant table, Dr. Johnson, in passing across the room, stopt to discover by what she was occupied; which he no sooner discerned, than he began see-sawing for a moment or two in silence; and then, with a ludicrous half laugh, peeping over her shoulder, he called out: "Ah ha! – Sam Johnson! – I see thee! – and an ugly dog thou art!"

He even extended his kindness to a remembrance of Mr. Bewley, the receiver and preserver of the wisp of a Bolt-court hearth-broom,[383] as a relic of the Author of the Rambler; which anecdote Dr. Burney had ventured to confess: and Dr. Johnson now, with his compliments, sent a set of the Prefaces to St. Martin's-street, directed,

"From the Broom Gentleman":
which Mr. Bewley received with rapturous gratitude...

[*Memoirs*, ii, 177-80]

...Dr. Johnson, in compliment to his friend Dr. Burney, and by no means incurious himself to see the hermit of Chesington,[384] immediately descended to meet Mr. Crisp; and to aid Mrs. Thrale, who gave him a vivacious reception, to do the honours of Streatham.

The meeting, nevertheless, to the great chagrin of Dr. Burney, produced neither interest nor pleasure: for Dr. Johnson, though courteous in demeanour and looks, with evident solicitude to shew respect to Mr. Crisp, was grave and silent; and whenever Dr. Johnson did not make the charm of conversation, he only marred it by his presence; from the general fear he incited, that if he spoke not, he might listen; and that if he listened – he might reprove.

Ease, therefore, was wanting; without which nothing in society can be flowing or pleasing. The Chesingtonian conceived, that he had lived too long away from the world to start any subject that might not, to the

Streathamites, be trite and out of date; and the Streathamites believed that they had lived in it so much longer, that the current talk of the day might, to the Chesingtonian, seem unintelligible jargon: while each hoped that the sprightly Dr. Burney would find the golden mean by which both parties might be brought into play.

But Dr. Burney, who saw in the kind looks and complacency of Dr. Johnson intentional good will to the meeting, flattered himself that the great philologist was but waiting for an accidental excitement, to fasten upon some topic of general use or importance, and then to describe or discuss it, with the full powers of his great mind.

Dr. Johnson, however, either in health or in spirits, was, unfortunately, oppressed; and, for once, was more desirous to hear than to be heard.

Mr. Crisp, therefore, lost, by so unexpected a taciturnity, this fair and promising opportunity for developing and enjoying the celebrated and extraordinary colloquial abilities of Dr. Johnson; and finished the visit with much disappointment; lowered also, and always, in his spirits by parting from his tenderly attached young companion.

Dr. Burney had afterwards, however, the consolation to find that Mr. Crisp had impressed even Dr. Johnson with a strong admiration of his knowledge and capacity; for in speaking of him in the evening to Mr. Thrale, who had been absent, the Doctor emphatically said, "Sir, it is a very singular thing to see a man with all his powers so much alive, when he has so long shut himself up from the world. Such readiness of conception, quickness of recollection, facility of following discourse started by others, in a man who has so long had only the past to feed upon, are rarely to be met with. Now, for my part," added he, laughing, "that *I* should be ready, or even universal, is no wonder; for my dear little mistress here," turning to Mrs. Thrale, "keeps all my faculties in constant play."

Mrs. Thrale then said that nothing, to her, was so striking, as that a man who had so long retired from the world, should so delicately have preserved its forms and courtesies, as to appear equally well bred with any elegant member of society who had not quitted it for a week.

Inexpressibly gratifying to Dr. Burney was the award of such justice, from such judges, to his best and dearest loved friend.

From this time forward, Dr. Burney could scarcely recover his daughter from Streatham, even for a few days, without a friendly battle. A sportively comic exaggeration of Dr. Johnson's upon this flattering hostility was current at Streatham, made in answer to Dr. Burney's saying, upon a resistance to her departure for St. Martin's-street in which Dr. Johnson had strongly joined, "I must really take her away, Sir, I must indeed; she has been from home so long."

"Long? no, Sir! I do not think long," cried the Doctor, see-sawing, and seizing both her hands, as if purporting to detain her: "Sir! I would have her Always come...and Never go! — "

When next, after this adjuration, Dr. Burney took the Memorialist back to Streatham,[385] he found there, recently arrived from Scotland, Mr. Boswell; whose sprightly Corsican tour, and heroic, almost Quixotic pursuit of General Paoli, joined to the tour to the Hebrides with Dr. Johnson, made him an object himself of considerable attention.

He spoke the Scotch accent strongly, though by no means so as to affect, even slightly, his intelligibility to an English ear. He had an odd mock solemnity of tone and manner, that he had acquired imperceptibly from constantly thinking of and imitating Dr. Johnson; whose own solemnity, nevertheless, far from mock, was the result of pensive rumination. There was, also, something slouching in the gait and dress of Mr. Boswell, that wore an air, ridiculously enough, of purporting to personify the same model. His clothes were always too large for him; his hair, or wig, was constantly in a state of negligence; and he never for a moment sat still or upright upon a chair. Every look and movement displayed either intentional or involuntary imitation. Yet certainly it was not meant as caricature; for his heart, almost even to idolatry, was in his reverence of Dr. Johnson.

Dr. Burney was often surprised that this kind of farcical similitude escaped the notice of the Doctor; but attributed his missing it to a high superiority over any such suspicion, as much as to his near-sightedness; for fully was Dr. Burney persuaded, that had any detection of such imitation taken place, Dr. Johnson, who generally treated Mr. Boswell as a school boy,[386] whom, without the smallest ceremony, he pardoned or rebuked, alternately, would so indignantly have been provoked, as to have instantaneously inflicted upon him some mark of his displeasure. And equally he was persuaded that Mr. Boswell, however shocked and even inflamed in receiving it, would soon, from his deep veneration, have thought it justly incurred;[387] and, after a day or two of pouting and sullenness, would have compromised the matter by one of his customary simple apologies, of "Pray, Sir, forgive me!"

Dr. Johnson, though often irritated by the officious importunity of Mr. Boswell, was really touched by his attachment. It was indeed surprising, and even affecting, to remark the pleasure with which this great man accepted personal kindness, even from the simplest of mankind; and the grave formality with which he acknowledged it even to the meanest. Possibly it was what he most prized, because what he could least command; for personal partiality hangs upon lighter and slighter qualities than those which earn solid approbation; but of this, if he had least command, he had also least want; his towering superiority of intellect elevating him above all competitors, and regularly establishing him, wherever he appeared, as the first Being of the society.

As Mr. Boswell was at Streatham only upon a morning visit, a collation was ordered, to which all were assembled. Mr. Boswell was preparing to take a seat that he seemed, by prescription, to consider as his own, next to Dr. Johnson; but Mr. Seward, who was present, waived his hand for Mr. Boswell to move further on, saying, with a smile, "Mr. Boswell, that seat is Miss Burney's."

He stared, amazed: the asserted claimant was new and unknown to him, and he appeared by no means pleased to resign his prior rights. But, after looking round for a minute or two, with an important air of demanding the meaning of this innovation, and receiving no satisfaction, he reluctantly, almost resentfully, got another chair; and placed it at the back of the shoulder of Dr. Johnson; while this new and unheard of rival quietly seated herself as if not hearing what was passing; for she shrunk from the explanation that she feared might ensue, as she saw a smile stealing over every countenance, that of Dr. Johnson himself not excepted, at the discomfiture and surprise of Mr. Boswell.

Mr. Boswell, however, was so situated as not to remark it in the Doctor; and of every one else, when in that presence, he was unobservant, if not contemptuous. In truth, when he met with Dr. Johnson, he commonly forbore even answering anything that was said, or attending to any thing that went forward, lest he should miss the smallest sound from that voice to which he paid such exclusive, though merited homage. But the moment that voice burst forth, the attention which it excited in Mr. Boswell amounted almost to pain. His eyes goggled with eagerness; he leant his ear almost on the shoulder of the Doctor; and his mouth dropt open to catch every syllable that might be uttered: nay, he seemed not only to dread losing a word, but to be anxious not to miss a breathing; as if hoping from it, latently, or mystically, some information.

But when, in a few minutes, Dr. Johnson, whose eye did not follow him, and who had concluded him to be at the other end of the table, said something gaily and good-humouredly, by the appellation of Bozzy; and discovered, by the sound of the reply, that Bozzy had planted himself, as closely as he could, behind and between the elbows of the new usurper and his own, the Doctor turned angrily round upon him, and clapping his hand rather loudly upon his knee, said, in a tone of displeasure, "What do you do there, Sir? – Go to the table, Sir!"

Mr. Boswell instantly, and with an air of affright, obeyed: and there was something so unusual in such humble submission to so imperious a command, that another smile gleamed its way across every mouth, except that of the Doctor and of Mr. Boswell; who now, very unwillingly, took a distant seat.

But, ever restless when not at the side of Dr. Johnson, he presently recollected something that he wished to exhibit, and, hastily rising, was running away in its search; when the Doctor, calling after him, authoritatively said: "What are you thinking of, Sir? Why do you get up before the cloth is removed? — Come back to your place, Sir!"

Again, and with equal obsequiousness, Mr. Boswell did as he was bid; when the Doctor, pursing his lips, not to betray rising risibility, muttered half to himself: "Running about in the middle of meals! — One would take you for a Branghton! —"

"A Branghton, Sir?" repeated Mr. Boswell, with earnestness; "What is a Branghton, Sir?"

"Where have you lived, Sir," cried the Doctor, laughing, "and what company have you kept, not to know that?"

Mr. Boswell now, doubly curious, yet always apprehensive of falling into some disgrace with Dr. Johnson, said, in a low tone, which he knew the Doctor could not hear, to Mrs. Thrale: "Pray, Ma'am, what's a Branghton? — Do me the favour to tell me? — Is it some animal hereabouts?"

Mrs. Thrale only heartily laughed, but without answering: as she saw one of her guests uneasily fearful of an explanation. But Mr. Seward cried, "I'll tell you, Boswell, — I'll tell you! — if you will walk with me into the paddock; only let us wait till the table is cleared; or I shall be taken for a Branghton, too!"

They soon went off together; and Mr. Boswell, no doubt, was fully informed of the road that had led to the usurpation by which he had thus been annoyed. But the Branghton fabricator took care to mount to her chamber ere they returned; and did not come down till Mr. Boswell was gone...

[*Memoirs*, ii, 187-97]

...Dr. Burney, when the Cecilian[388] business was arranged, again conveyed the Memorialist to Streatham. No further reluctance on his part, nor exhortations on that of Mr. Crisp, sought to withdraw her from that spot, where, while it was in its glory, they had so recently, and with pride, seen her distinguished. And truly eager was her own haste, when mistress of her time, to try once more to soothe those sorrows and chagrins in which she had most largely participated, by answering to the call, which had never ceased tenderly to pursue her, of return.

With alacrity, therefore, though not with gaiety, they re-entered the Streatham gates — but they soon perceived that they found not what they had left!

Changed, indeed, was Streatham! Gone its chief,[389] and changed his relict! unaccountably, incomprehensibly, indefinably changed! She was absent and agitated; not two minutes could she remain in a place; she scarcely seemed to know whom she saw; her speech was so hurried it was hardly intelligible; her eyes were assiduously averted from those who sought them, and her smiles were faint and forced.

The Doctor, who had no opportunity to communicate his remarks, went back, as usual, to town; where soon also, with his tendency, as usual, to view everything cheerfully, he revolved in his mind the new cares and avocations by which Mrs. Thrale was perplexed; and persuaded himself that the alteration which had struck him, was simply the effect of her new position.

Too near, however, were the observations of the Memorialist for so easy a solution. The change in her friend was equally dark and melancholy: yet not personal to the Memorialist was any alteration. No affection there was lessened; no kindness cooled; on the contrary, Mrs. Thrale was more fervent in both; more touchingly tender; and softened in disposition beyond all expression, all description: but in everything else, – in health, spirits, comfort, general looks, and manner, the change was at once universal and deplorable.[390] All was misery and mystery: misery the most restless; mystery the most unfathomable.

The mystery, however, soon ceased; the solicitations of the most affectionate sympathy could not long be urged in vain; – the mystery passed away – not so the misery! That, when revealed, was but to both parties doubled, from the different feelings set in movement by its disclosure.

The astonishing history of the enigmatical attachment which impelled Mrs. Thrale to her second marriage, is now as well known as her name: but its details belong not to the history of Dr. Burney; though the fact too deeply interested him, and was too intimately felt in his social habits, to be passed over in silence in any memoirs of his life.

But while ignorant yet of its cause, more and more struck he became at every meeting, by a species of general alienation which pervaded all around at Streatham. His visits, which, heretofore, had seemed galas to Mrs. Thrale, were now begun and ended almost without notice; and all others, – Dr. Johnson not excepted, – were cast into the same gulph of general neglect, or forgetfulness; – all, – save singly this Memorialist! – to whom, the fatal secret once acknowledged, Mrs. Thrale clung for comfort; though she saw, and generously pardoned, how wide she was from meeting approbation.

In this retired, though far from tranquil manner, passed many months; during which, with the acquiescent consent of the Doctor, his daughter, wholly devoted to her unhappy friend, remained uninterruptedly at sad and altered Streatham; sedulously avoiding, what at other times she most wished, a *tête-à-tête* with her father. Bound by ties indissoluble of honour not to betray a trust that, in the ignorance of her pity, she had herself unwittingly sought, even to him she was as immutably silent, on this subject, as to all others — save, singly, to the eldest daughter of the house; whose conduct, through scenes of dreadful difficulty, notwithstanding her extreme youth, was even exemplary; and to whom the self-beguiled, yet generous mother, gave full and free permission to confide every thought and feeling to the Memorialist.

And here let a tribute of friendship be offered up to the shrine of remembrance, due from a thousand ineffaceably tender recollections. Not wildly, and with male and headstrong passions, as has currently been asserted, was this connexion brought to bear on the part of Mrs. Thrale. It was struggled against at time with even agonizing energy; and with efforts so vehement, as nearly to destroy the poor machine they were exerted to save. But the subtle poison had glided into her veins so unsuspectedly, and, at first, so unopposedly, that the whole fabric was infected with its venom; which seemed to become a part, never to be dislodged, of its system.

It was, indeed, the positive opinion of her physician and friend, Sir Lucas Pepys, that so excited were her feelings, and so shattered, by their early indulgence, was her frame, that the crisis which might be produced through the medium of decided resistance, offered no other alternative but death or madness!...

[*Memoirs*, ii, 243-7]

A few weeks earlier, the Memorialist had passed a nearly similar scene with Dr. Johnson.[391] Not, however, she believes, from the same formidable species of surmise; but from the wounds inflicted upon his injured sensibility, through the palpably altered looks, tone, and deportment, of the bewildered lady of the mansion; who, cruelly aware what would be his wrath, and how overwhelming his reproaches against her projected union, wished to break up their residing under the same roof before it should be proclaimed.

This gave to her whole behaviour towards Dr. Johnson, a sort of restless petulancy, of which she was sometimes hardly conscious; at others, nearly reckless; but which hurt him far more than she purposed, though short of the point at which she aimed, of precipitating a change of dwelling that would elude its being cast, either by himself or the world, upon a passion that her understanding blushed to own; even while she was sacrificing to it all of inborn dignity that she had been bred to hold most sacred.

Dr. Johnson, while still uninformed of an entanglement it was impossible he should conjecture, attributed her varying humours to the effect of wayward health meeting a sort of sudden wayward power: and imagined that caprices, which he judged to be partly feminine, and partly wealthy, would soberize themselves away in being unnoticed. He adhered, therefore, to what he thought his post, in being the ostensible guardian protector of the relict and progeny of the late chief of the house; taking no open or visible notice of the alteration in the successor – save only at times, and when they were *tête-à-tête*, to this Memorialist; to whom he frequently murmured portentous observations on the woeful, nay alarming deterioration in health and disposition of her whom, so lately, he had signalized as the gay mistress of Streatham.

But at length, as she became more and more dissatisfied with her own situation, and impatient for its relief, she grew less and less scrupulous with regard to her celebrated guest; she slighted his counsel; did not heed his remonstrances; avoided his society; was ready at a moment's hint to lend him her carriage when he wished to return to Bolt Court; but awaited a formal request to accord it for bringing him back.

The Doctor then began to be stung; his own aspect became altered; and depression, with indignant uneasiness, sat upon his venerable front.

It was at this moment that, finding the Memorialist was going one morning to St. Martin's Street, he desired a cast thither in the carriage, and then to be set down at Bolt Court.

Aware of his disturbance, and far too well aware how short it was of what it would become when the cause of all that passed should be detected, it was in trembling that the Memorialist accompanied him to the coach, filled with dread of offending him by any reserve, should he force upon her any inquiry; and yet impressed with the utter impossibility of betraying a trusted secret.

His look was stern, though dejected, as he followed her into the vehicle; but when his eye, which, however short sighted, was quick to mental perception, saw how ill at ease appeared his companion, all sternness subsided into an undisguised expression of the strongest emotion, that seemed to claim her sympathy, though to revolt from her compassion; while, with a shaking hand, and pointing finger, he directed her looks to the mansion from which they were driving; and, when they faced it from the coach window, as they turned into Streatham Common, tremulously exclaiming: "That house…is lost to *me* – for ever!"[392]

During a moment he then fixed upon her an interrogative eye, that impetuously demanded: "Do you not perceive the change I am experiencing?"

A sorrowing sigh was her only answer.

Pride and delicacy then united to make him leave her to her taciturnity.

He was too deeply, however, disturbed to start or to bear any other subject; and neither of them uttered a single word till the coach stopt in St. Martin's-Street, and the house and the carriage door were opened for their separation! He then suddenly and expressively looked at her, abruptly grasped her hand, and, with an air of affection, though in a low, husky voice, murmured rather than said: "Good morning, dear lady!" but turned his head quickly away, to avoid any species of answer.

She was deeply touched by so gentle an acquiescence in her declining the confidential discourse upon which he had indubitably meant to open, relative to this mysterious alienation. But she had the comfort to be satisfied, that he saw and believed in her sincere participation in his feelings; while he allowed for the grateful attachment that bound her to a friend so loved; who, to her at least, still manifested a fervour of regard that resisted all change; alike from this new partiality, and from the undisguised, and even strenuous opposition of the Memorialist to its indulgence.

The "Adieu, Streatham!" that had been uttered figuratively by Dr. Burney, without any knowledge of its nearness to reality, was now fast approaching to becoming a mere matter of fact; for, to the almost equal grief, however far from equal loss, of Dr. Johnson and Dr. Burney, Streatham, a short time afterwards, though not publicly relinquished, was quitted by Mrs. Thrale and her family...

[*Memoirs*, ii, 249-53]

...A latent,[393] but most potent reason, had, in fact, some share in abetting the elements in the failure of the Memorialist of paying her respects in Bolt Court at this period; except when attending thither her father. Dr. Burney feared her seeing Dr. Johnson alone; dreading, for both their sakes, the subject to which the Doctor might revert, if they should chance to be *tête-à-tête*. Hitherto, in the many meetings of the two Doctors and herself that had taken place after the paralytic stroke of Dr. Johnson,[394] as well as during the many that had more immediately followed the retreat of Mrs. Thrale to Bath, the name of that lady had never once been mentioned by any of the three.

Not from any difference of opinion was the silence; it was rather from a painful certainty that their opinions must be in unison, and, consequently, that in unison must be their regrets. Each of them, therefore, having so warmly esteemed one whom each of them, now, so afflictingly blamed, they tacitly concurred that, for the immediate moment, to cast a veil over her name, actions, and remembrance, seemed what was most respectful to their past feelings, and to her present situation.

But, after the impressive reproach of Dr. Johnson to the Memorialist relative to her absence; and after a seizure which caused a constant anxiety for his health, she could no longer consult her discretion at the expense of her regard; and, upon ceasing to observe her precautions, she was unavoidably left with him, one morning, by Dr. Burney, who had indispensable business further on in the city, and was to call for her on his return.

Nothing yet had publicly transpired, with certainty or authority, relative to the projects of Mrs. Thrale, who had now been nearly a year at Bath; though nothing was left unreported, or unasserted, with respect to her proceedings. Nevertheless, how far Dr. Johnson was himself informed, or was ignorant on the subject, neither Dr. Burney nor his daughter could tell; and each equally feared to learn.

Scarcely an instant, however, was the latter left alone in Bolt Court, ere she saw the justice of her long apprehensions; for while she planned speaking upon some topic that might have a chance to catch the attention of the Doctor, a sudden change from kind tranquility to strong austerity took place in his altered countenance; and, startled and affrighted, she held her peace.

A silence almost awful succeeded, though, previously to Dr. Burney's absence, the gayest discourse had been reciprocated.

The Doctor, then, see-sawing violently in his chair, as usual when he was big with any powerful emotion whether of pleasure or of pain, seemed deeply moved; but without looking at her, or speaking, he intently fixed his eyes upon the fire; while his panic-struck visitor, filled with dismay at the storm which she saw gathering over the character and conduct of one still dear to her very heart, from the furrowed front, the laborious heaving of the ponderous chest, and the roll of the large penetrating, wrathful eye of her honoured, but, just then, terrific host, sate mute, motionless, and sad; tremblingly awaiting a mentally demolishing thunderbolt.

Thus passed a few minutes, in which she scarcely dared breathe; while the respiration of the Doctor, on the contrary, was of asthmatic force and loudness; then, suddenly turning to her, with an air of mingled wrath and woe, he hoarsely ejaculated: "Piozzi!"

He evidently meant to say more; but the effort with which he articulated that name robbed him of any voice for amplification, and his whole frame grew tremulously convulsed.

His guest, appalled, could not speak; but he soon discerned that it was grief from coincidence, not distrust from opposition of sentiment, that caused her taciturnity.

This perception calmed him, and he then exhibited a face "in sorrow more than anger." His see-sawing abated of its velocity, and, again fixing his looks upon the fire, he fell into pensive rumination.

From time to time, nevertheless, he impressively glanced upon her his full fraught eye, that told, had its expression been developed, whole volumes of his regret, his disappointment, his astonished indignancy; but, now and then, it also spoke so clearly and so kindly, that he found her sight and her stay soothing to his disturbance, that she felt as if confidentially communing with him, although they exchanged not a word.

At length, and with great agitation, he broke forth with: "She cares for no one! You, only—You, she loves still!—but no one—and nothing else!—You she still loves—"

A half smile now, though of no very gay character, softened a little the severity of his features, while he tried to resume some cheerfulness in adding: "As...she loves her little finger!"

It was plain by this burlesque, or, perhaps, playfully literal comparison, that he meant now, and tried, to dissipate the solemnity of his concern.

The hint was taken; his guest started another subject; and this he resumed no more. He saw how distressing was the theme to a hearer whom he ever wished to please, not distress; and he named Mrs. Thrale no more! Common topics took place, till they were rejoined by Dr. Burney, whom then, and indeed always, he likewise spared upon this subject.

[*Memoirs,* ii, 358-63]

List of Abbreviations

Anecdotes   *Anecdotes of the late Samuel Johnson, LL.D* [1786],
Hester Lynch Piozzi, pub. Alan Sutton (1984)

Barrett   see *Diary*

Bate   *Samuel Johnson*, Walter Jackson Bate (1984)

CH   *Johnson: The Critical Heritage*, ed. James T. Boulton
(1971)

Cecilia   *Cecilia, or Memoirs of an Heiress* [1782], ed. Peter
Sabor and Margaret Anne Doody (1988)

Clifford   *Hester Lynch Piozzi (Mrs. Thrale)*, James L. Clifford
(1941)

Complete Works   *The Complete Works of Thomas Chatterton*,
[Chatterton]   ed. Donald S. Taylor in association with Benjamin
B. Hoover, 2 vols (1971)

Correspondence   *Horace Walpole's Correspondence*, ed. W.S. Lewis
[Walpole]   *et al.*, 48 vols (1937-83)

Diary   *Diary and Letters of Madame D'Arblay*, ed.
Charlotte Barrett, with Preface and Notes by Austin
Dobson, 6 vols (1904-5)

Dictionary   *A Dictionary of the English Language*, Samuel
Johnson, 2 vols (1755)

Early Diary   *The Early Diary of Frances Burney, 1768-1778, with
a Selection from her Correspondence and from the
Journals of Her Sisters Susan and Charlotte Burney,*

	ed. Annie Raine Ellis, 2 vols (1913; original ed. 1889)
Eaves and Kimpel	*Samuel Richardson, A Biography*, T.C. Duncan Eaves and Ben D. Kimpel (1971)
Ellis	see *Early Diary*
Evelina	*Evelina, or the History of a Young Lady's Entrance into the World* [1778], ed. Edward A. Bloom, with the assistance of Lillian D. Bloom (1968)
FB	Frances Burney (1752-1840)
HLT	Hester Lynch Thrale (1741-1821)
Hawkins	*The Life of Samuel Johnson, LL. D.* , Sir John Hawkins (1787)
Hemlow	*The History of Fanny Burney*, Joyce Hemlow (1958)
Hill	*Boswell's Life of Johnson*, ed. G.B. Hill, revised and enlarged by L.F. Powell, 6 vols (1934-50)
Journal	*Johnson's Journey to the Western Islands of Scotland* [1775] *and Boswell's Journal of a Tour to the Hebrides with Samuel Johnson, LL.D.* [1785], ed. R W. Chapman (1970, original ed. 1924)
Leslie and Taylor	*Life and Times of Sir Joshua Reynolds, with Notices of some of his Contemporaries*, Charles Robert Leslie and Tom Taylor, 2 vols (1865)
Letters	*The Letters of Samuel Johnson, with Mrs. Thrale's Genuine Letters to him,* ed. R.W. Chapman, 3 vols (1952)
Letters (Piozzi)	*Letters to and from the late Samuel Johnson, LL.D.*, ed. Hester Lynch Piozzi, 2 vols (1788)
Life	*Life of Johnson*, James Boswell [1791], ed.

R.W. Chapman (revised ed. 1970)

Lives	*Prefaces, Biographical and Critical, to the Works of the English Poets* [1779-81], ed. G. Birkbeck Hill (1905)
Lonsdale	*Doctor Charles Burney*, Roger Lonsdale (1965)
Memoirs	*Memoirs of Doctor Burney, arranged from his own Manuscripts, from Family Papers, and from Personal Recollections*, Madame D'Arblay, 3 vols (1832)
Memoirs (Cumberland)	*Memoirs of Richard Cumberland, written by himself. Containing an Account of his Life and Writings*, 2 vols (1806, 1807)
Misc.	*Johnsonian Miscellanies*, ed. G.B. Hill, 2 vols (1897)
NED	*A New English Dictionary on Historical Principles*, ed. J.A.H. Murray, Henry Bradley, W.A. Craigie, and C.T. Onions (1884-1928; suppl. 1976)
PMLA	*Publications of the Modern Language Association of America*
Poems and Plays	*Oliver Goldsmith: Poems and Plays*, ed. Tom Davis (1975)
Plays	*Plays by David Garrick and George Colman, the Elder*, ed. E.R.Wood (1982)
Prior	*The Life of Edmund Malone*, Sir James Prior (1860)
Queeney	*The Queeney Letters, being letters addressed to Hester Maria Thrale by Doctor Johnson, Fanny Burney, and Mrs.Thrale-Piozzi*, ed. the Marquis Lansdowne (1934)
SJ	Samuel Johnson (1709-84)
Thraliana	*Thraliana, the Diary of Mrs. Hester Lynch Thrale (later Mrs. Piozzi), 1776-1809*, ed. Katharine C

Balderston, 2 vols (1942)

Tinker   *Dr. Johnson & Fanny Burney, being the Johnsonian Passages from the Works of Mme. D'Arblay*, ed. Chauncey Brewster Tinker (1912)

Walpoliana   *Walpoliana*, ed. John Pinkerton, 2 vols (1799)

Works   *The Yale Edition of the Works of Samuel Johnson*, (to date) 11 vols (1958-)

Notes

1. FB's affectionate nickname for Samuel Crisp (1708-83), a firm family friend and her first literary mentor. He was now in retreat at Chesington Hall (Chessington) in Surrey, although he had been a friend of the Duchess of Portland, Mrs. Elizabeth Montagu and David Garrick during the 1750s. His comments on the correct epistolary style influenced FB greatly: 'You cannot but know *that trifling, that negligence, that even incorrectness*, now and then in familiar epistolary writing, is the very soul of genius and ease; and that if your letters were to be fine-labour'd compositions that smelt of *the lamp*, I had as lieve they [travelled elsewhere]...Dash away, whatever comes uppermost...' (*Early Diary*, 2:41 [April 18, 1775]).

2. The title of an anonymous pamphlet (1767 – full title: *Lexiphanes, a Dialogue Imitated from Lucian*) that attempted to ridicule SJ's lexicography and the diction of the *Rambler* series. Boswell ascribed it to 'one [Archibald] Campbell, a Scotch purser in the navy' and described its effect as applying Johnson's ' "words of large meaning" ' to trivia 'as if one should put the armour of Goliath upon a dwarf' (*Life*, p. 386 [1767]). Its apparent purpose was to belittle the 'Babylonish Dialect which Learned Pedants much affect' (*CH*, p. 317).

3. Hester Maria (1764-1857), known to SJ as 'Queeney', after Queen Esther (See *Life*, p. 1049 [April 28, 1780]). For FB's revised opinion of her, see p. 12.

4. William Seward (1747-99). Known to have disappointed his father, the Mr. Seward of the prominent brewers, Calvert and Seward, by preferring literature to commerce. According to Boswell, he was 'well known to a numerous and valuable acquaintance for his literature, love of the fine arts, and social virtues' (*Life*, p. 813, n. [June 28, 1777]). Some of his *Anecdotes* (5 vols, 1795-7) are included in *Misc.*, 2:301-11.

5. Esther (1749-1832) and Susanna Burney (1755-1800) were both gifted players. As Esther often played at her father's concerts, the debutant must be Susan.

6. The Berg MS. breaks at this point. This phrase is supplied from the similar version at *Memoirs*, 2:91.

7. *best becomes*: A noun taken from the verb 'to become...III, to be congruous, appropriate...IX, to look well, comely of bearing' (*NED*). There is thus a fine irony in the phrase given SJ's actual appearance.

8. An addition to the MS., obscuring the original. Ellis suspected that SJ was originally described as having 'dirty fists' (*Early Diary*, 2:153).

9. SJ's appearance was often curious to others. For his near-sight, see Susan Burney's record of her first meeting with SJ at *Early Diary*, 2:255-6. Bate believes that the tics and convulsive movements were of a 'psycho-neurotic origin' (p. 125), rather than Boswell's St. Vitus' Dance (*Life*, pp. 105-6 [1739]). For an alternative profile, see *Thraliana*, pp. 189, 205.

10. SJ was often given to moods of great abstraction. Mrs. Thrale records Thomas Tyers' description of him as 'like the ghosts, who never speak till they are spoken to', a likeness so felicitous that SJ 'often repeated it' (*Anecdotes*, p. 94).

11. Tinker believed this an extreme statement, and repeats Charles Burney's account of SJ's listening to a performance of Queeney's in 1775. He was observed to listen very attentively while she played on the harpsichord, until suddenly he called out, 'Why don't you dash away like Burney?' (*Life*, p. 663); see also p. 615 (where Boswell concludes him 'dull of hearing'), p. 642 and *Anecdotes*, pp. 115, 122.

12. Johann Christian Bach (1735-82), son of J.S. Bach. He worked in London from 1759. The concerts referred to here are likely to have been the series with K.F. Abel, 1764-82.

13. 1, St. Martin's St. had once been Newton's residence.

14. SJ felt that he had no ear for music. Boswell dated him first 'affected by musical sounds' as late as 1780, when he and Bennet Langton attended a 'Freemason's funeral procession' at Rochester (*Life*, p. 1080). He confessed to Boswell in 1777 that he was 'very insensible to the power of musick' (*Life*, p. 874), although FB in the *Memoirs* claimed that the friendship with her father helped convert him from downright scorn to a consciousness of a gap in his education; see Lonsdale, pp. 64, 129 and 182, but also Hawkins, p. 318: '...it excites in my mind no ideas and hinders me from contemplating my own'.

15. The MS. shows a change from *dining-room* to *drawing-room* at this point, possibly because the former could have been considered vulgar. See SJ's distinction in the *Dictionary* between *Dining-Room*: 'The principal apartment of the house; the room where entertainments are made' and *Drawing Room*: 'The room in which company assemble at court'.

16. Elizabeth Montagu (1720-1800), the 'Queen of the Blues', was at this time one of the most celebrated Bluestockings of the London salons. See pp. 3 and 35-6 for an account of her personality. She wrote, anonymously, three of Lord Lyttelton's *Dialogues of the Dead* (1760) and a comprehensive *Essay on the Genius and Writings of Shakespeare* (1769), which SJ confessed not to have read all the way through (*Life*, pp. 413-14 [1769]). He likened her to Elizabeth I (*Anecdotes*, p. 93) and, after a rift (1781-3), he decribed her in 1784 as a 'very extraordinary woman', having a 'constant stream of conversation' which was 'always impregnated' (*Life*, p. 1278). Charles Burney, however, hated her (in his own 'sweet' way); see *Thraliana*, p. 136 [1777]).

17. David Garrick (1717-79) had retired from the stage the previous year, but agreed in February, 1777 to act out his old farce, *Lethe; or Aesop in the Shades* (1740), itself an episode from James Miller's *An Hospital for Fools* (rev. 1757). FB had sympathy for Garrick when she was summoned before the Queen in 1790 to recite George Colman, the Elder's, *Polly Honeycombe: A Dramatic Novel* (1760). She notes the 'tiresome and unnatural profundity of respectful solemnity' (*Diary*, 4:360).

18. *discriminate*: 'To mark with note of difference; to distinguish by certain tokens from another' (*Dictionary*), i.e. SJ's pen-picture of Garrick showed a fine attention to detail and strove to provide an original and exact likeness.

19. *candour*: 'Sweetness of temper; purity of mind; openness; ingenuity; kindness' (*Dictionary*), i.e. not pejoratively. Sir Joshua Reynolds (1723-92) felt that Garrick often appeared to be SJ's '*property*' in that he would 'allow no man either to blame or to praise Garrick in his presence, without contradicting him' (*Life*, p. 962 [April 17, 1778]).

20. SJ's most extended statements on Garrick's care of money can be found at *Life*, pp. 925-6 (1778). He was 'a liberal man', having 'given away more money than any man in England'. However, there may have been a 'little vanity mixed'. The implication is that the same could not be said of his 'domestick saving'.

21. SJ first knew the Thrales' Streatham home during his period of convalescence in 1766. Streatham Place, a large three-storey brick house, was set in a hundred acres. During the Thrales' Johnson years, the house was often refurbished, and a new library wing built. Susan Burney described it in August, 1779 as 'beautiful; worthy of the charming inhabitants. It is a little Paradise ... Cattle, poultry, dogs, all running freely about, without annoying each other' (*Early Diary*, 2:241).

22. That she was the author of *Evelina*.

23. Mary Cholmondeley, *née* Woffington (1729-1811), sister of the renowned actress, Peg Woffington, and married to the Earl of Cholmondeley's son (Horace Walpole's nephew). She was one of the most influential society hostesses of her generation and one of the first readers to praise *Evelina* publicly.

24. Marie-Jeanne Laboras de Mezières, Mme. Riccoboni (d. 1792), author of several sentimental novels, the most famous translated (as Frances Brooke) as *Letters from Juliet Lady Catesby* (1760).

25. The Branghtons live over their silversmith's shop on Snow-Hill. Evelina visits them often with Mme. Duval during her second stay in London. Snow-Hill ran between Holborn Bridge and Newgate. Mr. Smith lives in the same house. Sir Clement Willoughby joins Evelina's party when he comes upon her with the Miss Branghtons in the notorious 'dark walks' of Vauxhall Gardens (Vol. II, Letter xv, pp. 193-206).

26. Anna Williams (1706-83), SJ's blind housekeeper from 1752. He helped her publish her *Miscellanies in Prose and Verse* (1766), adding his own 'fairy tale' of "The Fountains" and including HLT's "The Three Warnings".

27. SJ was often given to mimickry. See below, p. 14 and his famous kangaroo hop: 'The company stared…nothing could be more ludicrous than the appearance of a tall, heavy, grave-looking man, like Dr. Johnson, standing up to mimic the shape and motions of a kangaroo. He stood erect, put out his hands like feelers, and gathering up the tails of his huge brown coat so as to resemble the pouch of the animal, made two or three vigorous bounds across the room!' (*Letters*, 1:241, n.).

28. This could be literally true. Boswell records several instances of SJ's feats of memory; see *Life*, pp. 30, 35, 1074-5.

29. William Melmoth's *Laelius: an Essay on Friendship* (1777).

30. The Prologue (not Epilogue) to Beaumont and Fletcher's tragedy, *Bonduca*, 'altered' by George Colman, the Elder, and produced at the Haymarket in July, 1778.

31. In 1775 SJ preferred him to Dryden in this regard; see *Life*, pp. 598-9.

32. John Wilkes (1727-97), the radical politician. Despite their immense political differences Wilkes and SJ twice dined together at the home of the publishers, Charles and Edward Dilly – on May 15, 1776 and May 8, 1781 (see *Life*, pp. 764-6, 1143-7). When, in 1763, the topic of Wilkes' writings came up, SJ found him an 'abusive scoundrel', who, whilst probably 'safe from the law', deserved to be visited by 'half a dozen footmen' to have him 'well ducked' (*Life*, p. 279).

33. Tinker notes (p. 20) that HLT could be alluding to an earlier remark of SJ's on Garrick (in 1775), that 'no man's face has had more wear and tear' (*Life*, p. 663).

34. 1719-89, SJ's biographer and literary executor. *The Life of Samuel Johnson, LL.D* appeared in 1787. He was awarded his knighthood in 1772 for his services as Chairman of the Middlesex Justices. An example of his thrifty ways was his charge on the Estate for coach hire in attending executors' meetings; see Prior, p. 426. His five-volume *History of Music*

(1776) was immediately overshadowed by Charles Burney's study (4 vols, 1776-89).

35. Unlikely to have been the famous Literary Club that Tinker identifies (p. 21), but rather the smaller Ivy Lane Club, which met every Tuesday at the King's Head in Ivy Lane, Paternoster Row, from 1749 to 1756.

36. Not an extraordinary event, as SJ all but abstained from drinking during the last twenty years of his life.

37. As FB points out, a word not found in the *Dictionary*. Boswell, when the Essex Head Club was formed in 1783, was to be included as he was a 'very *clubable* man' (*Life*, p. 1261).

38. In *Evelina* the heroine's low-born grandmother, once a 'waiting-girl at a tavern', and described by Mr. Villars, Evelina's guardian, as 'at once uneducated and unprincipled; ungentle in her temper, and unamiable in her manners' (Vol. I, Letter ii, p. 13).

39. *agreeability*: In the *Dictionary* 'agreeableness' is defined as either 'Consistency with; suitableness to' or 'The quality of pleasing', i.e. a positive social attribute, not just the power of being amenable.

40. The husband was her cousin, Charles Rousseau Burney.

41. Frances Reynolds (1729-1807), sister and companion to Sir Joshua Reynolds, and a professional painter in her own right. Her *Essay on Taste* was published in 1784, a work which SJ saw in draft form and judged to be 'full of very penetrating meditation, and very forcible sentiments' (*Letters*, no. 777, 2:476 [April 8, 1782]). Although almost completely supported by her illustrious brother, HLT found that she would not 'keep her Post by Flattery' and that she loved 'to hear her criticize Sir Joshua's Painting' (*Thraliana*, p. 79). FB found the cost great, noting that she seemed to exhibit 'an habitual perplexity of mind and irresolution of conduct, which to herself was restlessly tormenting, and to all around her was teazingly wearisome' (*Memoirs*, 1:332).

42. Her cousin and brother-in-law, mentioned above, n. 40.

43. Thomas Lowndes, the publisher of *Evelina*.

44. FB is evidently unaware of HLT's first impressions. On their first meeting in St. Martin's St. (March, 1777), she records that she was a 'graceful looking Girl', but that it was the 'Grace of an Actress not a Woman of Fashion'. The success of her writing 'embarrasses her Talk & clouds her Mind with scruples about Elegancies which either come uncalled for or will not come at all...' However, she was certainly a writer of merit and a girl of 'prodigious Parts' (*Thraliana*, p. 368).

45. Henry Thrale (1728/29-81) was probably beset in the long term by grief at the death of Harry, his nine-year-old son, (March 23, 1776). SJ certainly attributed his low spirits to this, writing to HLT (October 15, 1778): 'Is my master come to himself? Does he talk, and walk, and look about him, as if there were yet something in the world for which it is worth while to live?...All sorrow that lasts longer than its cause is morbid' (*Letters*, no. 583, 2:257). The Thrales had also just taken out a loan from Charles Scase (1709-92) to secure the brewery in adverse economic conditions. HLT put the melancholy down to 'the Influence of the bad Times upon his Business' and the fear that he would 'outlive *his* Fortune' (*Thraliana*, pp. 319-20). See also the letter to SJ, April/May, 1778 (no. 575a, 2:247-8).

46. The Rev. Mr. Tattersall, as revealed in the *Diary* entry for June 5, 1780 (1:388-9). The home and garden were crowded with 'the same paltry ornaments, the same crowd of buildings, the same unmeaning decorations, and the same unsuccessful attempts at making something of nothing'.

47. Bennet Langton (1737-1801) often received SJ at his estate in Lincolnshire. SJ felt that Langton had his children 'too much about him' (*Life*, p. 818 [1777]). See also p. 89.

48. These are financial affairs. Langton was notably profligate, without, SJ thought, much pleasure: 'He does not spend fast enough to have pleasure from it. He has the crime of prodigality, and the wretchedness of parsimony' (*Life*, p. 967 [1778]). See also *Thraliana*, pp. 105-6.

49. HLT's title for her husband. SJ was thus encouraged to address her as 'my mistress'.

50. Charles Burney described SJ's Streatham entertainments to Boswell in 1775, including mention of 'many long conversations, often sitting up as long as the fire and candles lasted, and much longer than the patience of the servants subsisted' (*Life*, pp. 661-2).

51. Richard Cumberland (1732-1811), the dramatist, was well known to SJ. HLT found him in 1777, 'a Man one cannot love' as 'his Delicacy is very troublesome, his Peevishness very teizing, his Envy very hateful...' (*Thraliana*, p. 135). He was the model for Sir Fretful Plagiary in Sheridan's *The Critic* (1779).

52. See above, p. 12.

53. *Cicerone*: 'a guide who shows and exhibits the antiquities of a place to strangers' (*NED*).

54. *tartar*: slang usage for one who is 'hard to beat or surpass in skill, an adept, a champion' (*NED*, sense III.b)

55. *toad*: again a very idiomatic word, near to *NED*'s sense III: 'mean-spirited . . . to fawn'.

56. The line is from the "Prologue" to *All For Love* (1678): 'Drink hearty Draughts of Ale, from plain brown Bowls,/ And snatch the homely Rasher from the Coals' (33-4). SJ is apologising for his idiomatic familiarity of speech – not for any innuendo.

57. In *Evelina* Lady Louisa Larpent is Lord Orville's sister. She lacks her brother's tact and sensitivity, however, and, when we are introduced to her in detail in Volume 3, is clearly distinguished by FB as a 'pretty but affected young lady' (Volume III, Letter ii, p. 281) who is 'so unamiably opposite' to her brother in her manners (Letter iii, p. 286).

58. Sir John Lade (1759-1838), one of HLT's nephews, some seven years younger than FB and so, in 1778, a minor. SJ composed a satire in 1780 on this 'rich, extravagant young gentleman's coming of age', where he inherited 'Pride and pleasure, pomp and plenty' and is characterised as 'Wild as wind, and light as feather' (*Life*, pp. 1388-9). In the class-list of her friends' "Beauties" drawn up by HLT in July, 1778, Lade scored 0 out of 20 for "Religion", "Morality" and "Scholarship". His highest mark was 10 for "Person & Voice" (*Thraliana*, p. 330).

59. *éloge*: a speech of praise or eulogium.

60. Miss Branghton's exclamation to her sister in Kensington Gardens: that Evelina had once danced with Lord Orville. Such an announcement suggests publicly that she claims a presumptuous friendship with nobility. The Letter ends with Mme. Duval and the Branghtons requisitioning Lord Orville's coach during a particularly violent rain-storm – much to Evelina's increasing horror and embarrassment (Vol. II, Letter xxiii, pp. 242-50).

61. i.e. one embroidered on a tambour or drum-shaped frame.

62. Sir Richard Jebb (1729-87), M.D., one of SJ's physicians.

63. For SJ "correct" usage was the essential basis for powerful and fully comprehensible expression. "Terms of Art", "Low" cant or the jargon of commerce eventually defeated the purpose of language, namely to help submit one's individual thoughts or sentiments to universal application and *vice versa*. In the *Rambler* papers, he attempted to 'refine our language to grammatical purity, and to clear it from colloquial barbarisms, licentious idioms, and irregular combinations' (*Rambler* no. 208, *Works*, 5:318-19, [March 14, 1752]) in the hope that meaning would be least obscured by form. The language of tradesmen resembled the 'garb appropriated to the gross employments of rusticks or mechanicks' which, in his "Life of Cowley", he felt would always demean 'the most heroick sentiments' (*Lives*, 1:58). His most unreserved praise for prosody was attracted by Addison's prose style, his 'genuine Anglicism' (*Lives*, 2:149-50).

64. Thomas Pennant (1726-98), a Welsh antiquarian and author of a *Tour in Scotland* (1771). SJ once differed (much to his instant regret) with Bishop Thomas Percy over Pennant's accuracy in his Northumbrian descriptions, especially that of the grounds of Alnwick Castle. Pennant was praised 'very highly' by SJ, whereas Percy believed that he had been disrespectful to his family estate. The heat of the difference brought instant repentance from SJ who, whilst conceding that Pennant was 'a Whig...; a *sad dog*', still believed that he was the 'best traveller' he had ever read as he 'observed more things than anyone else' (*Life*, pp. 931-3 [April 12, 1778]; see also p. 936 and *Journal*, pp. 307-8 [Sept. 17]).

65. John Montagu (1719-95), Commander-in-Chief at Newfoundland during the American campaign and now Vice-Admiral.

66. Guiseppe Marc' Antonio Baretti (1719-89), SJ's Piemontese friend. He was a teacher of Italian and prolific writer of Miscellanies. He had stayed with the Thrales from 1773 to July, 1776 as Queeney's Italian tutor. A quarrel with HLT terminated the appointment; see *Thraliana*, pp. 44-6 (May 28, 1777), for some indication of what lay behind the mimickry.

67. *The Good Natur'd Man* (1768) by Oliver Goldsmith (1728-74) has the reckless Honeywood in contrast to the melancholic Croaker, described by Sir William Honeywood, as possessing a 'mirth' that was 'an antidote to all gaiety' and an 'appearance' that had a 'stronger effect on [his] spirits than an undertaker's shop' (Act I, *Poems and Plays*, p. 9). Suspirius (the screech-owl) in *Rambler* 59 (October 9, 1750), 'goes on in his unharmonious strain, displaying present miseries, and foreboding more, . . . every syllable is loaded with misfortune, and death is always brought nearer to the view' (*Works*, 3:317). SJ wrote the "Prologue" to *The Good Natur'd Man*. For HLT's account of Goldsmith's moods, see *Thraliana*, pp. 80-4.

68. A consistent judgement; see his comment to Reynolds on the book's initial lack of appeal to publishers (*Life*, p. 969 [April 25, 1778]).

69. The 'poor Scotch poet' in *Evelina* who lodges with the Branghtons and has to default on his rent; see Vol. II, Letter xi, pp.173-9, for examples of his poetry. He is 'most unworthily, despised for being poor, and, most illiberally, detested for being a Scotchman' (pp. 177-8). Macartney's prose style may be flowery, but hardly colloquial; see Vol. II, Letter xx, pp. 225-31. In the third volume he is identified as Evelina's stepbrother.

70. *propriety*: '2. Accuracy; justice' (*Dictionary*).

71. Probably Rev. James Evans (d. c.1786), mentioned later in the *Diary*: 'Mr. Evans is a clergyman, very intimate with the Thrales, and a good-humoured and a sensible man' (1:318). He was Rector of St. Olaves, Southwark.

72. The Fullers were from the Sussex family of Rose Hill. The elder (d. 1777) was M.P. for Rye. See below for an account of the younger Rose Fuller, pp. 24, 42.

73. Miss Brown is later described as 'a most good-humoured, frank, unaffected, sociable girl' whom FB liked 'very much'. Apparently, both she and S[ophie] S[treatfield] were 'in fevers' in SJ's presence, 'from apprehension' (*Diary*, 1:209-10).

74. Her stepmother.

75. There is an abbreviated account of the same story in *Life*, p. 1144 [1781]). Tinker thought (p. 45) that FB had repeated the stanzas to Boswell, though the first two lines there run: 'When first I drew my vital breath,/ A little minikin I came upon earth...'.

76. Hill gives the reason for her acquittal in his edition of the *Life* (Hill, 4:103, n.), namely that 'the prosecutrix could not prove that the articles were hers'.

77. Dobson identifies this person as Mrs. Pilkington (Loetitia van Lewen – 1700-50), whose *Memoirs* were published in 1748 (*Diary*, 1:84).

78. Probably the acquaintances made during his nocturnal ramblings during the 1740s; see Bate, pp. 177-81.

79. Margaret Caroline Rudd had been tried for forgery in 1775 and acquitted.

80. d. 1767. A famous, or perhaps, notorious, beauty of the time, and the subject of at least six portraits by Reynolds.

81. FB refers back to Bet Flint's quatrain, above pp. 21-2.

82. He was M.P. for Streatham.

83. He was under contract for these essays for May 29, 1777. They finally appeared in March, 1779.

84. Charlotte Lennox, *née* Ramsay (1720-1804), author of *The Female Quixote* (1752). Having failed as an actress, she married an employee of William Strahan's (the printer of the *Dictionary*). SJ met her whilst she was in the process of finishing her first novel, *Harriet Stuart*. When it was finally published in December, 1750 (by John Payne), he organised 'a whole night spent in festivity' to celebrate her 'literary child', according to Hawkins (pp. 286-7). SJ was loyal to her throughout her literary career and wrote at least seven dedications for her. The most famous of these was that for *The Female Quixote* to which he also added a chapter (Book I, ch. xi). He also wrote the "Proposals" for the Quarto *Works* (1775). In some sort of return, it is likely that he consulted her *Shakespeare Illustrated* (1753-4) in the preparation of his edition.

85. James Harris (1709-80), the noted grammarian, whose major work was *Hermes; or a Philosophical Inquiry concerning Universal Grammar* (1751). His *Philological Inquiries* had just been published (1778). SJ thought him a 'prig, and a bad prig', although Boswell thought that this was more in reference to his '*manner* as a writer' (*Life*, p. 911 [1778]).

86. See above, p. 20.

87. HLT continues the anecdote to show SJ's capacity for charity. Seeing that Fuller 'thought him serious', SJ 'undeceived him very gently indeed' and set him right at length (*Anecdotes*, p. 44).

88. Hogarth's (1697-1764) *The Analysis of Beauty. Written with a view of fixing the fluctuating Ideas of Taste* (1753) met with Tinker's sharp verdict: 'An ill-considered book...which only yielded its opinionated author severe, though merited, censure' (p. 53). He may have had in mind Paul Sandby's caricatures, etched 1753-4, which ridiculed Hogarth's pleas for a more tolerant aesthetics, e.g. Sandby's 'A New Dunciad: done with a view of fixing ye fluctuating Ideas of Taste' or his view of a Temple of Diana set alight by a 'vile Ephesian to obtain a name' and who was endeavouring to undermine 'the ever sacred monument of all the best painters, sculptors, architects, etc.'. See William Sandby, *Thomas and Paul Sandby: Royal Academicians* (1892) for a full description and Johnson Ball, *Paul and Thomas Sandby: Royal Academicians* (1985), pp. 173-4. Cf. David Bindman, *Hogarth* (1981), pp. 151-60, and Ronald Paulson, *Hogarth: His Life, Art and Times*, 2 vols (1971), 2:167-88 for a more sympathetic assessment.

89. See above, p. 17 and below, pp. 32, 56-8. The resulting comedy (*The Witlings*) was suppressed by FB herself largely as the result of "Daddy" Crisp's advice that antagonising the Female Wits would be counter-productive; see Hemlow, pp. 130-8.

90. Richardson's (1689-1761) fear of rivals was notorious; see Eaves and Kimpel, pp. 292-305, 533-7. SJ corresponded with him from 1751, when he was warm and solicitous in his wishes for a successful reception for *Clarissa Harlowe* (1747-8); see *Letters*, no. 31 (1:35-6). It is to SJ we might turn when wishing to discover the origin of the commonplace that Richardson was vain: 'Richardson had little conversation, except about his own works, of which Sir Joshua Reynolds said he was always ready to talk, and glad to have them introduced' (*Life*, p. 1086 [1780]).

91. See above, p. 15 and below, p. 29.

92. *Rout*: '1. A clamorous multitude; a rabble...' (*Dictionary*). SJ could be referring to the needless noise and fuss they were making.

93. *Irene* is SJ's only play and widely regarded as a diploma-piece, 'to make some money and to establish his credentials' (Bate, p. 158). It concerns the fate of Irene, a Greek Christian slave, who is captured at the fall of Constantinople, and falls into the hands of the Sultan Mahomet, who becomes infatuated with her to the detriment of his whole rule. Irene refuses the safety of renouncing her faith for Islam and gives Mahomet no alternative but to execute her. Although completed in 1737, the play was not performed (and published) until 1749 at Drury Lane (as *Mahomet and Irene*) thanks to the support from its new manager, David Garrick. It ran for nine nights. SJ was the person most aware of its shortcomings. Bennet Langton remarked to Boswell in 1780 how, at a reading of the play 'at a house in the country', SJ did not stay until the end. When asked the reason why he had left so abruptly, he replied, ' "Sir,

I thought it had been better" ' (*Life*, p. 1068). SJ may well have read extracts that reflected on the weak and divided North administration and its prosecution of the American campaign, e.g. Demetrius' distaste at Greek faction:

> A thousand prodigies foretold it.
> A feeble government, eluded laws,
> A factious populace, luxurious nobles,
> And all the maladies of sinking state.
> (I. i. 36-9)

The French had signed a treaty of alliance and commerce with the Americans in February which produced ignominious failure for that summer's Carlisle Peace Commission. Leontius also rejects the 'lust of gold' that appears 'The last corruption of degenerate man!' (14-15), and which brings 'embattled nations at our gate' (23) according to Demetrius. Thus, both domestic and foreign policies are found wanting (*Works*, 6:113-14).

94. Produced in 1778. Arthur Murphy (1727-1805) was a friend of SJ's of long standing. His *Essay on the Life and Genius of Samuel Johnson* appeared in 1792. Boswell praised his 'talents, literature, and gentleman-like manners, [which] were soon perceived by Johnson and a friendship was formed which was never broken' (*Life*, p. 252 [1760]).

95. SJ is not supposed to have often read books through, and was sometimes incredulous that others did; see *Life*, p. 520 (1773).

96. Michael Lort, D.D. (1725-90), an antiquary and currently chaplain to the Bishop of Peterborough and Vicar at Bottisham, nr. Cambridge. His opinion would have weighed heavily with FB as he was 'reckoned one of the most learned men alive'. However, she also notes that his manners were 'somewhat blunt and odd, and [that] he is altogether out of the common road, without having chosen a better path' (*Diary*, 1:91).

97. Thomas Chatterton (1752-70). The Rowley MSS. were regarded as spurious by many. FB quotes Dr. H. Harrington's opinion that they were authentic in an entry for 1780 (*Diary*, 1:356-7). For SJ's view, see *Life*, pp. 752 (1776), and 1175 (1782) where Chatterton simply exhibits 'the resolution to say again what has once been said' (*Letters*, no. 766 [March 2], 2:464).

98. From February to April, 1770, Chatterton produced several satires inspired by his opposition to SJ's *The False Alarm*, published in January. In that pamphlet SJ defended the Commons' right to reject John Wilkes' (successful) election as M.P. for Middlesex. In *Kew Gardens* Chatterton exploits the prevalent Patriot myth that the country was actually run from there by Augusta, Princess Dowager of Wales and her supposed lover, the Earl of Bute, who granted SJ a state pension in 1762.

There, the 'mysterious Wings' of 'Inspiration' seem strangers 'to what rigid Johnson sings' (279-80). In *The Whore of Babylon* SJ's 'pension'd' muse is associated with the charnel-house: 'Whilst from his Fancy figures budded out / As Hair on humid Carcasses will sprout' (I.335-6), and, in *February; an Elegy*, it appears 'Drown'd in a butt of wine' (70); see also *Kew Gardens*, 279-98, *The Whore of Babylon*, I.307-36, and *Fables for the Court. The Shepherds*, 28-30 (*Complete Works*, 1: 512-42, 452-67, 447-50, 496-7).

99. See above, p. 19, n. 71.

100. Evelina's mother's maiden-name was Evelyn.

101. cf. SJ's comparison between Richardson and Fielding which gave the palm to the former who 'knew how a watch was made' whereas the latter merely told the hour 'by looking on the dial-plate'. Richardson drew 'characters of nature' but Fielding 'only of manners'. Boswell disagreed (*Life*, p. 389 [1768]).

102. By the elder Colman and Garrick (1766). One of the characters is named Fanny. HLT is mimicking the vulgar Mrs. Heidelberg's comment on her: 'Bless me! Why your face is as pale, and black, and yellow – of fifty colours, I pertest' (I.ii, *Plays*, p. 122). 'I wow and pertest' is her favourite oath.

103. There may be more warmth here than is apparent; see *Thraliana*, p. 368 for HLT's comments on her self-consciousness, p. 400 on her extreme sensitivity and p. 551 on her pride.

104. *maggot*: '2. Whimsy; caprice; odd fansy' (*Dictionary*).

105. Hannah More (1745-1833) had just seen her tragedy, *Percy* (1777), enjoy tremendous success, gaining her, with Garrick's help, as much as £750. The anecdote is repeated (with less credit to SJ) by Boswell (*Life*, pp. 327-8 [1784]) and *Anecdotes*, p. 84. SJ, in general, thought very well of her; see *Life*, p. 1278 [1784]).

106. Goldsmith, not Seward. See his *Retaliation, a Poem; including epitaphs on the most distinguished wits of this Metropolis* (1774): 'Who pepper'd the highest was sure to please' (112).

107. See above, p. 24.

108. See above, p. 1.

109. Sophia Streatfield (1754-1835) of Chiddingstone, Kent, was a noted beauty and Bluestocking, who throughout 1778 infatuated Henry Thrale; see Bate, pp. 548-50.

110. The visit to Warley Camp in Essex was in order to see Bennet Langton, Captain in the Lincolnshire militia. Langton's account can be found at *Life*, pp. 1001-4. Fears of a French invasion were high at this time.

111. For other instances, see above pp. 1-2 and 20.

112. Mrs. Desmoulins (b. 1716) was the daughter of SJ's godfather, Dr. Swinfen, and the widow of a writing-master. Besides their lodging, SJ gave her and her daughter an allowance of half a guinea per week, a 'twelfth part' of his pension (*Life*, p. 894 [March 20, 1778]). His domestic situation is rather feelingly described in a letter to HLT (November 14, 1778): 'We have tolerable concord at home, but no love. Williams hates every body, Levet hates Desmoulins and does not love Williams. Desmoulins hates them both. Poll loves none of them' (no. 591, 2:268).

113. Alexander MacBean (d. 1784) had been one of SJ's amanuenses in the compilation of the *Dictionary*. The 'dictionary' referred to above was MacBean's *A System of Ancient Geography* (1773), for which SJ wrote a Preface.

114. Robert Levett (1701-82), a surgeon, was the subject of SJ's ode *On the Death of Dr. Robert Levet* (1782). He had lived with SJ since 1763. He is celebrated as 'Officious, innocent, sincere, / Of ev'ry friendless name the friend' (7-8), whilst also being 'coarsely kind' (10). His quiet good nature is shown by his wide practice among the poor, reached by a long-distance walk each day. Whilst awkward and uncouth, SJ valued him highly: 'a very useful and very blameless man' (*Life*, p. 1172 [January 17, 1782]).

115. Poll Carmichael was identified by Tinker as the 'poor woman lying in the street, so much exhausted that she could not walk'. SJ took her to his home upon his back, 'where he discovered that she was one of those wretched females who had fallen into the lowest state of vice, poverty, and disease'. She was consequently taken into the household (*Life*, p. 1313 [June, 1784]).

116. 'Mr. Burke...doats on it: he began it one morning at seven o'clock, and could not leave it a moment; he sat up all night reading it' (*Diary*, 1:107).

117. Reynolds' offer and the imposition on his nieces can be found at *Diary*, 1:107.

118. SJ hated deceptions of all kinds, impressing 'upon all his friends the importance of perpetual vigilance against the slightest degrees of falsehood' (*Life*, p. 900 [March 31, 1778]).

119. The first twenty-two *Lives* were published in four volumes in March, 1779. The full title was *Prefaces, Biographical and Critical, to the Works of the English Poets*. The "Life of Cowley" was sent to press in December, 1777.

120. Rev. John Norris (1657-1711), rector of Bemerton, was known for his mystical brand of religion. SJ's summary of his argument in *The Theory and Regulation of Love* (1688) is accurate.

121. e.g. SJ's interruption of the conversation between Richardson and Hogarth in 1740, when still an unknown; see *Life*, pp. 106-7, for his invective against George II.

122. John Gregory, (1734-73), M.D., Professor of Medicine at Edinburgh University. His letters, *A Father's Legacy to his Daughters*, were published posthumously in 1774.

123. See below, pp. 38-9. This was Montagu House in Portman Square.

124. *bandeau*: 'A narrow band or fillet worn by women to bind the hair or as part of a head-dress' (*NED*).

125. i.e. the King's birthday when it was the custom to wear new clothes in celebration.

126. An alternative spelling for Lade. Lady Mary Lade (?1753-1802) was HLT's sister. In the ratings out of 20 devised in July, 1778, Lady Mary scored 15 for "Good Humour" and 18 for "Useful Knowledge", but only 6 for "Conversation" and 3 for "Ornamental Knowledge" (*Thraliana*, p. 331).

127. HLT commented on SJ's mature style that it became 'so natural to him, and so much like his common mode of conversing, that [she] was ... but little astonished when he told [her], that he had scarcely read over one of those inimitable essays [the *Ramblers*] before they went to the press' (*Anecdotes*, p. 134).

128. *trim*: 'to make neat or adjust' (*Dictionary*).

129. *Hudibras* (1663-78), Pt.I, Canto i, 55-6: '...he never scanted / His bounty unto such as wanted'.

130. *mag*: 'to chatter, talk' (*NED*).

131. See above, pp. 31-2.

132. S.N.H. Linguet (1736-94), a French political writer. Charles Burney had lent a volume of his complete works to Mrs. Montagu who in turn had lost it (*Diary*, 1:121).

133. The most prominent example of this was when, in 1781, HLT praised Dudley Long (afterwards North, 1748-1829), as 'a gentleman distinguished amongst his acquaintance for acuteness of wit', according to Boswell. SJ's reply was to admonish her for her immoderate praise: 'Mr. Long's character is very *short*. It is nothing. He fills a chair. He is a man of genteel appearance, and that is all. I know nobody who blasts by praise as you do; for whenever there is exaggerated praise, every body is set against a character...' (*Life*, p. 1129).

134. July 5-September 30, 1774. The visit was cut short due to the dissolution of Parliament. Henry Thrale had to return to the Southwark house and campaign. HLT's Welsh journal can be found in A.M. Broadley, (ed.), *Dr. Johnson and Mrs. Thrale* (1910), pp. 158-219. There is also a reprint there of SJ's tour diary. One of the most recurrent items of friction was over the appreciation of the landscape. Henry Thrale would linger to take in the whole effect, whereas SJ, to whom distant vistas often seemed a blur due to his near-sight, preferred to glance at a book; see Clifford, pp. 114-16 and Bate, pp. 476-7.

135. *cutter*: 'a sharply disconcerting remark'.

136. For Rose Fuller, see above, p. 24. Stephen Fuller was his uncle.

137. Not a particularly gentle comment. In *Evelina* Mr. Smith inhabits the Branghtons' house in Snow Hill, near Holborn, and Evelina comments that he 'seems very desirous of appearing a man of gaiety and spirit; but his vivacity is so low-bred, and his whole behaviour so forward and disagreeable, that I should prefer the company of *dullness* itself...to that of this *sprightly* young man'. (Vol. II, Letter xi, p. 178).

138. George Romney (1734-1802), whose first major sitter was Richard Cumberland, the 'first, who encouraged him to advance his terms [in 1768], by paying him ten guineas for his performance' (*Memoirs* [Cumberland], 2:213).

139. Sir Richard Jebb (1729-87) was Henry Thrale's physician. HLT lamented that there was 'no true Affection, no Friendship in the Sneakers & Fawners: tis not for Obsequious Civility that [she delighted] in Johnson, Hinchcliffe, Sir Richard Jebb or Piozzi' (*Thraliana*, p. 470 [January 10, 1781]).

140. Jeremiah Crutchley (1745-1805), later M.P. for Horsham, Sussex. He was supposed 'by those that knew his Mother & her Connections, to be Mr. Thrale's natural son, & in many Things he resembles him, but not in Person; as he is both ugly & aukward' (*Thraliana*, p. 497 [May 17, 1781]).

141. Henry Smith (?1756-89), of New-House, St. Albans. He was Henry Thrale's cousin and one of the executors of the estate. According to HLT, in June, 1781, he was 'a ductile Minded Creature' (*Thraliana*, p. 499, n. 1).

142. Sir John Lade; see above, p. 16.

143. Mr. Crisp lodged with Kitty Cooke's aunt. She was noted for her oddities of speech.

144. *Castalian stream*: 'the stream on Mt. Parnassus, sacred to the Muses'.

145. Dug at Thrale's direction at Streatham Place in 1777, in imitation of Duck Island in St. James' Park; see Clifford, p. 165.

146. i.e. the list of guests.

147. Cf. pp. 1-2, 33, 81.

148. A local schoolmaster; see *Thraliana*, p. 101 (June, 1777).

149. The famous tour with Boswell made in August-September, 1773. SJ's *Journey to the Western Islands of Scotland* was published in 1775.

150. Alexander Pope's *The Rape of the Lock* (1714), Canto III, 152. The description is of the aethereal Sylphs – who do not possess Lady Ladd's bearing.

151. See above, p. 36, where the two are considered to be of similar build.

152. One of SJ's most settled beliefs; see Boswell's report of his conversation with Allan Ramsay (1713-84) in 1779: ' "We are all agreed as to our own liberty; we would have as much of it as we can get; but we are not agreed as to the liberty of others: for in proportion as we take, others must lose. I believe we hardly wish that the mob should have liberty to govern us. When that was the case some time ago, no man was at liberty not to have candles in his windows." RAMSAY. "The result is, that order is better than confusion." JOHNSON. "The result is, that order cannot be had but by subordination." ' (*Life*, pp. 1017-18). See also *Life*, pp. 514, 601. HLT, in summing up his 'singularities', noted 'that though a man of obscure birth himself, his partiality to people of family was visible on every occasion; his zeal for subordination warm even to bigotry; his hatred to innovation, and reverence for the old feudal times, apparent, whenever any possible manner of shewing them occurred' (*Anecdotes*, p. 135). This is an uncharitable view, for see the less extreme explication of Feudal Order propounded at *Life*, pp. 857-9 (September 20, 1777) or p. 681 (March 10, 1776, 'for I am for leaving a quantity of land in commerce, to create industry, and keep money in the country').

153. SJ often made use of this same summer-house to read, work and form pious resolutions (*Life*, pp. 1170-1 [August 9, 1781]).

154. From a letter to "Daddy" Crisp, January, 1779.

155. *Warley: a Satire* (1778) by the Rev. George Huddesford (1749-1809), published anonymously and dedicated to Reynolds, provided a solution to the latter's query as to the authorship of *Evelina* by naming 'dear little Burney'. FB's horror at the satires on her that might now proliferate no doubt intensified whenever she remembered her father's distress at the publication of George Veal's scabrous parody of his *Tours* called *Musical Travels through England* (1774); see Hemlow, pp. 135-6.

156. Miss Dorothy Young from Lynn had been a close friend of the first Mrs. Burney.

157. Robert Bremner (d. 1789), a music printer and publisher.

158. The heroine of SJ's fairy-tale, "The Fountains", contributed to Anna Williams' *Miscellanies* (1766).

159. See above, p. 38.

160. This extract is from a letter to Susan Burney, dated January 11.

161. See above, p. 4.

162. Sir Philip Jennings-Clerke (c.1722-88), Whig M.P. for Totnes, in Devon, and a political friend of Henry Thrale's, who helped him canvass in 1780. During the Gordon Riots in June, 1780, he managed to secure the brewery's 'Counting House Bills, Bonds, etc.' at Chelsea College. HLT found 'nothing particular to recommend him but good plain sense & Manners highly polished – a Civility of a very fine sort it is though, always gentle & never obsequious, – the Manner of an old Horse Officer entirely, & not too ceremonious neither' (*Thraliana*, p. 372 [March 1, 1779]). See too SJ's notice of Clerke's 'very rich laced ruffles' and his 'appearance of a gentleman of ancient family' which led him to conclude that 'ancient ruffles and modern principles [did] not agree' (*Life*, p. 1128 [April 1, 1781]).

163. The Bill was directed against Court and aristocratic patronage in the Commons and, as such, forms part of a national concern for Reform outside Parliament, the initial aims of which were to limit the sovereign's spending and re-found the Constitution on its genuine first principles; see Eugene Charlton Black, *The Association: British Extra-Parliamentary Political Organization, 1769-1793* (1963), pp. 1-82, and H.T. Dickinson, *Liberty and Property: Political Ideology in Eighteenth-Century Britain* (1977), pp. 195-231, for the full context.

164. Henry Thrale won his bet: 'March 10...Sir Ph. J. Cl--ke brought forward the bill for excluding contractors with government from sitting in the house; which was rejected by a majority of 41' (*Gentlemen's Magazine*, vol. 49, p. 575 [December, 1779]). This was only a temporary set-back as the Bill was successfully re-introduced in March, 1782 and passed both houses; see *Diary*, 2:82.

165. See above, p. 26, n. 94.

166. The failure of *The Witlings* is usually ascribed to its satiric particularity, i.e. the pillorying of the *bas bleus*, especially Mrs. Montagu in the character of Mrs. Smatter – not FB's meekness.

167. FB had been asked if she knew any Latin, and she had had to confess her ignorance; see *Diary*, 1:207.

168. Presumably, a 'castle in the air'.

169. The play was *The Good Natur'd Man*. The play was hissed, even though it eventually played for ten consecutive nights. Goldsmith still went along that evening to the Literary Club and, on his own admission, 'chatted gaily among his friends, as if nothing had happened amiss'. However, when everyone had left except SJ, he 'burst out a-crying, and even swore' that his writing career was at an end (*Anecdotes*, pp. 109-10).

170. i.e. June 24.

171. Both Pope and FB completed these works when they were twenty-five, although *Windsor Forest* was started when the former was sixteen.

172. In his "Life of Pope" SJ takes issue exactly with Pope's 'desire of diversity', although he admired at the same time his 'variety and elegance' (*Lives*, 3:225).

173. These 'peculiar circumstances' appear to have been FB's great shyness aided by the lack of strong parental support in her education. As Hemlow points out, her early reticence provoked only neglect (pp. 13-23). Dr. Burney records the early FB as possessing 'a great deal of invention and humour in her childish sports' in private, but when 'in company', she remained 'silent, backward, and timid, even to sheepishness' and that, because of the serious set of her features, she was named 'The Old Lady' from the age of eleven (*Memoirs*, 2:168). One unkind effect of this was that, unlike both her sisters, she was not sent to France to acquire the language. This could also have been due to Dr. Burney's fear that FB may turn to Roman Catholicism under the influence of her grandmother. FB had, therefore, to devise her own curriculum. For her reading and its ethical orientation, see Hemlow, pp. 18-22 and her 'Fanny Burney and the Courtesy Books', *PMLA*, lxv (1950), 732-61.

174. Lowndes had, obviously, not yet paid FB the extra £10 owing on the appearance of the third edition; see *Memoirs*, 2:151.

175. Thrale had suffered a stroke on June 8; see *Thraliana*, pp. 389-90.

176. To Ashbourne to see John Taylor and Lichfield to see Lucy Porter (May 22-June 28); see *Letters*, nos. 616-623.1 (2:288-98). HLT was to suffer a miscarriage in early August. Throughout this period of extreme stress, both SJ (initially) and FB, more generally, found little favour with her. SJ had been away on the road during the crisis and FB's reticence had by now become occasionally irritating; see Clifford, pp. 175-8, *Thraliana*, p. 390: 'Johnson is away – down at Lichfield or Derby, or God knows where, something always happens when *he is away*' and *Thraliana*, p. 400 (August 15): 'Fanny Burney...makes me miserable in too many Respects – so restlessly & apparently anxious lest I should give myself Airs of Patronage, or load her with the Shackles of Dependance – I live with her always in a Degree of Pain that precludes Friendship'.

177. See the letter to John Taylor (August 3) where SJ appreciates the healthy regime at Ashbourne: 'My Nights grew better at your house, and have never since been bad...Of the last fifty days I have taken mercurial physick, I believe, forty, and have lived with much less animal food than has been my custom of late' (*Letters*, no. 627, 2:300-1).

178. *fag*: 'To grow weary; to faint with weariness' (*Dictionary*). The work is drudgery and so taxes her.

179. This passage is taken from a letter to Mr. Crisp (July 30). FB is rebuking him for backsliding in his 'intended reformation as to diet and exercise' (*Diary*, 1:254).

180. The reference is to his letter to Mrs. Thrale of October 28: 'The two younglings; what hinders them from writing to me. I hope they do not forget me' (*Letters*, no. 640, 2:316). The date of this passage is some time between then and November 3, the date of the next entry.

181. The letter is dated April 11, when SJ finds Queeney 'a good Girl' for writing him a letter, yet also claims that 'if Burney said she would write, she told you a fib. She writes nothing to me. She can write home fast enough'. The letter continues: 'I have a good mind not to let her know, that Dr. Bernard, to whom I had recommended her novel, speaks of it with great commendation, and that the copy which she lent me, has been read by Dr. Lawrence three times over. And yet what a Gypsey it is. She no more minds me than if I were a Branghton' (*Letters*, no. 657, 2:339-40). SJ was not only disturbed by Thrale's second stroke (February 21), but also the death (March 11) of Topham Beauclerk, his friend since 1752.

182. Dr. Edward Barnard (1717-81) was not only Provost of Eton but also the Canon of Windsor.

183. Dr. T. Lawrence (1711-81) was SJ's physician and President of the London College of Physicians.

184. Although most unwell, Thrale was canvassing for re-election in the Autumn as M.P. for Southwark.

185. This marks the cooling of relations between SJ and the Thrales. HLT's view was that, as they were taking FB, they did not have an extra room for him at Bath. SJ was to spend nearly the whole summer working on the *Lives of the Poets* at Bolt Court, Fleet Sreet, whilst the Thrales were at Brighton. SJ's letter of April 6 betrays some of this unease: 'Do not let new friends [Piozzi?] supplant the old, they who first distinguished you have the best claim to your attention' (no. 654, 2:334).

186. FB is writing from London to HLT (July 8).

187. From an undated letter to HLT.

188. Now Milton Street. Grub Street is defined by SJ as 'originally the name of a street near Moorfields in London, much inhabited by writers of small histories, dictionaries, and temporary poems; whence any mean production is called *grubstreet*' (*Dictionary*); see Pat Rogers, *Grub Street: Studies in a Subculture* (1972) for a fuller account.

189. SJ describes the Gordon Riots (June 2-7) at *Life*, pp. 1053-7.

190. From a letter to HLT of August 16.

191. Tinker is correct in assuming (p. 119) that these must consist of proof-sheets as two volumes of the *Lives* were dispatched to HLT in July; see *Letters*, no. 690, 2:385 [August 1]). The last six *Lives* were published in 1781.

192. 'Whatever Prior obtains above mediocrity seems the effort of struggle and of toil. He has many vigorous but few happy lines; he has every thing by purchase, and has nothing by gift' ("Life of Prior", *Lives*, 2:209).

193. FB could be referring either to Gay's pastoral burlesque, *The Shepherd's Week* (1714), or his later, more orthodox, pastoral drama, *Dione* (1720). *The Shepherd's Week* is praised for its realism. Its intention (suggested by Pope) that, 'if it be necessary to copy nature with minuteness, rural life must be exhibited such as grossness and ignorance have made it', is foiled to some degree by the execution where 'the effect of reality and truth became conspicuous' (*Lives*, 2:61). *Dione* bored SJ: 'A Pastoral of an hundred lines may be endured; but who will hear of sheep and goats, and myrtle bowers and purling rivulets, through five acts' (2:69).

194. From the Journal, December 6.

195. Thrale was recovering from a severe attack of influenza contracted during the last two days of his stay at Brighton and which had grown suddenly worse during the journey home. HLT felt it was 'an Apoplexy succeeded by a Carbuncle' (*Thraliana*, p. 464 [December 10]).

196. From a letter to Dr. Burney, December 11.

197. FB's own note: 'The Bodleian librarian had placed *Evelina* in his noble library, to the author's astonished delight'.

198. Pope's *Epistle to Jervas* (1727), 9, where the last word is 'name'.

199. From the Journal, late May, 1781.

200. Sophia Gast, "Daddy" Crisp's sister.

201. Jeremiah Crutchley; see above, pp. 43-4.

202. Thrale had died on April 4; see *Diary*, 1:468-71.

203. See p. 62.

204. HLT was in the midst of settling her husband's estate. On May 31, David Barclay, a Lombard St. banker, had bought up the business, but that was only one problem settled out of several; see Clifford, pp. 201-5.

205. H.W. Bunbury (1750-1811), the caricaturist. FB was later to become well acquainted with him; see *Diary*, 3:303-5, 323-5 (August/September, 1787).

206. John Cator (1730-1806), a timber merchant of London and Beckenham, and one of Thrale's executors.

207. Probably Thrale's sister.

208. SJ's biography of George, First Lord Lyttelton (1709-73) was the last of the series and one taken on unwillingly as he considered that there were others closer to the subject who could provide a better piece. SJ had, however, been acquainted with him since his days with Cornelius Ford at Stourbridge (1726). Possibly because of Lyttelton's Whig sympathies the relationship could well have been a cool one. Bishop Percy certainly dated their animosity to these meetings and their 'colloquial disputes' (*Misc.*, 2:208). There is no suggestion directly from SJ that there is any sexual jealousy involved concerning Hill Boothby (this despite HLT's suggestion, erroneously indicating Molly Aston, to Boswell, *Life*, p. 1108 [1781]). Hannah More felt sorry that SJ had 'lost so much credit' by the "Life", for 'he treats [Lyttelton] almost with contempt; makes him out a poor writer, and an envious man' (*Misc.*, 2:193). Apparently, the main offence was taken at SJ's calling him 'poor Lyttelton'; see *Thraliana*, p. 622, and *Life*, pp. 1109, 1114. Horace Walpole commented that 'Mrs. Montagu and all her Maenades intend to tear him limb from limb for despising their moppet' (*Correspondence*, 29:97 [January 27, 1788]).

209. These can be found in SJ's "Life of Shenstone". William Shenstone (1714-63) attended Pembroke College, Oxford, from 1732 (three years after SJ) which may have predisposed him in his favour. From 1745, he had the care of his estate and grounds at the Leasowes as a near-neighbour to Lyttelton at Hagley Hall. As Shenstone 'improved' his inheritance, Lyttelton's 'empire [appeared] spacious and opulent' which 'led those at Hagley to grow envious'. Visitors to Lyttelton were conducted 'perversely to inconvenient points of view'. SJ concluded that 'where there is emulation there will be vanity, and where there is vanity there will be folly' (*Lives*, 3:351-2).

210. *dunned*: to dun – '1. To claim a debt with vehemence and importunity' (*Dictionary*).

211. Pepys' letter to Mrs. Montagu (August 4, 1781) makes it clear that the reconciliation was a superficial one. Pepys accepts the apology for himself, but cannot do so on Lyttelton's behalf: 'But what hurts me all this while is, not that Johnson should go unpunished but that our dear and respectable friend should...be handed down to succeeding generations under the appellation of poor Lyttelton' (*Misc.*, 2:417). For SJ's perspective, see *Anecdotes*, pp. 64-5. A possible reason for his heat in argument might be a jealous qualm about Pepys, once praised so liberally by HLT ('...you praised that man with such disproportion, that I was inclined to lessen him, perhaps more than he deserves' [*Life*, p. 1129, April 1, 1781]).

212. FB may have been nettled by Crutchley's obvious favour for Queeney – which astounded HLT, as they were both near-relations, half-brother and -sister. For the quarrel between FB and Crutchley, see *Diary*, 1:479-86, 489-90. For HLT's view, see *Thraliana*, pp. 496-7. In September, she began 'to wish in good earnest that Miss Burney should make Impression on Mr. Crutchley; I think she honestly loves the Man, who in his Turn appears to be in Love with some one else – Hester, I fear! Oh that would indeed be unlucky!' (*Thraliana*, p. 505).

213. June 28.

214. SJ confessed on April 5, in a letter to HLT, that 'No death since that of my Wife has ever oppressed me like this' (*Letters*, n o. 717, 2:415).

215. FB is throughout her Journal addressing Susan Burney.

216. July 30.

217. Lady Frances (Fanny) Burgoyne (*née* Montagu, d. 1788), daughter of the second Earl of Halifax and wife of Sir Roger Burgoyne (d. 1780). HLT rated her as scoring 17 out of 20 for "Worth of Heart", "Person, Mien and Manner", and "Useful Knowledge", but only two for "Good Humour".

218. The visit by SJ and HLT had been to Jeremiah Crutchley's house at Sunninghill Park; see *Diary*, 2:22-6.

219. *amain*: 'With vehemence; with vigour' (*Dictionary*).

220. Richard Musgrave (1746-1818, created a Baronet in 1782), M.P. for Lismore. His *Memoirs of the Rebellions in Ireland* was published in 1802. HLT met him in Bath and wrote to SJ at Bolt Court (May 21, 1776), describing him as 'rich, young, handsome, hotheaded & I fancy vicious enough: not however without some parts & some Literature, & has an enthusiastick Regard for you' (*Letters*, no. 482a, 2:135); see also *Thraliana*, pp. 220 (where he is dubbed 'Mercury' [December, 1777]) and 548 (where he proposes to HLT [November, 1782]).

221. Reynolds' portrait, now in the Tate Gallery.

222. SJ was insomniac at the time; see below, p. 74.

223. *The Private Life of Lewis XV*, trans. from the French (of Mouffle d'Angerville) by J.O. Justamond (1781).

224. *Joe Miller's Jests; or the Wit's Vade-Mecum. Being a Collection of the most Brilliant Jests; the Politest Repartees; the most Elegant Bon-Mots, and the most pleasant Short-Stories in the English Language...* (1739).

225. Musgrave had obviously not encountered SJ's *Taxation No Tyranny* (1775).

226. August 27.

227. Tinker suggests (p. 138) that this correspondent recalled the continuation of Richardson's *Pamela*.

228. 'Snow Hill' may well be derived from *Evelina*, the Branghtons' address.

229. September 3.

230. i.e. Capt. Mirvan.

231. Presumably, because he is Scottish.

232. See above, p. 71.

233. From Pope's *Essay on Criticism* (1711), 298.

234. September 14.

235. A letter from FB to "Daddy" Crisp.

236. Pasquale Paoli (1725-1807), the Corsican patriot who fled to England after the end of the Corsican War of Independence in 1769. Boswell's *Account of Corsica* was published in 1768. SJ found that Paoli 'had the loftiest port of any man he had ever seen' (*Life*, p. 410 [October 10, 1769]); cf. *Misc.*, 2:16.

237. In Corsica, 1765. See Murray McLean, *Corsica Boswell: Paoli, Johnson and Freedom* (1966), pp. 82-91 and Frederick Pottle, *James Boswell: The Earlier Years, 1740-1769* (1966), pp. 247-83.

238. In Paoli's pidgin, probably a "Thief".

239. Tinker believes (p. 148) that this was probably Charles Byrne (8ft. 4in.) who was to die in Cockspur St. in 1783.

240. The visit to Brighthelmstone (now Brighton) lasted from October 7 to November 20; see *Life*, pp. 1188-91. SJ disliked the resort, but this was not the major reason for any synthetic gaiety. In August, HLT had broken the unwelcome news to SJ that she was to let the Streatham house to Lord Shelburne for three years, and then take her three daughters to the Continent (with Piozzi as it turned out). SJ's leave-taking is described below, pp. 118-19. SJ appeared to take it well; according to HLT (August 22), he seemed to think 'well of the Project & wished [her] to put it early in Execution' – which piqued her after all her care of him. He is taken to think it 'a prudent Scheme, & goes to his Book as usual. This is Philosophy & Truth; he always said he hated a *Feeler*' (*Thraliana*, pp. 540-2). The visit to Brighton appeared as his virtual farewell to the Thrales and his happiest and most settled years; see Clifford, pp. 209-14 for HLT's comments and Bate, pp. 566-72, for a more sympathetic reading of the inner turmoil behind his external nonchalence.

241. i.e. relief from SJ's implicit censure. FB confesses in her Journal for August 12 at Chessington that she knows of HLT's plans (*Diary*, 2:95-6) and HLT records FB's suspicion that she is in love with Piozzi in September (*Thraliana*, p. 544).

242. HLT's mother's maiden name was Cotton. Henry Calveley Cotton (d. 1837) was the sixth and youngest son of Sir Lynch Salusbury Cotton, her Uncle.

243. "Booby" Swinnerton from Hanley, Staffs. FB is later to describe him as 'very sweet-tempered, and good, and soft-hearted; but alas! he is also soft-headed' (*Diary*, 2:115 [November 4, 1782]).

244. *Cecilia, or Memoirs of an Heiress* was published by Tom Payne in five volumes on June 12, and immediately sold out. The Harrel family take in Cecilia Beverley when she is orphaned, but their wild and extravagant social life disturb her greatly. Mrs. Harrel had been one of her best friends, but, it is pointed out, had, 'no pretensions to the wit or understanding of her friend' (Book I, ch. iii, p. 21). Cecilia soon grows fatigued at this incessant round of pleasure, and 'to grow weary of eternally running the same round, and to sicken at the irksome repetition of unremitting yet uninteresting dissipation' (Book I, ch. vii, p. 53). Thanks to his gambling debts, Mr. Harrel eventually commits suicide.

245. October 28.

246. Rev. Dr. John Delap (1752-1812), rector of Lewes, Sussex, is described at length by FB in the entry for May 28, 1779 as silent, a man 'of deep learning, but totally ignorant of life and manners' (*Diary*, 1:222). He had pretensions to being a playwright, HLT having supplied the prologue to *The Royal Suppliants* (1781). Of his next play, a tragedy: *The Captives* (1786), Kemble records that the Drury Lane first night audience roared with laughter (Prior, p. 126). On one of the early occasions that the Thrales met SJ (June, 1766), at Johnson's Court, they found him on his knees before Delap, 'beseeching God to continue to him the use of his understanding' (*Misc.* 1:423); see also *Anecdotes*, p. 57. The Thrales then first introduced SJ to their Streatham household for a convalescent stay of three months.

247. Charles Selwyn (1715-94) was a retired banker from Down Hall in Essex. FB first met him in October, 1779 and described him as 'uncommonly good, full of humanity, generosity, delicacy, and benevolence', even if possessed of no 'brilliancy' (*Diary*, 1:300).

248. cf. Reynolds' observation on SJ's compulsive sociability: 'The great business of his life...was to escape from himself; this disposition he considered as the disease of his mind, which nothing cured but company' (*Life*, p. 106 [1739]).

249. Philip Metcalfe (1733-1818) was a friend SJ had encountered at Reynolds' house. He saw much of him this Autumn, 'being pleased at once with his excellent table and animated conversation' (*Life*, p. 1191 [October 10, 1782]).

250. The party was given by HLT on October 29 at Brighthelmstone.

251. SJ's great desire to 'talk for victory' was derived, according to Boswell, to his settled notion that conversation was 'a trial of intellectual vigour and skill' (*Life*, p. 1150 [May, 1781]; see also p. 528 [April 30, 1773]).

252. *Essay on Criticism*, 297-8. SJ may here have merely decided to 'talk for victory' as his "Life of Pope" finds the *Essay* almost flawless as 'it exhibits every mode of excellence that can embellish or dignify didactick composition' (*Lives*, 3:228).

253. Jane Elizabeth Leslie, Countess of Rothes (d. 1810), married Dr. (later Sir) Lucas Pepys in 1772, i.e. she was William Pepys' sister-in-law.

254. Elizabeth Shelley (*née* Woodcock, d.1808) was the second wife of Sir John Shelley (d. 1783), once Keeper of the Tower records, and a Privy Councillor.

255. For a fuller account, see *Diary*, 2:124-7.

256. i.e. concerning the propriety or otherwise of HLT and FB dancing together instead of just sitting out the evening's entertainment.

257. The visit to Chichester (plus Petworth and Cowdry) took place from November 8 to 10 during which SJ took notes; see *Works*, 1:348-9.

258. November 7.

259. SJ first met William Gerard Hamilton (1729-96), M.P. for Wilton, and Chancellor of the Irish Exchequer, in Brighthelmstone during November, 1779. FB comments on him, including his nickname, "Single-Speech Hamilton", earned when a brilliant maiden speech in 1755 was followed by no other. He was 'extremely tall and handsome' yet had 'an air of haughty and fashionable superiority' being 'intelligent, dry, sarcastic, and clever' (*Diary*, 1:308).

260. Capt. Molesworth Phillips (1757-1832), one of the heroes of Capt. Cook's last expedition, had married Susan Burney at the start of the year (January 10); see Hemlow, pp. 146-7, 285-91.

261. November 12.

262. November 18-19.

263. When Cecilia retires to Bury St. Edmunds on being forced to separate from Mortimer Delvile, Mr. Albany becomes her adviser in her charitable schemes. He is a man with a tragic and a foolish past, now rapidly making amends by living for the good of the poor, and who suggests to his mistress a practical system of aid that does not pauperize its recipients. The 'unappeasable remorse' that calls forth the 'high-flown language' is due to his guilt at forsaking his first love, the 'daughter of a villager' and 'child of simplicity' that he had first met whilst at University (Book VIII, ch. ix, p. 705). Cecilia suspects that his 'reason had been impaired' because of 'his flightiness, wildness, florid language, and extraordinary way of life' (p. 708).

264. Hon. Mary Monckton, Countess of Cork (d. 1840), daughter of Viscount Galway. She was famous for her literary parties: 'she is one of those who stand foremost in collecting all extraordinary or curious people to her London conversaziones, which...mix the rank and the literature, and exclude all beside' (*Diary*, 2:123). She is described by FB as 'between thirty and forty, very short, very fat, but handsome; splendidly and fantastically dressed...her rage of seeing any thing curious may be satisfied, if she pleases, by looking in a mirror' (2:124 [November 10, 1782]).

265. Margaret Cavendish Holles Harles (1714-85), only child of Edward, second Earl of Oxford. William, second Duke of Portland had died in 1762.

266. Mary Granville Pendarves Delany (1700-88) had been a widow since the death of Patrick Delany in 1768. After the death, she lived with the Duchess of Portland and was finally pensioned by George III. In her youth she was a great friend of Swift's; in age, she frequented many Blues gatherings and introduced FB to the royal family.

267. Mr. Crisp.

268. On November 12, Reynolds had apparently suffered 'a paralytick attack, of sufficient severity to alarm his friends seriously' (Leslie and Taylor, 2:380). After a short stay at Bath, he had returned to London by December 4.

269. Frances Macartney (d. 1789), author of the *Ode to Indifference* (1777). She married Charles Burney's friend, Fulke Greville, in 1747. For the occasion of the poem, see *Thraliana*, p. 136 (August-September, 1777). See below, pp. 107-8.

270. Edmund Burke (1729-97) was at the time Paymaster-General of the forces in the Rockingham-Shelburne coalition government that had come to power in March of that year. He was actively involved in framing legislation on the economic reform of government. FB had first met him in June and was immediately impressed: 'He is tall, his figure is noble, his air commanding, his address graceful; his voice is clear, penetrating, sonorous, and powerful...' (*Diary*, 2:91). He had first met SJ at Garrick's in 1758 and was one of the earliest members of the Club. Whilst never *political* companions, there was mutual admiration between them. SJ thought him an 'extraordinary man [whose] stream of mind [was] perpetual' (*Life*, p. 696 [March 21, 1776]). He married Jane Nugent, daughter of his physician, in the winter of 1756-7. She is supposed to have renounced her Catholicism on her marriage. FB always found her agreeable company; see *Diary*, 2:233.

271. He thought that the masquerade was too long (Book II, ch. iii, pp. 103-28) and disliked 'Morrice's part of the Pantheon' (Book IV, ch. vi, pp. 281-8). He also wished that the conclusion were 'either more happy or more miserable' (*Diary*, 2:139). Mr. Morrice acted as Mr. Monckton's spy and informant concerning Cecilia's suitors at the Harrels.

272. Horace Walpole disagreed for he felt that 'she has laboured far too much to make all her personages talk always in character' (*Walpoliana*, 1:39). Burke, however, took this to be a virtue; they may have been 'too numerous', but they comprehended 'an incredible variety...; most of them well planned, well supported, and well contrasted with each other' (*Diary*, 2:93 [July 29, 1782]).

273. Burke had obviously heard about the sum of £250 that had been paid for the copyright of *Cecilia*. Many said, according to Charlotte Burney, that 'she ought to have had a thousand' (*Early Diary*, 2:307).

274. Mr. Briggs, in *Cecilia*, is one of her three guardians. After Harrel's suicide, she fails to last a day with the miserly Briggs, who could 'by parsimony, vulgarity, and meanness, render riches contemptible, prosperity unavailing, and oeconomy odious' (Book V, ch. viii, p. 374).

275. A very different scenario from the covert composition of *Evelina*. For the Chessington writing period, see Hemlow, pp. 142-5.

276. Sarah Siddons (*née* Kemble, 1755-1831) had returned in triumph to the London stage on October 10 less than two months before this conversation. Her debut in 1775-6 at Drury Lane had been a failure, but since then she had toured the provinces with conspicuous success.

277. See above, p. 82.

278. There is no record that SJ ever saw Sarah Siddons act. She visited him in October, 1783, at which meeting he vowed he would 'once more hobble out to the theatre' if she would play Catherine in *Henry VIII*. The part was hers only after his death (*Life*, p. 1251 [October, 1783]).

279. The occasion was probably the benefit for Frances Abington (1737-1815) at Drury Lane (March 27, 1775). Boswell remarked that 'as he could neither see nor hear at . . . a distance from the stage, he was wrapped up in grave abstraction, and seemed quite a cloud, amidst all the sunshine of glitter and gaiety' (*Life*, p. 598).

280. Probably December 17.

281. Boswell confessed in 1783 that SJ was given to an occasional 'fit of *narrowness*'. SJ joined him in this confession: 'He has now and then borrowed a shilling of me; and when I asked for it again, seemed to be rather out of humour. A droll little circumstance once occurred: as if he meant to reprimand my minute exactness as a creditor, he thus addressed me; – "Boswell, *lend* me sixpence – *not to be repaid* " ' (*Life*, p. 1213 [1783]).

282. December 27.

283. Elizabeth Cumyns (*née* Thornton), a childhood friend of HLT's who ran a tough boarding school in Kensington; see *Thraliana*, p. 291 (April-May, 1778).

284. January 10.

285. FB's younger brother, a schoolmaster.

286. William Doughty (d. 1782). The print is dated June 24, 1779. In Hawkins' collection of Apophthegms and Sayings from SJ's *Works*, the engraving and thus Reynolds' canvas displays 'the appearance of a labouring working mind, of an indolent reposing body' (*Misc.*, 2:10).

287. See also the letters (mainly to HLT) for a fuller picture of SJ's affliction (nos. 847-61, 3:32-46). The attack had occurred on the morning of June 17. In his house there was only the blind and ailing Anna Williams, so extra help was needed. The 'querulous letter' he dispatched to HLT on 19 June provides an indication both of the degree of the estrangement and the depth of SJ's need – 'I am sitting down in no chearful solitude to write a narrative which would once have affected you with tenderness and sorrow, but which you will perhaps pass over now with the careless glance of frigid indifference' (no. 850, 3:34). Although HLT now rented a house as near to Bolt's Court as Argyll St., they had hardly met at all throughout the preceding Winter or Spring. For HLT's side of the affair (herself in remorse at having to have had Piozzi sent away on January 27 due to her daughters' dissent), see *Thraliana*, pp. 568-74. There are few entries on SJ.

288. Tinker points to a probable confusion in dates here. Barrett places this passage immediately before the June 19 entry and dates it as February 23. The references to SJ's stay with Bennet Langton at Rochester (July 10-23) and then with William Bowles at Heale, near Salisbury (August 28-September 18 [see *Life*, p. 1244]) obviously place it as much later. Tinker provisionally dates this conversation as July 15, believing it to be originally part of the *Diary* entry for 2:218-22, where the page corresponding to p. 221 in the Berg MS. is missing.

289. Richard Owen Cambridge of Twickenham (1717-1802), known as a wit and, by Boswell, a *fortunate senex* for his fashionable villa (Cambridge House, near Richmond Bridge), 'excellent library, which he accurately knows and reads', his pictures and circle of friends (*Life*, p. 1216 [1783]).

290. See above, p. 12.

291. William Bowles (1755-1826), son of the Canon of Salisbury and a member of the Essex-Head Club. Bowles, who at the time had never met SJ, simply asked if he would like to visit him (*Letters*, no. 871-2, 3:56-7). SJ enjoyed the stay enormously; see *Life*, pp. 1244-8.

292. Extract from a letter to Queeney at Bath, October 25, 1783, where FB is counselling moderate dissent, and even that she relent in her opposition to HLT's attachment to Piozzi.

293. Jeremiah Crutchley, the implication being that he would not be able to keep the secret from SJ.

294. Rev. Samuel Hoole (1758-1839), ministered to SJ during his last days; see *Misc.*, 2:157-60, and *Life*, p. 1387.

295. Which occurred on September 6, during SJ's stay with Bowles. In his letter to Charles Burney (September 20), his 'domestick companion' is praised for her many 'acquisitions' and her 'universal' curiosity, where she took part in 'every conversation' (*Letters*, no. 882, 3:70).

296. A common occurrence. Dr. W. Maxwell recounted the following to Boswell in 1770: 'About twelve o'clock I commonly visited him, and frequently found him in bed, or declaiming over his tea...He generally had a levee of morning visitors, chiefly men of letters...and sometimes learned ladies' (*Life*, p. 437).

297. From a letter to Queeney. Hemlow gives a full account of the secrecy behind the correspondence at pp. 174-83. The *Diary* at this point is also uncharacteristically cryptic; see the entry for November 22: 'I am sorry not to be more explicit, but I should not give you more pleasure if I were. I can only now tell you that I love Mrs. Thrale with a never-to-cease affection, and pity her more than ever I pitied any human being; and if I did not blame her, I could, I should, I believe, almost die for her!' (*Diary*, 2:229-30).

298. The original letter is no. 902 (3:100-1). FB supplies the title of the discovered book for her Journal entry.

299. SJ was habitually forgetful about both books he had borrowed and those he had lent. In the *Memoirs* FB reports Garrick's SJ imitation on receiving his quarto Petrarch. In the midst of a 'Greek ejaculation, and a couplet or two from Horace', the volume ('Russia leather, gold border, and all!') was flung to the floor and the care of the 'housemaid's morning mop' (*Memoirs*, 1:352-3).

300. FB's sister.

301. Hester Chapone (*née* Mulso, 1727-1801), once the friend of Samuel Richardson. She wrote four 'billets' in *Rambler* 10 and later was to be the author of the famous *Letters on the Improvement of the Mind* (1774). SJ quoted some of her poetry in the *Dictionary* under the entry of 'Quatrain'; see Frances Reynolds' comments, *Misc.*, 2:252. For her friendship with Richardson, see Eaves and Kimpel, pp. 343-9.

302. FB wrote at the foot of the letter, 'FB flew to him instantly and most gratefully' (*Diary*, 2:283).

303. In the *Memoirs*, FB (as Mme. D'Arblay) identifies this as an allusion to a remark made by SJ when Elizabeth Montagu resented his "Life of Lyttelton" (*Memoirs*, 2:357, n.).

304. '*Lear*: I tax not you, you elements, with unkindness', *King Lear*, III, ii, 16.

305. Her brother.

306. Francesco Sastres (*fl.* 1776-1822), Italian teacher and translator. SJ left him a bequest of £5 'to be laid out in books of piety for his own use' (*Misc.*, 1:447) and an Italian visit for both of them was planned (*Misc.*, 2:459).

307. This is the record of a conversation at Mrs. Vesey's on 9 December.

308. The younger Owen Cambridge, the Rev. George (1756-1841), prebendary of Ely. He proved to be a favourite of FB's by refraining from embarrassing praise of *Cecilia*. HLT thought him 'an Admirer' of FB's as early as April, 1783 (*Thraliana*, pp. 562-3). For a full account of their friendship, see Hemlow, pp. 187-93.

309. The Essex Head Club. Details of the rules of its foundation and SJ's determination to battle through ill-health to attend are described in *Life*, pp. 1264-5, 1344.

310. See *Spectator* 9 (March 10, 1710) for the rules of the Two-Penny Club.

311. See above, pp. 64-7.

312. See above, pp. 64-7.

313. SJ's tone is restrained, but never unfriendly: 'You have, Madam, the satisfaction of having alleviated the sufferings of a Woman of great merit both intellectual and moral...hat I have not written sooner, you may impute to absence, to ill health, to any thing rather than want of regard to the Benefactress of my departed Friend' (*Letters*, no. 884, 3:73-4).

314. December 16.

315. He had probably suffered a coronary thrombosis soon after attending a meeting of the Essex Head Club. He described it as 'a spasmodick asthma so violent, that with difficulty I got to my own house ... The asthma is not the worst. A dropsy gains ground upon me; my legs and thighs are very much swollen with water' (*Life*, p. 1265). See also his letters to HLT, (no. 917, 3:113 [December 13]) and John Taylor (no. 918, 3:114, [December 20]).

316. See his letters to HLT (no. 922, 3:119 [December 31]) and to John Taylor (no. 923, 3:120, [January 4, 1784]). The open 'blister' on his chest was to ease his breathing.

317. The fear was grounded less on the wish to avoid pain than on the fear of extinction. At Charles Dilly's (April, 1778), SJ grew irritated at Anna Seward's conception of death as 'only a pleasing sleep without a dream' and retorted that it was 'neither pleasing, nor sleep; it is nothing. Now mere existence is so much better than nothing, that one would rather exist even in pain, than not exist' (*Life*, p. 950). He wrote to HLT on December 31, describing his great 'need of entertainment; spiritless, infirm, sleepless, and solitary, [he was] looking back with sorrow and forward with terrour' (*Letters*, no. 922, 3:119).

318. From an undated letter to Queeney, where FB voices her growing fear of losing HLT's friendship for ever and where she also regards Piozzi as the true culprit in the affair. The Marquis of Lansdowne dates it as early April.

319. Dr. Arthur Collier (d. 1777) of Doctor's Commons who had once been HLT's tutor.

320. Sophy Streatfield, who had waited all her life for the Rev. Dr. Vyse and dismissed all others.

321. SJ acknowledges the gift of the 'magnificent Fish' in the morning of April 19 and 'in the afternoon [Mrs. Thrale's] apology for not sending it' (*Letters*, no. 954, 3:156).

322. This is probably a reference to SJ's negro servant, Frank Barber (1745-1801). He lived next door to SJ from 1776, but, with his wife and two young daughters, moved in with him after Anna Williams' death (September 6). FB would therefore be anxious not to impose on his family.

323. Martha Hall (c.1707-91) was a Methodist preacher, and was said by Boswell to resemble John Wesley 'both in figure and manner' (*Life*, p. 1136 [April 15, 1781]).

324. See above, p. 93.

325. Near Mickleham in Surrey and home of William Locke (1732-1810) and his wife Frederica Augusta (*née* Schaub), both to become FB's dearest friends. Boswell concluded that Locke's 'knowledge and taste in the fine arts' was 'universally celebrated' (*Life*, p. 1096 [1781]). FB had been re-introduced to the family in April and the summer had seen a firm friendship flourish.

326. This tour of Lichfield and Ashbourne (July 13-November 16) was the last that SJ made. The letters from this period highlight the physical courage that lay behind the bare facts of this pilgrimage. On October 13, he wrote to William Heberden, one of his physicians, that, in Ashbourne, he was 'oppressed very heavily by the asthma; and [that] the dropsy had advanced so far, that [he] could not without great difficulty button me at my knees' (*Letters*, no. 1022, 3:235).

327. Elizabeth ('Tetty') Porter had died in 1752.

328. Queeney Thrale, who had chosen to be estranged from her mother on her re-marriage (to Piozzi) on July 23; see Clifford, pp. 228-31.

329. Ann Yearsley (1752-1806) or 'Lactilla', sold milk from door to door. Hannah More was shown her poetry by her cook and set about correcting it. Subscribers were sought for an edition of her work, which finally appeared in the Autumn of 1784 (although the title-page is dated 1785). FB and her father subscribed. After dispensing with More's patronage, Yearsley continued to publish. Her novel, *The Royal Captives*, appeared in 1795.

330. James Woodhouse (1735-1820). SJ first came to the Thrales to meet Woodhouse in 1765; see *Thraliana*, p. 159 and *Misc.*, 1:232-3. SJ recommended Addison's works to the poet on that occasion 'as a model for imitation' (*Anecdotes*, p. 56). SJ felt contempt for those who favoured his poetry and claimed that it 'was all vanity and childishness' and a provision of 'mirrours of their own superiority' (*Life*, pp. 443-4 [1770]).

331. Frank Barber.

332. Dr. George Strahan (1744-1824), the Vicar of St. Mary's, Islington and Rector of Little Thurrock in Essex. He published SJ's *Prayers and Meditations* (1785). He was the son of SJ's friend and early printer, William Strahan.

333. Dr. Richard Warren (1731-97). SJ refused to dull his intellect, as he had 'prayed that [he would] render up [his] soul to God unclouded'. Boswell confirmed that this was true to the very end (*Life*, p. 1390).

334. An extract from a letter to Frederica Locke which was begun on Sunday, December 7 and completed December 11. Barrett places it *before* the preceding passage. However, I have followed Tinker in placing it in its chronological, not textual, order.

335. Dr. Richard Brocklesby (1722-97), SJ's principal physician in his last illness; see Bate, pp. 584-6.

336. Mr. Strahan.

337. Arthur Murphy remembers that he made 'translations of Greek epigrams from the Anthologia' and composed Latin epigraphs for his parents and brother. 'Eternity presented to his mind an aweful prospect, and, with as much virtue as perhaps ever is the lot of man, he shuddered at the thought of his dissolution' (*Misc.*, 1:445).

338. *Lady Macbeth*: '...He grows worse and worse./Question enrages him...' (Act III, iv, 116-17).

339. Bennet Langton told Boswell of this visit; see *Life*, pp. 1384-5.

340. The Drs. Rose (1719-86) and J. Gillies (1747-1836) were famous Classical scholars. Dr. Garthshore was a physician. Rose was master of Chiswick School, a contemporary of Charles Burney's.

341. Probably, 'to begin a conversation'.

342. This is possibly the wife of Tom Davies, (?1712-85), an ex-actor and bookseller of Covent Garden, who first introduced Boswell to SJ in May, 1763. Mrs. Davies 'had been celebrated for her beauty' (*Life*, p. 276).

343. From a letter to Dr. Burney of September 24, 1785, from Norbury Park.

344. These are the *Prayers and Meditations... Composed by Samuel Johnson, LL.D., and published from his manuscripts by George Strahan*. The fifth edition (1817) may be consulted in *Misc.*, 1:1-124.

345. This is a conversation with Queen Charlotte, which took place at the home of Mrs. Delany in 1785. FB happened to be visiting there and she was subsequently invited for a Court interview in June, 1786.

346. The *Life* was announced in the *Journal of a Tour to the Hebrides*, published in September.

347. A passage from FB's journal (February 26, 1787). FB was then one of Queen Charlotte's dressers. She reports herself in conversation with the Queen's French reader, known throughout the Journal as 'Mr. Turbulent' (Charles de Guiffardière).

348. See above, p. 23.

349. Published in February, 1787.

350. A journal entry for July 13, 1787. FB's phrase here is an indication of her growing nostalgia for the life outside Court ritual; see *Diary*, 3:161 (January 16) : 'Now, therefore, I took shame to myself, and *Resolved to be happy*...To be patient under two disappointments now no longer recent; – to relinquish, without repining, frequent intercourse with those I love; – to settle myself in my monastery, without one idea of ever quitting it'.

351. Dr. James Beattie (1735-1803). FB had been talking of his character: 'pleasant, unaffected, unassuming, and full of conversible intelligence' (*Diary*, 3:281). She had especially appreciated his *The Minstrel* (1771-4) and his *Essay on Truth* (1770).

352. i.e. Dr. Percy.

353. Elizabeth Juliana Schwellenberg, a German fellow-attendant on the Queen and FB's immediate superior at the Queen's toilette.

354. HLT was lost to FB after the quarrel over her marriage to Piozzi.

355. HLT's *Letters to and from the late Samuel Johnson, LL.D.* were finally published on Saturday, March 8, 1788. FB regretted that no effort was made to mitigate SJ's more robust qualities.

356. No. 302, *Letters* (Piozzi), 1:212.

357. No. 465, *Letters* (Piozzi), 1:381.

358. No. 512, *Letters* (Piozzi), 2:4-5; see above, p.1.

359. This is an extract from the entry for February 13 which describes the trial of Warren Hastings (1732-1818) on corruption charges for offences whilst Governor-General in India. William Windham (1730-1810) was elected (Coalition) M.P. for Norwich in 1784 and was a friend of both SJ and Burke. FB found him 'one of the most agreeable, spirited, well-bred, and brilliant conversers I have ever spoken with' (*Diary*, 3:419). He attended the dying SJ (*Life*, p. 1330).

360. *Poetae Graeci Heroici per Henricum Stephanum*; see *Life*, p. 1381. In the Appendix F to Hill's *Life*, 4:440, he records that two days earlier, SJ had donated him a New Testament as well.

361. From the Journal, October-November, 1790.

362. See above, p. 102.

363. FB's health had begun to give way under the excessive confinement as the Queen's dresser: 'I was ill the whole of this month [October], though not once with sufficient seriousness for confinement... A languor so prodigious, with so great a failure of strength and spirit, augmented almost hourly, that I several times thought I must be compelled to excuse my constancy of attendance; but there was no one to take my place' (*Diary*, 4:427); see also Hemlow, pp. 215-16. She had drawn up her terms of resignation in the summer and submitted them in December. Boswell was hard at work on the *Life*, which finally appeared on May 16, 1791; see Frank Brady, *James Boswell: The Later Years, 1769-1795* (1984), pp. 413-21.

364. His eyesight had begun to deteriorate with the obscuring of vision in his left eye on July 13, 1789, which spread to the right in October. By November 5, 1791, he was almost totally blind.

365. *Reflections on the French Revolution* was finally issued in November, 1790.

366. It appeared on May 16, 1791.

367. One of Boswell's party-pieces. Hannah More, in 1781, once had to stand as umpire in a 'trial of skill' between himself and Garrick 'which could most nearly imitate Dr. Johnson's manner'. Boswell was successful 'in familiar conversation', but Garrick won it 'in reciting poetry' (*Misc.*, 2:195).

368. i.e. to FB, November 17, 1784 (*Letters*, no. 1036, 3:248).

369. *rhodomontading*: 'To *Rodomontade*: to brag thrasonically; to boast like Rodomontade [a character from Ariosto]' (*Dictionary*).

370. 'I dined yesterday at Mrs. Garrick's, with Mrs. Carter, Miss Hannah More, and Miss Fanny Burney. Three such women are not to be found; I know not where I could find a fourth, except Mrs. Lennox, who is superior to them all' (*Life*, p. 1278 [May 15, 1784]).

371. June 1, 1792.

372. Bennet Langton was one of Boswell's readiest sources of information: 'My worthy friend Mr. Langton, to whom I am under innumerable obligations in the course of my Johnsonian History' (*Life*, p. 701 [March 22, 1776]).

373. See above, pp. 1-4.

374. Richard Fulke Greville (c.1717-c.1806), of Wilbury House and grandson of Fulke Greville, fifth Baron Brooke, was Charles Burney's first patron. For the range of his accomplishment and spendthrift ways, see Lonsdale, pp. 14-16. His *Maxims, Characters, and Reflections* (1756) was, according to Boswell, 'entitled to much more praise than it has received' (*Life*, p. 1300 [June 12, 1784]). For Frances Greville, see p. 83.

375. i.e. Dr. Burney.

376. Perhaps the first instance of this persona can be seen in Charles Churchill's characterisation of SJ as 'Pomposo' in *The Ghost* (1762), Book II, 'whose very name inspires an awe,/ Whose ev'ry word is Sense and Law' (*CH*, p. 357).

377. See above, pp. 2, 93.

378. The *Lives of the Poets*.

379. Boswell believed in the *Life* (p. 1009 [February, 1779]) that they were entrusted to him.

380. 'He told us, "almost all his *Ramblers* were written just as they were wanted for the press; that he sent a certain portion of the copy of an essay, and wrote the remainder, while the former part of it was printing. When it was wanted, and he had fairly sat down to it, he was sure it would be done" ' (*Life*, p. 747 [April 12, 1776]); cf. *Life*, p. 145 [March, 1750]).

381. A self-reference by Mme. D'Arblay.

382. Reynolds portrayed SJ in at least seven portraits. It is likely that this is William Doughty's mezzotint (pub. 1779) of the painting provided for Henry Thrale's library at Streatham (c.1772 - now in the Tate Gallery).

383. This is derived from a brief entry in 1760 in the *Early Diary*: 'Mr. Bewley [1726-83] accepted as a present or relic, a tuft of his hearth-broom, which my father secretly cut off, and sent to him in a frank. He thinks it more precious than pearls' (1:176). Burney is quoted directly by Boswell concerning this gift which was culled from SJ's chambers in the Temple – 'being shewn into the room where he was to breakfast, finding himself alone, he examined the contents of the apartment, to try whether he could undiscovered steal anything to send to his friend Bewley, as another relick of the admirable Dr. Johnson. But, finding nothing better to his purpose, he cut some bristles off his hearth-broom, and enclosed them in a letter to his country enthusiast, who received them with due reverence. The Doctor was so sensible of the honour done him by a man of genius and science' (*Life*, p. 1170 [July 17, 1781]).

384. Crisp had retired there over twenty years before.

385. Tinker concludes that this event is likely to have occurred on Monday, March 29, 1779.

386. Not just due to Boswell's persona. In 1779, SJ was seventy and Boswell thirty-nine.

387. Charles Burney's opinion of Boswell was never high, but he, on the evidence of the *Life*, could sometimes take issue with SJ e.g. see *Life*, p. 983 [May 8, 1778]). For the relations between SJ and Boswell, see Richard B. Schwartz, *Boswell's Johnson: A Preface to the Life* (1978), pp. 3-18, and Frank Brady, *James Boswell: The Later Years, 1769-1795* (1984), pp. 426-39.

388. *Cecilia* was finally published in July, 1782. In order to complete it, FB obeyed her father's advice to quit Streatham's distractions and immure herself at St. Martin's Street, from late October, 1780 to February, 1781. By the end of January, 1781, a draft of the first volume was completed; see Hemlow, pp. 142-7. HLT at this time called Charles Burney a 'Blockhead . . . to be always sending for his Daughter home so! . . . Johnson is enraged at the silliness of their Family Conduct' (*Thraliana*, p. 502 [July 7, 1781]).

389. Thrale had died in April.

390. HLT's ill-health seems not to have been obvious. On April 17, she reports herself 'well in Health, & *very* sound of Heart, notwith-standing the watchers & the Wagerlayers' who wished to marry her off (*Thraliana*, p. 531).Her guilty secret was her growing affection for Piozzi, an affection kept from SJ until well after the leave-taking from Streatham. For the extent of FB's knowledge at this time, see Clifford, pp. 210-15, and Hemlow, pp. 170-3.

391. FB has just described her father's farewell from Streatham.

392. The full reason for the cooling of the friendship was not known to SJ until July, 1784; for the exchange of letters between them, see *Letters*, nos. 969a – 970.2, 3:172-6. Boswell's account is at *Life*, pp. 1190-1, including SJ's prayer.

393. Tinker believes (p. 234) that FB has transposed some events from November, 1784 to a year earlier. The letter complaining of FB's absence was sent on November 19, 1783, yet Tinker feels that before HLT's unequivocal announcement of her attachment to Piozzi, SJ's resentment would not have been so bitter. He, therefore, concludes the date to be November, 1784.

394. June 16, 1783.